(twelve)
£12·00
4r

The Kynoch Press

the anatomy of a printing house

1876–1981

The Kynoch Press

the anatomy of a printing house

1876–1981

CAROLINE ARCHER

The British Library and Oak Knoll Press, 2000

Dedication

This book is dedicated to my father
JOHN WILLIAM ARCHER
a typographer and teacher
who gave me a love for printing
and who provided the motivation
and inspiration behind this book

It is my great regret
he did not live to see it completed

© 2000 Caroline Archer

FIRST PUBLISHED 2000 BY

The British Library   Oak Knoll Press
96 Euston Road   310 Delaware Street
London NW1 2DB   New Castle, DE 19720
UK   USA

British Library Cataloguing in Publication Data
A CIP Record for this book is available from The British Library

Library of Congress Cataloging-in-Publication Data

Archer, Caroline, 1961–
    The Kynoch Press: the anatomy of a printing house, 1876–1981/Caroline Archer
        p. cm.
Includes bibliographical references and index.

ISBN 0 7123 4704 6   (The British Library)
ISBN 1-58456-046-0   (Oak Knoll Press)

1. Kynoch Press–History. 2. Printing–Great Britian–History–19th Century.
3. Printing–Great Britian–History–20th Century. I. Title

Z232.K93 A74 2000
686.2'0941–dc21   00–050193

Designed and typeset by the author

Printed in England by St Edmundsbury Press, Bury St Edmunds

Contents

Acknowledgements

I would like to acknowledge the assistance provided by the following institutions in the preparation of this book:

Birmingham Central Reference Library; Birmingham Museum of Science; Birmingham and Midland Institute; Birmingham Proof House; BBC Written Archives, Reading; The Bodleian Library, John Johnson Collection, Oxford; The British Library, London; Cambridge Bibliographical Society; Imperial Chemical Industries (ICI), London; Imperial Metal Industries (IMI) Birmingham; The Imperial War Museum, London; Manchester Metropolitan University Library; The Ministry of Defence Pattern Room, Nottingham; The Monotype Corporation, Surrey; The Royal Armouries, Leeds; The St Bride Printing Library, London; The Type Museum, London; The Typographical Association, Birmingham; The University of Reading, Department of Typography and Graphic Communication; Victoria and Albert Museum, London; West Herts College Library, Watford.

My thanks also go to the following individuals:

Roger Almond (IMI); Hazel Archer; Duncan Avery (Monotype Hot-Metal); Colin Baines (Kynoch Press); Len Boulton (Kynoch Press); Michael Clapham (Kynoch Press/ICI); David Cockbill (Kynoch Press); Roger Denning (Kynoch Press); Len Harvey (Kynoch Press); Wallis Heath (Kynoch Press); Michael Hope; David Hopewell (Kynoch Press); Beryl Hunter; Dick Hurst (Kynoch Press); Roy Kilminster (Kynoch Press); Alex King (Kynoch Press); Paul Luna (The University of Reading); Craig McCracken; James Mosley (St Bride Printing Library); Bert Pace (Kynoch Press); Bill Pardoe; Nigel Roche (St Bride Printing Library); Ian Rogerson (Manchester Metropolitan University); Sheena Russell (ICI Library); Margaret M. Smith (The University of Reading); Michael Twyman (The University of Reading); Sue Walker (The University of Reading).

Introduction

My original intention had been to write about the work of the Birmingham School of Printing and its one-time head, Leonard Jay, but work on Jay had already been done and it seemed futile to duplicate research. However, when looking at Jay I noticed the names of several Midlands printers who frequently donated prizes to the School: Eberneezer Baylis, Buckler and Webb, Silk and Terry and the Kynoch Press were all regular sponsors. The latter name caught my attention as a possible subject for a book.

The Kynoch Press, part of the ICI group of companies, was a name with which I was very familiar. My father had worked at the Press as a journeyman compositor from 1945 until 1948, and often recalled his time there and talked proudly of its reputation. To find whether this reputation was merely a result of his rose-tinted reminiscences or whether it was more widely acknowledged, I asked several typographic historians and practitioners for their opinions of the Press. All said it was a first-class, lively outfit which had produced fine work to a standard which was worth paying a bit extra for. But although the Press was highly regarded, it was also something of an enigma about which few people had any information. The Press has remained curiously undocumented, not least because tangible, documentary information is difficult to find. Standard typographic literature makes infrequent reference to the Press, and any commentary that does exist is usually confined to the period pre-1939. Trade literature is equally sparing in its reporting with only a few references to the Press in publications such as *The British Printer* or *Litho Weekly*, nor does the Press receive much coverage from *The Penrose Annual, The Monotype Recorder* or *Typographica*. There is scant mention of it in trade directories and general advertising issued by the Press itself is virtually non-existent. However, some patchy and uncoordinated internal company documentation survives, and the ICI in-house magazine contains news reports and editorials on the Press which cover a period of 70 years. But the greatest insight into the workings of the Press has come through talking with past employees. This book pulls together this wide-ranging and disparate material in an attempt to tell the story of the Kynoch Press, although this is by no means a company history. Some of the employee interviews that I undertook have been extracted and are included in the book because they help show the Press as a living, working entity with a distinct personality. These employee 'oral histories' have provided an invaluable insight into the spirit of the Press, have been tape recorded and transcribed for posterity, and are lodged with the Department of Typography and Graphic Communication at the University of Reading where they form a separate appendix to my Ph.D thesis on the Kynoch Press out of which this book has evolved.

A clue to the personality of the Kynoch Press was apparent through the typefaces it chose to stock. The Press was particularly innovative in its type selection, and in the inter-war years can be credited with starting the fashion for English nineteenth-century revival types, and after the war it remained in the typographic vanguard. Appended to this book are some tables which give full details of what typefaces were available at the Kynoch Press and some comparisons are made with those types held at the rival firms of Percy, Lund Humphries and the Curwen Press. A more extensive study of what typefaces were available at the Kynoch Press and several other British and European printers in the period 1900 to 1980 forms an appendix to my thesis.

It is not just the typefaces which revealed the workings and personality of the Press, but the customers that went to the Press for their work are also very telling. The Press had a diverse range of clients who employed it to work on a range of publications, from fine books to commercial leaflets, from complicated techno-scientific publications to foreign language setting. At the end of this book there appears a catalogue of work produced by the Press; it is by no means exhaustive, but is there merely to provide an indication of some of the more important projects with which it was associated.

I decided to write the story of the Kynoch Press, not just because it had an interesting and original history, nor because it produced high-quality innovative work, but because by documenting its life, some light is shed on how a British printing house adapted itself to major changes in the printing industry. The Kynoch Press traded for just over 100 years and experienced two major printing revolutions: the move from hand- to machine-composition and on to photo-composition; and the transition from letterpress to offset-lithographic printing.

Over a period of 100 years, the Kynoch Press developed from an

unknown in-plant printing house into a business with a widely acknowledged reputation for quality, originality and enterprise in the areas of
composition, press-work, typographic and graphic design. This reputation was maintained from the early 1920s until the Press was closed in
1981.

The Press developed its reputation in four, distinct, phases. From
1876 until 1900 it was an in-house printer which worked exclusively at
the behest of its parent and produced material which was typographically representative of many printing houses of the period. At the
beginning of the twentieth century, the Press started to attract outside
clients and emerged from obscurity through its early adoption of
Caslon Old Face and by its practice of 'purist' typography. During the
inter-war period of 1922 to 1939 the Press considerably expanded its
reputation and increased its external clientele. It modernised its production and moved away from hand- to machine-composition and
installed a unique range of founders' types. During this period the Press
was one of only a few printers who produced the sort of classical typography for which it developed a reputation. In the post-war years,
between 1945 to 1981, the Press underwent a second technological revolution. It moved away from machine- to photo-composition, from letterpress to offset-lithographic printing. Alongside these technological
changes the Press re-structured its organisation, developed a specialised
product and brought more modern ideas to its approach to design.

Between 1945 and 1981, the Press successfully managed to change
from a craft-based to a technology-led printing house. It developed both
a product and an image for itself which were appropriate to post-1945
trade. It moved away from the conservatism of the pre-war years and
progressed towards increasingly international and more modern ideas.
This change could be seen in three areas: production; organisation and
services; and design.

Before 1939, methods of production at the Press were largely dependent upon art and the human hand and eye. Composition and printing
were performed both by hand and machine, but decisions on the quality
of typesetting and reproduction were usually subjective. The Press successfully transformed its methods of production into a technological
process with the installation of offset-lithographic printing and an in-
house graphic reproduction department in 1952, followed by computer-
assisted typesetting in the late 1960s and photo-composition in the early
1970s. Post-1945, the Press moved its print production away from subjective art and towards a rational and measurable science which had its

foundations in the laboratory rather than the studio. Printing at the Kynoch Press became a modern process.

Prior to 1939 the organisation and structure of the Press was not as developed as it became after 1945. Before 1939, the Press staff were expected to diversify their skills: salesmen doubled-up as layout artists and compositors assumed the role of typographers. There was a merging of occupational boundaries, and it was not until after 1945 that some skills became acknowledged as independent professions. After 1945 there was a greater degree of professionalism at the Press. As a result of evolving technologies and increased competition from the rest of the printing industry, the Press was forced (like many others) to make its services more specialised: a sales-force was established as a necessary, independent and vital part of the business and dedicated sales people were recruited; professional typographers or graphic designers emerged at the Press and were employed as part of its fully equipped service and by the 1960s the Press had become one of the rare breed of designer-printers. Alongside the recruitment of new professionals, the Press was also forced to find a product by which to promote itself. It was no longer acceptable merely to be a general commercial printer; survival dictated the development of a specialist service and the Press established Kynoch International Print (KIP) to promote its 'printing for export' service. The Press extended its horizons towards Europe, it became international in complexion and attitude and through KIP it educated its clients in the importance of design for foreign markets.

Before 1939 the Kynoch Press was vernacular in its approach to design: it favoured indigenous rather than continental typefaces; was dependent upon the influence of the book on its work; used familiar imperial paper sizes; employed domestic artists on its publications; and was an adherent of essentially British design movements. After 1945 the Press successfully moved away from the parochial conservatism of the pre-1939 period to a more liberal and international attitude towards design. Its work was freed from the conventions of book production and it developed original solutions more appropriate for the genres with which it worked. Modern ideas, influenced by Jan Tschichold, could be seen in many publications after 1960: continental sans serif types were used for a more contemporary and international 'look' to design; the DIN series of paper sizes were increasingly used; new substrates were experimented with; designers from abroad, or with an international perspective, were seconded to the Press for various projects; and it found inspiration from design movements in America and Europe.

Despite re-equipping for modern production, finding a product appropriate to post-1945 trade and developing a design language which was contemporary and international, the Press failed to maintain a footing in the post-war printing industry. A victim of the parent company that brought it success and of the economic depression in the United Kingdom in the 1980s, the Press was an unfortunate casualty of circumstances, going the way of many medium-sized commercial printing houses. It finally ceasing trading in 1981.

Chapter 1

1876–1981
FOUNDATIONS
background to the Kynoch Press

From its birth in 1876 to its demise just over a century later, the Kynoch Press of Witton in Birmingham remained a constituent part of an industry whose interests were very different from that of printing. It was an industry whose early development was dependent upon the character and enthusiasm of one man, George Kynoch, whose ability to succeed in his chosen field was the result of being infected by the enterprising spirit of one particular city, Birmingham. Over the course of a century, and as a result of successive mergers and takeovers, the company considerably expanded from its humble workshop origins and went on to form a substantial element of the mighty Imperial Chemical Industries. The Press, a component part of the company, was swept along with the tide of expansion, always maintaining its identity and autonomy in its daily life, but finding its fate to be inextricably tied to the roller-coaster existence of the parent company. It is, therefore, useful to take a brief look at the remarkable man, his company and the city, who were to form the backdrop to the Kynoch Press.

George Kynoch[1] was an immense and colourful man—immense in every sense of the word and in all aspects of his nature. He was the founding father of a vast industrial empire which manufactured, amongst many other items, ammunition percussion caps, and as an international business man Kynoch was *persona grata* with the imperial heads of both Europe and the British Empire. He was also a local dignitary, a zealous patron and president of Aston Villa Football Club and a Conservative Member of Parliament for Aston. In addition, George Kynoch was the impetus behind the printing house of the Lion Works at Witton, Birmingham. The printing house started as an unpretentious endeavour, but grew into a successful enterprise that came to withstand a century of industrial, technological and social revolution.

All larger-than-life figures leave behind fertile ground upon which to build legends and George Kynoch is no exception, for he was, in every sense of the word, a big man with a towering personality who climbed dangerously high and fell ignominiously low. A century after his death there remains little solid documentation of his life, but a received wisdom and colourful folklore successfully perpetuate his reputation.

Large and bearded, sporting a cravat and wearing a rose in his lapel, George Kynoch cut a formidable and extravagant figure as he strode through his ammunition factory flourishing a cane. He inspired both awe and affection, instilled confidence and ignited people's motivation. An indefatigable 'doer', he was an inspired, if not measured, businessman who was undeterred by his failures and exalted by his successes. George Kynoch was a societal, mercantile and industrial entrepreneur, an arch-nonconformist who excelled in a city populated by religious, political and instinctual nonconformists. He was a maverick and an adventurer who pursued any avenue, however bizarre, which promised excitement or fortune. Wealth and social status were the objectives he sought and achieved without compromise. However, his inexhaustible energy encouraged him to take unacceptable moral and financial risks. Accompanying his insatiable lust for fame and fortune, Kynoch had a commensurate passion for the fleshly, and stories abound of his numerous liaisons with girls from his ammunition works—encounters which sometimes produced unwished-for progeny. Fable also recounts Kynoch's generous paternity payments, made available by way of restitution, to the unfortunate girls in their weekly pay-packets and of the additional payments to those poor unfortunates who had given birth to twins! George Kynoch, acknowledged as a man of ambition and determination, who exuded charisma, was not wholly without humanity.

This is how received wisdom paints the Kynoch portrait.

The known facts of George Kynoch's life record that he was born on 22 August 1834 at Peterhead, on the easternmost point of the Aberdeenshire coastline, in Scotland. His humble origins, as the youngest son of a journeyman tailor, gave no intimation of the unpredictable and noteworthy career that lay before him, nor was his coastal-backwater childhood an obvious preparation for life in the land-locked industrial city of Birmingham—a city where he was to find fame and fortune on an international scale.

George Kynoch received what education was available to him from the local National School, but he aspired to greater things and was frustrated by his limited schooling and restricted horizons and left home at the earliest opportunity, making his way south towards England. George Kynoch went first to Glasgow where he worked in an insurance office and then to Worcester, in the English Midlands, where he was employed as a bank clerk. He arrived in Birmingham in 1852 where he took a job as a ledger clerk in a large bank. England's industrial heartland changed Kynoch's fate, stimulated his desire for success and wealth, and opened his eyes to an abundance of new opportunities.

By the nineteenth century, Birmingham was a long-established industrial town whose well-entrenched manufacturing foundations excited Kynoch's imagination.[2] Birmingham, city of a thousand trades, produced small items made of iron such as nails, bits and bridles, cutlery and small-wares known as 'toys' which were found in homes throughout Europe and America. It also manufactured small-arms. The city was a seething mass of industry and George Kynoch must have found Birmingham very much as Mr Pickwick did:

> the murky atmosphere, the paths of cinders and brick dust, the deep red glow of the furnace fires in the distance, the volumes of dense smoke issuing heavily forth from high toppling chimneys, blackening and obscuring every thing around; the glare of distant lights, the ponderous wagons which toiled along the road, laden with clashing rods of iron, or piled with heavy goods—all betokened their rapid approach to the great working town of Birmingham . . . .The streets were thronged with work-people, the hum of labour resounded from every house, lights gleamed from the long casement windows in the attic stories and the whirl of wheels and the noise of machinery shook the trembling walls.[3]

This drama of industrial production excited George Kynoch's imagination and lured him away from his conventional and staid profession as a bank clerk. Industrial Birmingham showed Kynoch an alternative means of working, another method by which a fortune might be made; it was the antithesis of banking, it fired his imagination and enticed him away from convention and predictability. George Kynoch felt immediately at home in the city and traded-in his old skills for new talents.

During the nineteenth century Birmingham underwent such rapid industrial expansion that its output could not be met by the native population alone. A well organised and affluent town, Birmingham offered social and working conditions which attracted émigrés from across the country, including such famous names as Avis, Baskerville, Chamberlain, Hector, Hutton and Scoffield. In moving to Birmingham George Kynoch followed in the footsteps of a number of Scottish immigrants such as James Watt who invented the steam-engine, William Small who discovered the properties of oxygen and William

Murdoch, the inventor of coal-gas lighting; all were men who settled in Birmingham and who made significant contributions to the wealth and reputation of the city and by whom the nation as a whole prospered. George Kynoch was also to make his mark on Birmingham, Europe and the Empire.

In the mid-nineteenth century Birmingham was the centre of the gun-making trade. Alongside the production of small-arms were the ancillary industries of cartridge and percussion cap manufacturing and it was to this lucrative but perilous world that George Kynoch was drawn. In 1856 George Kynoch, at the age of twenty-two, joined the percussion cap business of Pursall and Phillips, a small enterprise based in Whittall Street in the heart of Birmingham's gun-makers' quarter. The company was one of the many hundreds of small workshops which populated the city. No records exist as to Kynoch's employment (it was probably a clerical post) but Kynoch instinctively realised the small-arms industry was one which could make him very wealthy.

In 1859 the Whittall Street factory was destroyed by an explosion all too common in the ammunition business. The accident killed nineteen employees and a number of passers-by, many others suffered injury and much of the surrounding property was damaged. The factory was re-built, but the deprecations of the city fathers and the coroner, the censorious comments in the press and the disapprobation of the local community forced Pursall and Phillips to move out of the city. In 1861 Mr Pursall applied for a licence to build a factory at Witton, three miles north-west of Birmingham. The licence was granted and George Kynoch was placed in charge, becoming works proprietor twelve months later in 1862. George Kynoch the hired-hand had rapidly become the master. The works were re-named Kynoch and Co., but were known locally as the Lion Works, after the stone statue of a lion straddling the factory gates. There is no record of how Kynoch equipped himself with the knowledge and financial wherewithal to become proprietor, but his marriage to Helen, daughter of Samuel Birley, a wealthy local jeweller, may have provided him with the necessary money, and for technical knowledge he probably relied upon his instinctive talent, quick intelligence and abounding self-confidence. George Kynoch's business grew with astonishing speed into an industrial empire immense by contemporary standards and soon world-famous for its sporting and military ammunition.

In 1862, the Witton site occupied a four-acre plot in a rural setting surrounded by babbling brooks, smiling meadows and green trees, but it did not remain a rural idyll for long as the area quickly became urbanised by the Kynoch works whose presence introduced the first chimney stacks to the area, considerably increased the local population and brought the first public cemetery to the district in anticipation of further fatalities! The Witton works eventually grew into a 250-acre site.

From the beginning, business was rapid and profitable. Orders were secured from several foreign powers and a large commission came from the British government for percussion caps for use in the new British Army Enfield rifle.[4] The significance of this commission was that it stimulated Kynoch's interest in metals as raw material, prompting him to set up his own brass-rolling mill, the product of which was used in the manufacture of Kynoch's most successful enterprise—brass cartridges. The Kynoch factory expanded rapidly and by the early 1880s it was manufacturing 400,000 cartridges a day. To handle the work-load, the original twelve employees had expanded to 800 people who worked on a site so vast that it had its own transport system, hospital and fire service.

In 1883, twenty-one years after opening his factory, George Kynoch's empire had reached its zenith. The humble Glasgow clerk had become the owner of Britain's second-largest ammunition factory. He was potentate over an ammunition works which had grown to the proportions of a small town and which possessed all those facilities commensurate with town life and which was not dissimilar to that described by George Bernard Shaw in his play *Major Barbara*:

> It is almost a smokeless town . . . of slender chimney shafts, beautifully situated and beautiful in itself. The best view of it is obtained from the crest of a slope about half a mile to the east, where the high explosives are dealt with. The foundry lies hidden in the depths between, the tops of its chimneys sprouting like huge skittles into the middle distance. Across the crest runs an emplacement of concrete, with a fire-step, and a parapet which suggests fortification, because there is a huge cannon . . . peering across it at the town . . . the parapet stops short of the shed, leaving a gap which is the beginning of the path down the hill, through the foundry to the town.[5]

George Kynoch's empire was not restricted to Birmingham; he had extended his domain to Liverpool, Glasgow and London and additionally to over thirty cities world-wide. George Kynoch became fabulously wealthy as he supplied ammunition to wars around the globe and because he was always willing to 'give arms to all men who offered an honest price for them, without respect of person or principle'.

As Kynoch's industrial reputation grew, he found new commitments both within Birmingham public life and in national politics. His

appetite for political and public service demanded an increasing proportion of his time and money. To finance his external interests George
Kynoch took the disastrous step of converting his business into a limited
company.

In 1884, George Kynoch received a substantial fee for the sale of his
business which was re-named Kynoch and Co. Ltd. He was retained as
the Managing Director and a board of six London-based directors was
appointed. Within a year the company went into decline as it lost lucrative government contracts due to defective quality control arising from
George Kynoch's diminished presence on the Witton site and remote-
control management by directors in London. The business developed
an escalating overdraft which was aggravated by George Kynoch using
company money for private undertakings, unable to understand that
the company's revenue was no longer his own personal fund.

He had been too long the master to become a happy servant.

By 1888 the shareholders realised that all was not well with Kynoch
and Co. Ltd. They concluded that the lack of co-operation between the
Managing Director and the rest of the board was the key to the company's decline and recommended the abolition of the role of Managing
Director with the appointment of a Local Board with more frequent

An artist's impression of
the Kynoch works
in 1886.

visits by the Main Board to Birmingham. In December 1889 George Kynoch's links with the company were severed as he resigned on grounds of ill-health and left for self-imposed exile in South Africa. He died, fourteen months later on 28 February 1891, in Johannesburg, aged 57 years, owing his company thousands of pounds. The self-made potentate had finally fallen from grace, a pitiful end for a man with so many gifts.

With Kynoch's departure, the company passed through the most perilous months of its history with a huge trading loss, a reputation for poor workmanship, inadequate supervision and low morale. But in 1888 a new Managing Director was appointed—Arthur Chamberlain, brother to Joseph, Liberal Member of Parliament and uncle to both Neville, Conservative Prime Minister and Joseph Austen, Conservative Foreign Secretary.

Arthur Chamberlain[6] had great ambition for the company which was now named Kynoch Ltd. He was as far removed from his flamboyant predecessor, George Kynoch, as could be imagined, for where Kynoch had the looks and actions of a grand impresario, Arthur Chamberlain was altogether more austere in his appearance. With the thunderous sermons of Birmingham's nonconformist pulpit weighing on his conscience, Chamberlain's character was proud and severe, he was quarrelsome and had a single-minded determination which checked any inclination to intemperance. He was an individual with great drive, who inherited the family characteristics of honesty, ruthless ability and chilly ruggedness, characteristics he used to good effect when he attempted, and succeeded, in resurrecting the company's dwindling fortunes. Arthur Chamberlain guided the company for nearly 25 years, bringing to the business a high degree of mercantile aggression and radically increasing the company capital. Chamberlain had a policy of making the works independent of outside suppliers: he established for Kynoch Ltd a manufacturing basis which was wholly self-sufficient, broadened company activities and responded to an increased demand for explosives by developing more factories.[7] By the end of the nineteenth century, Kynoch Ltd was the world's largest producer of cordite, the explosive material used for propelling bullets.

The Great War of 1914–18 concentrated the efforts of Kynoch Ltd on the production of small-arms ammunition. The factory was enlarged and the personnel was increased to 18,000. In 1914 Arthur Chamberlain died and was succeeded by his son Arthur Chamberlain junior. Despite the war frenzy, plans were being made behind the scenes for adapting to conditions after the end of the conflict. Before the Great

War the British explosives industry was operated by seventeen major producers with twenty-three subsidiaries at home and abroad. It was evident that peace-time conditions could not support all these producers and an explosives merger was proposed. In November 1918 Curtis Harvey, Kynoch Ltd, Ely Brothers, Bickford Smith, Nobel Explosives and twelve other much smaller companies amalgamated to form Explosive Trades Ltd. In 1921, Explosive Trades Ltd became Nobel Industries which was responsible for all Britain's gunpowder, explosives, detonators and ammunition. Kynoch Ltd had become a constituent part of a great organisation.

In the 1920s, the Kynoch factory at Witton went through lean times. Desperate efforts were made to secure a market, find suitable commodities for production and to convert Kynoch's large works into peace-time activities. Nobel Industries rationalised all the United Kingdom's non-ferrous metal manufacturing on the Kynoch site which also became the largest producer of sporting ammunition in the United Kingdom. An unlikely but very successful department opened at Witton for the manufacture of Lightning zip-fasteners, and Amalgamated Carburettors Ltd (Amal) evolved into another highly successful arm for the company.

By 1926 business was flourishing, but there were plans for a company which would dwarf even Nobel Industries. The new company, Imperial Chemical Industries (ICI) was an amalgamation of Brunner Mond and Co. Ltd, Nobel Industries Ltd, United Alkali Co. and the British Dyestuffs Corporation Ltd. There were many reasons behind the merger. Each company was reliant upon the same set of raw products and the waste product of one company was often the raw material for another. By uniting the companies each could share resources and benefit from administrative, commercial and technical economies, and advances could be both shared and exploited. ICI was a worldwide organisation with nearly 170 offices around the globe, all of which helped in the progress of the Empire, but its production capacity lay with its eleven British manufacturing units, termed Divisions (Alkali, Billingham, Dyestuffs, Explosives, General Chemicals, Leathercloth, Lime, Metals, Paints, Plastics and Salt Division), which were, in a sense, separate companies. In the course of 64 years, George Kynoch's business had become an integral part of the largest company in the British Empire. When war ended in 1945, ICI expanded with the addition of four divisions (Central Agricultural Control, Pharmaceuticals, Terylene Council and Wilton). ICI was then operating from over 80 factories across the

United Kingdom and employing 80,000 people in the production of 12,000 different products.

With the formation of ICI, priority was given to metal manufacturing in Birmingham. In 1928 Witton became the headquarters for the Metals Group of ICI and in 1929 the name of Kynoch was banished in favour of ICI (Metals). In 1930, ICI (Metals) absorbed three more metal-producing firms of considerable size making the Group the largest producer of non-ferrous metals in the country. During World War II, ICI (Metals) was a hive of activity with the number of employees at Witton exceeding 20,000 and with an additional 26 production units in twenty locales. In 1945 arrangements were made for ICI (Metals) to go into voluntary liquidation; it ceased to exist as a separate organisation and was renamed ICI Metals Division. Changes were made once again in 1962 when ICI Metals Division became a new operating company— Imperial Metals Industries (Kynoch) Ltd (IMI), the first time the name of Kynoch had been included in the company title for nearly 40 years. It was a wholly-owned subsidiary of ICI, administered by a new holding company IMI Ltd which now exists as IMI plc and which was the last banner under which the Kynoch Press operated.

This was the environment in which the Kynoch Press worked. It was a world very different from that occupied by its rivals. Unlike its competitors, the Press was never a family concern governed by the intimate, personal hand which directs a family business, it was never in the managerial hands of one individual for very long, there was no continuity of management and it performed against an ever shifting backdrop. The Press was not an independent, autonomous trade printer with sole control over its destiny; it was firmly linked into another industry. This association with manufacturing could have proved a disadvantage which kept the printing office forever tied to a vast but routine range of domestic work. In fact, the Press grew steadily over the years, expanding in size, scope and facilities, matching its parent in development and establishing a reputation as a first-class printer. It may be argued that this happened because of, rather than in spite of, its close dependence on the world of manufacturing. Companies of the stature of Kynoch Ltd, Nobel, ICI and IMI which operate in the cruelly competitive world of international trade have no room for sidelines which bring them neither profit nor prestige. For the Press to survive, it had to prove itself either as a viable commercial proposition, or as a press with a reputation that would provide the services and the goods which matched the same outstanding quality as was demanded of all other ICI products.

Chapter 2

1876–1899
GEORGE KYNOCH
formation of the Kynoch Press

George Kynoch established his printing house in about 1876. In doing so, Kynoch indulged himself in what both Thomas Carlyle and William Thackeray saw as two of 'the three elements of modern civilization: gunpowder, printing and the Protestant religion'.[1] Printing and explosives were two industries which always happily co-existed in the heart of Birmingham's gun-makers quarter, with both the gunsmiths and the printers being dependent upon the same raw material—metal.

From the outset, Kynoch and Co. needed printing in great quantity and the work was distributed amongst several local printers, but the vast majority went to Silk and Terry of Warstock Road, Birmingham,[2] and here it remained for fifteen years until 1876 when George Kynoch abruptly severed the contract. The agreement was concluded, if legend is to believed, and there is no lack of circumstantial evidence, when George Kynoch's eye for the ladies led him to try his luck with a local music-hall actress. Unfortunately, he found he had a rival in the shape of his trusted printer. The printer won the lady but lost the Kynoch account when, in a fit of pique as a result of his defeat, George Kynoch withdrew his orders from Silk and Terry and decided to print his own material.

Not many printers in the nineteenth century would have admitted to owing their origins to *l'amour*, that most unpredictable of human urges, but so runs Kynoch legend.

Alternatively, if George Kynoch started rolling his own brass in order to control the quality, supply and price of the raw material for his cartridges, he may also have started his printing and box-making shop for the same reasons. The work required by the main business represented a substantial order for any printer and a sizeable bill for Kynoch and Co. George Kynoch would probably have viewed starting his own in-house printers both as a means of saving money, and a way of introducing into the company domain an area of production which, when with Silk and Terry, was beyond his control. It was an unusual move, for printing was not an industry in which George Kynoch was well-versed, but lack of knowledge never deterred him from pursuing any venture which took his fancy. Some of George Kynoch's other peripheral activities suffered untimely and ignominious deaths, but the printing house was destined to survive as an outstanding success.

In about 1876, whether through devilment, inspiration or good business acumen, George Kynoch started his printing house. It was not yet called the Kynoch Press, but it traded under the consonant title of The Printing Office of the Lion Works, a name which gave it status and gravitas, but which also firmly defined its ownership. From the beginning, the Press was merely regarded as an element of a greater whole.

The Printing Office of the Lion Works was founded in unceremonious circumstances.[3] There is no record as to the precise location of the original printing house other than that it started business at Witton in an unprepossessing shed which was cramped and inadequate. By 1896 the Press had been transferred to equally confined accommodation in a stable attic adjoining the railway line on the perimeter of the Witton site, but in 1898 the Press was moved to more centrally located, ground-floor accommodation where the new buildings were large and bright with space for a composing room, press room, stereo plant and a small book-binding section.[4]

George Kynoch also set up a Paper Box factory which was managed by the Press and which was located close-by in what was known as Shed 13. The foreman of the Paper Box factory was Mr Neal who had been recruited, along with all his own equipment, in 1871. Management of the Paper Box factory remained with the Neal family for several decades, for when Mr Neal retired he was succeeded by his son. The Paper Box factory produced rigid boxes, and later folding boxes, for the ammunition, fog signals and other commodities manufactured by Kynoch and Co., but commissions also came from businesses outside Witton. Warwick House, costumier and millinery makers of Birmingham, came to Paper Box for their packaging, work which must have provided a charming antidote to that generally required of Mr Neal and his assistants.

Kynoch and Co. also opened a paper mill in Ireland for the manufacture of vast quantities of the firm yet elastic paper used for sporting cartridges. The cartridge paper was transported from Dublin to the Port of London on the S.S. *Kynoch* or the S.S. *Anglesey*, the two cargo vessels owned by Kynoch and Co. Ltd and euphoniously referred to as the 'fleet'; the paper was then conveyed by canal to Birmingham and into the Kynoch Press, which then printed the cartridge wrappers. Although the Kynoch mills were primarily for the manufacture of cartridge paper, the company also launched its own range of burnt sienna paper called 'Irish Parchment', which became a product particularly popular in Ireland.

Initially, the Kynoch Press employed eight people: a foreman who was in charge of the printing house, one compositor, and four others including a wood-engraver, a man, a woman and a boy, but by the end of the nineteenth century, the number of staff had greatly increased. Mr R. Fryer, a Kynoch man to the backbone and one of the longest-serving employees of the company, was appointed to the curious role of manager of both the printing house and the sporting ammunition department—the Press was not yet large enough, or of sufficient importance, to warrant the dedicated attention of a single individual.[5]

The Kynoch Press started out with a meagre collection of machinery: two old platens worked by hand, a hand-press and one small power-assisted cylinder machine.[6] When it was relocated to the stable attic, the two platens and the cylinder machine were retained but the hand-press was replaced by four small platen presses worked by power. The plant was expanded in 1897 when a litho machine was bought for £130 and two small Allen presses at £38 each arrived in the printing department. When the Press moved once again in 1898, the original power-assisted cylinder machine was replaced by a Bremner cylinder machine which was twice its size. The composing room was equipped with three frames of the customary range of lively, if extraneous, Victorian types which ranged from the exotic through to the monstrous and which were common currency in composing rooms across the country. The type frames included a selection of faces for text setting such as Cheltenham, Caledonian and Windsor, and display types from the foundries of Miller and Richard and Caslon including Milanese, Monumental and a collection of floral letters. The stereo and book-binding section were equipped with a wooden ruling machine, a punching machine and other stereo and book-binding equipment.

The Press was primarily required to print the wrappers for the sporting and military cartridges produced by Kynoch and Co. In addition, it printed the large variety of material connected with the running of the main business, or the private needs of George Kynoch including advertising material, pamphlets, stationery and an abundance of ephemera.

Two posters produced by the Kynoch Press at the end of the nineteenth century. They demonstrate the eclectic range of type faces in use at the Kynoch Press at that time.

By the close of the nineteenth century, the Press had progressed to printing more than just utilitarian material for the ammunition works.

The first of many ammunition catalogues published and printed by the Press was issued in 1897.[7] The catalogues gave the Press an opportunity to produce technical material of both substance and quality. The catalogues were an inventory of products and prices but they also served as technical reference manuals and were the first of their kind in the ammunition and small-arms industry. Multifarious in size, but always landscape in format, they were brimming with information which was illegibly composed in Caledonian italic set to a measure too long for the type size, and typically accompanied by borders and decoration. Illustrated throughout and printed in anything up to ten colours, they were expensive productions, impressive ambassadors for the business, and the first real test of Kynoch Press production standards.

In 1899, work began on *The Kynoch Journal*, a technical publication which involved some complexity of setting as well as skill in printing.[8] *The Kynoch Journal* contained articles, both technical and popular, on all aspects of shooting and included features on contemporary ammunition developments made at the Kynoch Works. A full-time editor, J. F. P. Lewis, was employed on the *Journal*, the production of which ran to 36 issues and appeared bi-monthly until 1904 when it was reduced to quarterly appearances. Its typography was a combination of the professional and the home-spun. Fronted by a title-page with hand-drawn lettering which showed its nineteenth-century roots and a pen-and-ink drawing by Raoul, the text was professionally and competently composed in Old Style and De Vinne. It was sold on subscription for 3*s.*, a sum which the Press claimed merely covered the cost of production which was particularly high because of the substrate and the number of half-tone blocks required. *The Kynoch Journal*, like the ammunition catalogues, was an expensive, solid and commendable example of early Kynoch Press printing.

The Press also produced a considerable stream of commemorative literature to mark the occasion of visiting dignitaries, and numerous menus and programmes were printed to celebrate retirements, long-service awards and festive staff dinners. The first of these programmes was produced in 1896 for G. Kynoch and Co.'s annual staff dinner and smoking concert. Although printed at 'Kynoch's Private Printing Office' it was designed and illustrated by a member of Kynoch and

LEFT
The cover of the
first edition of
The Kynoch Journal,
issued in 1899.
The illustration, by Raoul,
is of the entrance to
Kynoch's Lion Works
at Witton.

RIGHT
The cover to the
programme for
G. Kynoch and Co's
annual staff dinner and
smoking concert of 1896.
Designed by
George H Stacey,
it was printed at Kynoch's
Private Printing Office.

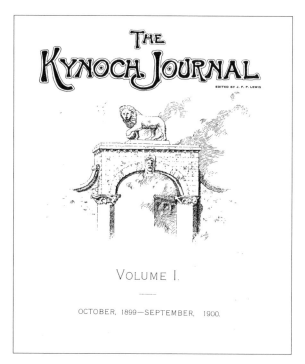

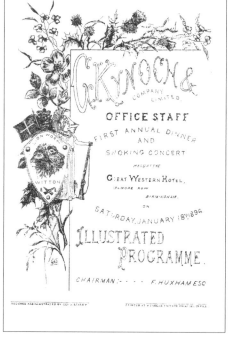

Co.'s own staff, George H. Stacey, in the flamboyant style of an enthusiastic amateur, but subsequent commemorative literature received a
more professional treatment.

By the end of the nineteenth century the Kynoch Press had grown
into a busy printing house which served an industrial empire. It was
recognised as an important part of the Works and a department of
which the main company was justifiably proud:

> It has, like all other departments connected with the name of Kynoch, grown
> very rapidly of late years, and is at the present moment one of the best-equipped
> offices of its kind in Birmingham. It prints the whole of the scores of millions of
> sporting cartridge cases sold by the Sporting Department every year, besides all
> the stationery and advertising matter for the several works. No work is too great
> or too small for it, a thousand price lists being turned out with the same precision
> as a dozen labels. Take away this department from the Witton works and a void
> would be left which would be hard to fill. [9]

But the Press was, as it always would be, merely a department of the
main business and totally beholden to the parent company for work.
The Press had no need to seek external work because the needs of the
main business ensured it worked to capacity and as the cost of printing
was absorbed into the over-heads of the parent this provided the Press
with a cushioning which freed it from any obligation to make a profit. A
comfortable position to be in, but it was a relationship in which the Press
was necessarily subservient to the needs of the Company, wholly dependent upon it for resources, and dangerously reliant upon it for its success.

Chapter 3

1900–1921

DONALD HOPE

expansion of the Kynoch Press

Between 1900 and 1921 the main company underwent changes of such great magnitude that the Kynoch Press was forced to either adapt with its parent or perish. By 1921, the Press had not only expanded to accommodate the ever increasing needs of its demanding parent, but it had also started to establish an identity of its own, develop its independence, and to source and gather work from the hitherto unexplored outside world.

Arthur Chamberlain, successor to George Kynoch as Managing Director of Kynoch Ltd, was father to eight daughters. In 1900 the fourth of his progeny, Bertha, married Donald Hope who was then 31 years old.[1] It was Chamberlain's practice to place his sons-in-law into any one of the many companies in which he had an interest. Kynoch Ltd was the largest of Chamberlain's enterprises and in 1901 he made Donald Hope a part-time director of the Company with particular responsibility for the Kynoch Press.[2]

H. Donald Hope was born in Birmingham in 1869. He attended King Edward VI Grammar School, Birmingham, followed by Wolverhampton Grammar School. At the age of eighteen, he started work in the family business of Henry Hope and Sons of Birmingham, manufacturers of metal windows and their accessories, hothouses, conservatories and central heating.[3] Donald Hope was tall, dark and strikingly good-looking with a stylish demeanour and dapper appearance and he demonstrated a proclivity for fine clothes, monocles and Turkish cigarettes. He was an exotic and cultured figure with a refined intellect. To his family he was a remote and unusual father and husband, but to his many friends and business associates he was a kindly, honourable and gentle man who had a mercantile and industrial instinct which was balanced by an appreciation of the refined arts and a natural love for, and interest in, human beings, as his obituary writer on the *Birmingham Post and Mail* wrote:

> . . . a man absolutely devoid of pretence or affectation. It is common knowledge that his was a first-class intelligence, active in directing the great firm that bears his name. But as he rigorously shunned publicity, only his family and friends had the opportunity of knowing him as an assiduous reader and collector of fine books, an enlightened lover of the visual arts. [4]

Hope's appreciation of art and design came from several sources. As an adolescent he learned draughting skills whilst watching his father who, by all accounts, had an unsurpassed ability as a draughtsman. The workshops at Hope's Windows had gained for themselves a reputation as champions of the designs and spirit of John Ruskin and William Morris and for this reason their work was much sought-after around the world, particularly in America. Hope's associations with architectural firms in Birmingham and London further exposed him to contemporary views of arts and crafts and he was particularly influenced by the ideas of William Haywood, a young architect and partner in the Birmingham architectural practice of Buckland and Haywood whom Hope's had commissioned to design their bronze alphabets. In the evenings Donald Hope studied drawing at the Birmingham School of Arts and Crafts,[5] and his interest in fine art and design was further developed through his friendship with Whitworth Wallis, Keeper of the Birmingham Museum and Art Gallery. Most important were his associations with the Birmingham Guild of Handicraft[6] which had been founded in 1880 and whose aim was: 'to supply handmade articles superior in beauty of design and soundness of workmanship to those made by machinery; and to make only such as shall give just pleasure both to the craftsman and to the buyer of them'. Under Arthur Gaskin and James Richardson Halliday, the Guild printed fine books and magazines, and it was here that Hope developed his interest in design for, and production of, printing. The relationship between the Guild and Donald Hope was strong, for Henry Hope and Sons formed one of the few points of contact between the trades and the artist-craftsmen of the Guild, they were one of a limited number of commercial firms which played a part in the movement. It was also at the Guild that Hope was introduced to the political, religious and artistic beliefs of the nonconformist Unitarian families who were at the core of both the Guild and Birmingham life, and it was here that he met the Chamberlain family.

With his practical and theoretical experience of art, craft and industry,

Donald Hope came to believe that the decorative arts could and should be applied to industrial mass production and that such an alliance might raise public taste. What Hope lacked was the opportunity to put his beliefs into practice, but with his appointment to Kynoch Ltd a ready-made vehicle was at hand in the shape of the Kynoch Press.

Donald Hope was an uncharacteristic choice for a part-time director of Kynoch Ltd, but his enthusiasm for the sporting shot made the company an appropriate environment for Hope, and his interest in design made him suited for, amongst other duties, taking responsibility for the Kynoch Press, which was an inheritance for which the main company had little understanding. At the Press, Hope found he was in a position to test out his theories on design, and that these theories could be implemented by a printing house which he could control to an extent not possible when working with external suppliers. The Press was to be Donald Hope's typographic experiment, but it was an unlikely vehicle for such a trial because it was a printing house whose staple diet was the production of ammunition boxes and utilitarian literature which gave little opportunity for typographic experimentation. But under Donald Hope the Press started to develop an enviable, but justifiable, reputation for being at the forefront of the printing revival not just in Birmingham, but the country as a whole.

When Donald Hope arrived at the Kynoch Press it was a thriving element in an expanding industrial empire. The expansion of the main company brought an increase in work for the Press and this in turn necessitated an increase in the workforce. The Press had become of sufficient importance to need a knowledgeable and sympathetic controlling figure-head. Hope was in a position to inspire change, but his time was limited for he was seldom at Kynoch's for more than two days a week, frequently being called away on business for the main company, travelling to America, Canada and South Africa. He also lacked experience as a hands-on printer and this meant that the practical work had to be delegated to another. The increasing volume of work and the degree of specialist knowledge required to run a printing house necessitated the recruitment of a full-time Press manager, and in November 1903 Mr J. C. Forbes was appointed to the job. Forbes was an experienced printer, having come into contact with new approaches to printing when he was employed at a printing house in the United States. It is almost certain that during his frequent trips to the United States that Donald Hope had seen, and been impressed by, American printing. It is also probable that Hope had met Forbes on one of his trips to America and persuaded him to return to England and to come and work at the Kynoch Press in order to assist Hope with his typographic vision. Between them, Hope and Forbes set about to change the face of printing at the Kynoch Press:

> With the advent of Mr J. C. Forbes as manager, who had the backing of Mr Donald Hope, a keen disciple of good typography and progress, a new epoch in the method of printing was developed from experience gained by Mr Forbes in America. This was known as a purist style in which Caslon type of varying sizes was used with telling effect, also the American idea of balancing colour. No longer was it permissible for compositors to set a different style of type for each line. The Kynoch Press pioneered this class of work in this country. Mr Forbes left the Press in 1913, but he laid the foundation of good printing. [7]

In 1913, Mr Forbes was replaced by his deputy, Mr C. S. Cowling, who was Press manager until 1921.

Donald Hope sought to update the Kynoch Press by installing modern equipment and encouraging contemporary attitudes towards printing. He first turned his attention on the composing room and it was in this department that the Kynoch Press was to perform a quiet, but startling, typographic revolution, one which was to place it apart from its contemporaries and competitors. The first change was in 1901 when Donald Hope started a programme of clearing-out and replacing the types held at the Press. He ordered the quaint and archaic nineteenth-century faces to be consigned to the melting-pot and, on the advice of Emery Walker, Hope re-equipped the composing room with the clean and classical lines of Stephenson Blake's Caslon Old Face, a reasonable book type of legible design which was installed as a counter-balance to the unreasonable advertising letters, frequently of illegible design, which filled the Press type racks in the early years of the twentieth century. Caslon, a revival from the eighteenth century, had been resurrected in the 1840s by the Chiswick Press, and although its popularity was slowly spreading, its use amongst ordinary printers in 1901 was not extensive. When Donald Hope brought Caslon into the composing room, the Kynoch Press was the first printer in Birmingham to re-introduce the face into its racks. Caslon was a type which was to be blessed with longevity, and it was in use at the Press from the time of its acquisition until it ceased trading in 1981. It was a face which was to prove very popular, and it established the reputation of the Press by aligning it with American purist typographic ideas, thereby placing it in the vanguard of British printing in the early years of the twentieth century and bringing it to the attention of a number of discerning customers. When

Hope purchased Caslon Old Face, he inadvertently lay the foundation stones for the future passion for type revival at the Press.

The composing room was further modernised when, on 8 April 1920, the Press invested in Monotype composition equipment. The installation consisted of four composition casters, two super-casters and three keyboards. The Press chose not to equip itself for machine composition until some years after its nearest rivals (Cowell's installed Monotype in 1903, Lund Humphries 1903, Curwen Press 1906, CUP 1913). Having dispensed with its archaic range of nineteenth-century founders' text faces and having set up a typographically advanced plant furnished with Founders Caslon, Garamond and Baskerville, the Press was not going to commit itself to a mechanical composition system which was only manufacturing the dated range of Clarendons and Cheltenhams that the Press had so recently jettisoned. It was only when Monotype, under the guidance of Stanley Morison, introduced its range of classical revival typefaces that the Press committed itself to machine composition.

Progress in the composing room was also matched by some modernisation in the press room when, in 1918, the Press bought its first Miehle printing press, the most modern machine of its kind that was available.

Up until Hope's arrival the Press had only produced uninspired utilitarian literature, but the material was proficiently produced and complex and varied enough to need versatile compositors and pressmen. It was not the class of work with which Donald Hope could make his design experiments and the Press was in need of a greater range of material with which to display its new Caslon typeface. Donald Hope helped the Press to extend its range of work by bringing Henry Hope's own trade catalogues to the Press.[8] Henry Hope's published literature was in desperate need of a typographic overhaul because it was so illegible in its use of nineteenth-century typefaces and exotic ornamentation as to be wholly unreadable and unquestionably impractical. When production of their literature was transferred to the Press this gave both the Kynoch Press and Henry Hope's the opportunity to revise completely their respective typographic approaches.

Hope's material was aimed at architects, particularly those who shared the company's design beliefs, and Henry Hope's felt their publicity should be an extension and reflection of these beliefs. The first publications produced by the Press for Hope's Windows saw a change in typographic style for both the Press and Hope's. The catalogues produced for Henry Hope by the Press in the early 1900s were composed

using the newly introduced Caslon Old Face, a signal to customers that both Henry Hope's and the Kynoch Press were at the forefront of contemporary typographic thought. The work was of a high quality with considered composition, excellent press work and six-colour printing reproduced on well-chosen material. In the early 1920s, the firm launched a consciously collectable and wholly delightful series of catalogues. Produced to a constant 202 x 130 mm each catalogue had the appearance of a diminutive book and was set in the newly released Monotype Garamond. All the catalogues were vibrantly and charmingly illustrated by a Mrs G. Barraclough whose richly coloured illustrations were reproduced in six colours using either a stencil process or Ben Day tints.[9] Today these catalogues retain the same warmth of feeling and colour that accompanied their first publication, fulfilling Henry Hope's claim that although they made very good windows, what they really excelled at was the production of catalogues, as Hope's son later wrote:

Well, we always considered that our catalogues, both from the point of view of design and from the point of view of containing really useful information, that our catalogues were streets ahead. Ahead of any of our competitors. I think, in fact, that Crittalls catalogues were modelled to some extent on ours. We all, of course, looked at each others catalogues, and to some extent copied them. By the time our catalogues had really got launched in the very early 1900s, I don't think there was anyone [producing such attractive catalogues]. . . Crittalls were concentrating on developing windows for the housing market and doing extremely well with the standard window. They, like us, were influenced very considerably by the kind of clients they happened to have. They went in for a style, very much more with sans serif, which was rather advanced in the early 1920s . . . I was very much surprised when I found that people were selling old issues [of our catalogues]. We were always very proud of our catalogues, we spent a lot of time overseeing them. They were really developed in the twenties. The entire catalogue was done in-house then trotted round to Kynoch's saying 'print this!' The layouts as well as the actual words and the technical drawings were all done by our own staff.[10]

Henry Hope's was also important to the Press for another reason: their work helped to lay the foundations of external business at the Press and to give it publicity in the world beyond Birmingham. They introduced the Press to British print-buyers and saved it from the insularity which is the burden of the in-house printer. This was very important, for a time was fast approaching when the Press could not wholly depend upon its parent for work. External clients were difficult for the

A double-page from a Hope's catalogue of the early 1920s. Vibrantly and charmingly illustrated by Mrs Barraclough, they were delightful and consciously collectable items of publicity.

A "HOPE" METAL CASEMENT

The ideal window for comfort in a Country House.

FEW people who have not lived in a house fitted with Hope's Casements can appreciate the comfort which they provide. "Casements" to the general public too often signify leakage and draught—not to mention the constant inconvenience caused by a contrivance which can only be set open at fixed points, at rather wide intervals. A Hope Metal Casement is designed and built to exclude rain and wind, to open and close without effort and to provide ventilation in all weathers. A little air is provided in the simplest manner by Hope's patent handle, which sets the casement open about 1 in. without rattling, while their non-projecting sliding stay, by the simple action of a thumb screw, sets the casement open rigidly at any other angle desired, and is an effectual safeguard against breakage in a gale. The illustration on the opposite page shows a side-hung casement of best quality, in a mullioned window, glazed with leaded glass and provided with the handle and stay described above. This class of casement is recommended for dwelling houses and similar buildings where weather tight and everlasting windows are desired. They are made to open inwards or outwards, with suitable fittings for all conditions.

Press to find, for not only did the Press have the problem of being thought of as the exclusive property of Kynoch Ltd, but it was located in the heart of an ammunition site which rendered it out of bounds to the general public and also served to remove it from the mainstream design movements of London.

Although the Press was keen to be recognised by the outside world it did little to promote its services. The first item of self-advertising was a small publication called *An Example of Printing from the Kynoch Press* issued in February 1919, a small, quarter-bound booklet describing the war effort made at Kynoch's Birmingham factory between 1914 and 1918 which had previously been issued on behalf of Kynoch Ltd under the title *War Work at Kynoch's*. The *Example* was a typographically considered publication set in Caslon with generous margins and printed in two colours on a toned, laid, stock with deckle-edging. It was a commendable example of the sort of classical typography being produced by the Press and represented its initial, tentative steps to advertise itself, albeit while hiding behind its parent's coat-tails. The intended recipients of the booklet are unknown, but it may be assumed that they were the clients and associates of Kynoch Ltd who might have been encouraged to place work with the Press. It provided a simple demonstration of its ability as a printer, and was intended for a limited and targeted audience.

The arrival of Donald Hope and the adoption of Caslon Old Face was soon reflected in the main company literature. In 1904, the design of *The Kynoch Journal* was changed to reflect the typographic convictions of Hope and his manager. The nineteenth-century type of previous issues was replaced with Caslon Old Face and the reader was presented with clean, clear, crisp pages of the sort of purist typography which was already winning the Press a reputation for being a pioneer of the newly emerging typographic style. *The Kynoch Journal* was superseded in 1918 by *The Kynoch Journal of Technical Research* which was published by Nobel Industries with the intention of providing a permanent record of the progress made by the company in order to promote the general advancement of the company through shared information. Published by Kynoch Ltd from the Central Research Laboratories at Witton and printed by the Kynoch Press, the *Journal* was intended primarily for private circulation amongst company staff. The publication ran to three volumes and was produced to a high standard: printed on unbleached Arnold paper with embossed text pages, commissioned illustrations and five-colour printing in full leather binding, this was no ordinary house-journal. Typographically, it was poised and restrained and the elegantly

THE

KYNOCH

JOURNAL

CONCERNING

GUNS AND AMMUNITION

Vol. V.   Jan.-Dec., 1904

THE

KYNOCH

JOURNAL
of
TECHNICAL RESEARCH

Printed & Published by
Kynoch Limited
Birmingham

The changing typographic style of *The Kynoch Journal.* The journal of 1904 [left] is set in Caslon type which has been competently arranged though lacking in some of the finer points of spacing and positioning. The journal of 1919 [right] again uses Caslon, but displays greater sensitivity to spacing.

proportioned pages composed in Caslon showed greater sensitivity to spacing than the earlier *Kynoch Journal.* All the conventions of high-quality, limited-edition book-work were applied, perhaps inappropriately, to what was a strictly scientific publication. It was to be a few more years before a typographic style was developed specifically for application to technical publications.

The increase in work generated by the main company coupled with a burgeoning client list necessitated an increase in staff at the Press which by the end of Hope's tenure, had grown to 45 people. The Press staff were, however, from an industry very different to that of the rest of the Witton site and needed the protection of a union sympathetic to their trade. In 1920, the Typographic Association was recognised by the directors of the main company and the Press became a society shop with all employees in both the machine and composing rooms taking membership of the trade association. Kynoch Press membership of the Typographic Association numbered thirteen men in December 1920; a year later, as a reflection of the speed of growth at the Press, this had doubled to 27.[11] It was also at this time that the Kynoch Press was moved to larger accommodation by the main entrance to the Kynoch Works, a building which was to be home to the Press for over 60 years.

The Kynoch Works as they appeared in 1896. The premises occupied by the Kynoch Press at that time are indicated by the darkened roof on the left. By 1922 the Press occupied the buildings shown by the darkened roofs on the right.

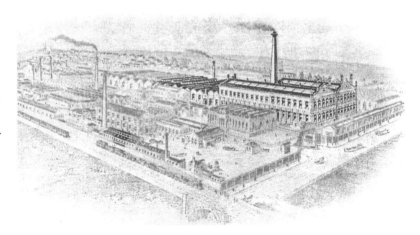

In the opening decades of the twentieth century the main company had been vastly expanded. Over the same period, the Kynoch Press had been enlarged to meet the needs of its parent, but its role as a captive printer was no longer straightforward. The Kynoch Press had been established to print the packaging for the ammunition produced by Kynoch Ltd, but following a series of mergers this company had ceased to exist by the turn of the century and the Press had become the inheritance of a series of new companies: Explosive Trade Ltd and Nobel Industries. The new owners were not the procreators of the Press and had less comprehension of its work than might otherwise have been the case; the Kynoch Press no longer found itself in the ownership of a benign business which had a personal interest in its welfare but it was a constituent part of a much larger organisation with interests very different from printing. As a result, during the 1914–1918 war the main works nearly closed the Press as it was not integral to the main business, but it was reprieved and just six to eight compositors were retained for essential war work in connection with the production of military ammunition. This was to be the first of several threats to the survival of the Press.

Donald Hope resigned from the board of Kynoch Ltd on 27 June 1922 and at the same time he resigned from the Kynoch Press, having transformed the small jobbing printing house into one of the finest printers in the country, bringing it to the fore-front of printing both in the Midlands and nationally.

Chapter 4

1922–1933
HERBERT SIMON
building a business of repute

Donald Hope's resignation from the Kynoch Press was accompanied by that of Mr Cowling. As he had done on previous occasions, Hope turned to Emery Walker for advice as to whom to appoint as the next manager of the Press. Walker recommended that Herbert Simon, a young man recently returned to England from the United States, would be an admirable choice for the post and so, in February 1922 Herbert Simon[1] became the third full-time manager of the Kynoch Press. Simon was a man of modesty and temperance and an advocate of simplicity. His staff gave him their unflinching loyalty and by his ordinary, kindly and upright character, he earned their trust and affection. Simon was known as a sympathetic manager, punctilious and reasonable, but he was also a hard task-master who vigorously pursued excellence with the minimum of fuss and without thought of glory:

> Herbert Simon could have been taken for a rather old-fashioned pedant, for his manner and his conduct, indeed his whole approach to people and to living was of a quality rarely found in our contemporary society. He set himself the highest standards of professional performance and human behaviour and quite reasonably looked for those same qualities in everyone with whom he came in contact. Here was an attribute which created a unique human relationship with those who worked for him both at Kynoch and at Curwen, a master and man relationship which he would never have admitted to, but which made his management so human and so successful. Herbert was very much a product of his own generation. Rebellious to the extent to which any ardent Fabian would go, fanatical for the new order of industrial design which he helped the DIA to bring about, and zealous for the perfection of manufacture which made him scathingly critical of what he [latterly] saw as slipping standards and confused motives in his own printing industry.[2]

Simon was a friend and patron to many artists, giving encouragement to talent and hard work in whatever field it showed itself. He was also a cricket enthusiast and a regular spectator at the Edgbaston Test Match, and like Eric Gill and Stanley Morison he had an interest in industrial archaeology and railways. Simon gave expression to his interest in trains through his authorship of *The Puffin Book of Locomotives*, and his life-long fascination with the industrial revolution found an outlet in the printing of books like *Old Euston* and *The history of the Southern Railway*.

Herbert [Bobby] Simon was born in 1898 to an affluent, middle-class, Jewish émigré family who, when they arrived in England in the middle of the nineteenth century, settled in Sale on the Lancashire–Cheshire borders. His father, Louis, was a scholarly cotton merchant and his mother, Louisa, was the sister of the artists William Rothenstein and Albert Rutherston. Herbert was the younger brother of Oliver Simon who was also to make a name for himself as director of the Curwen Press in London. Simon's childhood was permeated with the ideas of the arts and crafts movement and his parents were members of the Ancoats Brotherhood, an organisation which gave William Morris and his contemporaries a platform from which to speak to the people of the north-west of England. Simon recalled that his family had a puritanical outlook on life and expected high standards from all family members, and so Herbert followed his career with the requisite seriousness and sobriety expected of him, and to a standard which ensured he would make a great and lasting contribution in his chosen profession of printing.

In 1919, Herbert Simon was discharged from the British Army following active service in France. Having no idea of a career, he went to New York to join the family cloth business. It was while he was in America that Oliver wrote enthusiastically to Herbert about his newly discovered interest in printing:

> Both Harold [Curwen] and I were fervent worshippers at the shrine of printing and talked for a time of little else and we must have been terrible bores to some of our companions. But our enthusiasm was not without its response. We made new friends both direct and by post. My letters certainly affected my brother Bobby [Herbert], who was in our uncle's cotton business in New York, with dazzling prospects of wealth. My consistent enthusiasm acted upon him like rays of a distant lighthouse and, so directed, he threw up his job and entered a printing-house as an ordinary compositor.[3]

Herbert found work in the famous and reputable American printing house of William Edwin Rudge in Mount Vernon, New England. Herbert worked under Bruce Rogers who gave him a comprehensive grounding in all aspects of printing and encouraged him in his apprecia-

tion of typography as it developed on both sides of the Atlantic, as one
of Herbert's letters to Oliver reveals:

1920

My Dear Oliver

Very many thanks for your letter and the very interesting specimen of printing.

I spent about an hour with Bruce Rogers going over these and the ones you
sent me previously. Rogers got really enthusiastic about them and told me he is
going to show them to people who insist on declaring that 'no good printing is
being done in England at present'. . . in return he is sending you interesting specimens from the best American shops. I think this would be an excellent thing and
most interesting to all concerned.

I am beginning to get an insight into estimating now and hope later on to
make a very thorough study in this very important branch.

Good type, good machines, good estimating and enthusiasm seem to me,
when mixed, to be a solid keystone for a first-class shop.

Wishing you again all success during the coming year and much happiness,

With love from Bobby.[4]

Herbert Simon returned to England at the end of 1921 after nearly
three years with Bruce Rogers. On his return he applied for a position
at the Cambridge University Press but was considered too young for the
post; however, Emery Walker re-directed Simon to the Kynoch Press.
In February 1922, at the age of 24 years, he was appointed manager of
the Press on an enviable annual salary of £600, plus five per cent on
net profits, and a £100 annual performance bonus.

Like Donald Hope and Mr Forbes before him, Herbert Simon was a
devotee of purist typography and a product of the American typographic movement and was, therefore, an ideal successor to continue
the tradition of clean, clear typography already implemented by Hope
and Forbes. He also came to the Press with ambitious and clearly
defined ideas for its development. He was intent on building up the
external clientele, expanding the range of work and raising the quality
of output with the intention of turning the Kynoch Press into one of
the leading fine printing houses in the country.

. . . I had seen enough in the United States to realise that no better building material existed for a small printing press than good quality work. I therefore set out
quite deliberately to produce well planned and good quality business printing.
There were many hurdles to overcome but at the very beginning I explained my
purpose to the overseers and leading hands and through their untiring efforts
some measure of success was obtained. Later on it became a matter of balancing
real craftsmanship with reasonably fast production times. We did not feel justified
in offering good, straightforward commercial printing at high prices. Indeed it

was felt that if it could not be produced at normal rates that it had better not be done at all. We were not a 'private press' concerned with the printing of *de luxe* editions. In course of time we gathered a splendid band of craftsmen who took a very real pride in their work. We all became more and more absorbed in printing technique and through this there grew up quite naturally a 'team spirit.' It has no balance sheet value, but to us it represented our most treasured asset. My own general interest in the trade has waxed greater every year and I feel that there is a splendid future for those houses which are bold enough to talk and think in terms of quality. If the organisation is sound and there is proper co-ordination between staff and the works then 'price' will as a rule look after itself.[5]

To fulfil his ambitions for the Kynoch Press, Herbert Simon had to expand and modernise its equipment, increase the work-force, update its accommodation and reorganise its administrative structures to cope with the anticipated increase in external work and the growing requirements of the parent company. Under the management of Herbert Simon, the Press employed over 170 men and women in Birmingham and grew to comprise nine departments: in Birmingham there was a production office, composing room, Monotype room and foundry, press room, bindery, reading room, library and the paper box factory. In addition there was a sales and design office based in ICI's London headquarters.

The Kynoch Press in Birmingham was located in one of the oldest buildings in the Kynoch works, next to the main entrance of the site. It occupied the ground- and first-floor of the original military ammunition factory, an area which was well in excess of 43,000 square feet. The building was a self-contained unit and provided the Press with ample space. The administrative offices were re-built in 1928 and they gave the clerical staff spacious, modern, purpose-built accommodation which itself was a fine example of modern industrial design, and which provided Herbert Simon with an office space which was beautifully equipped with Gordon Russell furniture:

> The new offices of the Kynoch Press are worthy of mention as they reflect the growth of the printing works from a small press for printing ammunition labels to an up-to-date factory capable of anything from a ticket to a bound illustrated catalogue of over 1,000 pages. Six years ago the clerical work of the Press was done in one small office. As the Press increased its activities it was found necessary to sub-divide the staff, so a new suite of offices has been erected which, all are agreed, is a great improvement on the old quarters. Here there is ample room. The up-to-date fittings add to the spaciousness and create an atmosphere of business-like simplicity that is far pleasanter to work in than the dust catching extravagances of many an office.[6]

The composing-room

'The Kynoch Press
compositors using
the splendid equipment
put at their disposal.'

*The Kynoch Press
advertising literature, 1929*

The composing room was the focus of much of Herbert Simon's attention and he went to a great deal of trouble to ensure that it could provide customers with a singular range of hand- and machine-set typefaces and that the department was staffed with capable and sympathetic compositors who were able to execute the most complex of typographic specifications, and as the Press's literature explained, its compositors could help:

> . . . the user of printing to achieve distinguished publicity . . . every printer must study typography, and even go so far as to make it his hobby. He must gather around him craftsmen who can intelligently interpret the ideals of the House to the benefit of the customers . . . The responsibility for setting types to the best advantage rests with the composing room. All business printing can be set out in an infinite variety of ways and it requires the intelligence of the finest craftsmen to decide upon the setting which will be most appropriate for each particular subject. Kynoch Press compositors are highly-skilled men, and have been carefully trained.

Simon equipped the Kynoch type racks with an original range of nine-teenth-century English revival founts which were supplemented by some unusual twentieth-century continental founts used for display work. Ludlow equipment was bought for semi-mechanical composition work and was stocked with a selection of sans serif faces of English design. The Monotype room was also enlarged with additional casters, supercasters and keyboards, and matrices for many popular text faces were purchased.[7] The foundry was treated to a new two-hundred-weight metal furnace and a complete nickeling plant. By 1933 there were 39 people working in the composing room, including 23 composi-tors, three Monotype keyboarders, one Monotype caster, two overseers, four readers, three apprentice compositors and three apprentice Monotype operators. It was, and would continue to be, the largest com-posing room in Birmingham.[8]

Situated next to the composing room was the reading department which was headed by Mr Bastow, a mathematics graduate from Cambridge with a formidable general knowledge and unquestionable proof-reading ability. Mr Bastow was later succeeded by his son as head reader. The complexity of work produced by the Press necessitated an authoritative reading department which could raise the standards of composition through superlative copy preparation and proof correcting across a wide spectrum of work from complicated scientific publications to foreign language composition.

> . . . over the years Bastow had become a fount of knowledge. And of course, his fanaticism. Copy would be prepared by him before anyone, anyone saw it. He would look at the total—literacy, content, capitalisation, consistency of the man-uscript, so he'd carefully prepare that. He, or his readers, would read every stage of the galley, . . . and it was read again on press. So, in all, the average book, brochure, or whatever, would certainly be read half-a-dozen times, quite apart from the client. So literacy and accuracy was of tremendous importance.[9]

The printing department was also subject to much development and the main board at the Kynoch Works gave Herbert Simon sufficient money for the economic running of the press room which was trans-formed with the addition of several printing machines, including: one Miehle No 1 quad demy press with external pile delivery (£1,365); two Miehle No 6 demy machines (£725 each); two automatic horizontal crown folio machines complete with electrical equipment (£275 each); and two Victoria platen model A presses complete with electrical con-trols and counting apparatus (£390 the pair). By 1933 the Press had 21 printing machines of various sizes with automatic paper feeders, and

The Machine-room

'The secret of good machin-
ing lies in the employment of
good presses combined with
painstaking 'make-ready'.
The men who are chosen
to work the Kynoch Press
presses are keen on their
job, and it is a point of
honour with them to
produce really creditable
results. The Press gives them
the best machines available.'

*The Kynoch Press
advertising literature, 1929*

eleven modern platen-presses all of which were driven by individual
machine power which replaced the over-head belt-driven shafting
which had previously supplied power to the presses. The department
was staffed by 22 pressmen, including one apprentice printer.

Under the supervision of its manager, Mr Hoggs, new accommodation
was built for the binding department and £3,616 was spent on expanding
its equipment with the addition of a Monitor wire-stitcher; a Krause super
high-speed guillotine; a Mansfield book trimming and looping machine;
and four folding, punching, gumming and perforating machines. Len
Boulton, a sixteen year-old apprentice in the bindery remembers:

> When I first went there it [the bindery] was about half the length of this room.
> More like an enlarged passage than a room! They had taken over the Lightning
> fastners. Lightning fastners had moved upstairs. Then Lightning fastners had a
> place built so we took over the upstairs. There was a lot of stuff moved and walls
> knocked down and we had a new enlarged bindery. We finished up with quite a

The Bindery

'This department's duty is
to finish the various jobs
coming from the machine
room. The range of their
work is enormous.
It may be a simple folder,
forms to perforate and
make-up into pads,
or it may be an account
book, half-bound red basil;
or it may be a *de luxe* edition
of a book to be sumptuously
bound in full calf, bevelled
boards and gold block.'

*The Kynoch Press
advertising literature, 1929*

nice layout. There were about eight men, and I should think about, roughly, fifteen girls employed in the bindery. It was an average [size] bindery.

In 1925 the Press started a library which was run by a committee of
Press and external representatives and which had the financial backing
of ICI. In five years it expanded from 22 books and a membership of
seven, to over 500 books and periodicals and a membership exceeding
50. The library formed an archive of Press work and gave staff the
opportunity to keep abreast of modern trade developments.

The Kynoch Press also had offices in Imperial Chemical (IC) House,
Millbank, and High Holborn, London. The office functioned both as a
studio and a sales office and was established 'for the convenience of our
London customers . . . all matters are expeditiously dealt with by this
office. The staff are ready at all times to furnish layouts and offer advice
on typographic layout' and the selection of suitable materials for the job.

The design and sales office came under the guidance of both Harry

Carter who was based in Birmingham and Noel Carrington in London; they were assisted by Messers R. J. Beeching, C. R. Hiles and A. Poore, layout artists, and Charles Wormall, photographer, all of whom were in London. Harry Carter came to the Press in 1929 after serving time as a learner at the Monotype Works. It was a productive time at the Press for Carter, who was typographically responsible for two type specimen books and a series of Kynoch Press Notebook and Diaries. He also designed a Russian type [Monotype series 1692R] and a fount of Hebrew and was part-author with Herbert Simon of *Printing Explained*, a popular text book which was published by the Dryad Press of Leicester in 1931, and which was printed by the Kynoch Press. Noel Carrington was an energetic and imaginative salesman who moved to the Kynoch Press in 1928 having worked for Oxford University Press in India and *Country Life* in London. Carrington did much to encourage new business to the Press.

Under Herbert Simon design at the Press became a concerted and separate service performed by staff dedicated to the task of typographic layout; it was not, as it was in many other printing houses of the period, left to interested amateurs or roving salesmen, but was a distinct and professional skill and a defining feature of the Press. The London office was also home to a sales department which helped the Press find and maintain clients in the south of England and keep in close contact with its customers from the ICI combine via the Central Publicity Office which was next to the Kynoch Press in IC House. Between them Simon, Carter and Carrington captured many prestigious business and publishing accounts[10] through personal contacts made at the Double Crown Club, of which Herbert Simon was a founding father (along with his brother Oliver and others in 1926) and which Carter and Carrington regularly attended as members. The Design and Industries Association [DIA] was another organisation which received the support of Herbert Simon and the Kynoch Press and which also had two great allies from within ICI: Colonel Millman, ICI Chairman, and Commander H. S. H. Ellis who was ICI's Publicity Manager. Both men were exponents of the principles of the DIA and contributed to raising the standard of work in the Press through their enthusiasm for design in industry and their appreciation of good work. A Birmingham branch of the DIA was started by Noel Carrington who encouraged university professors, retailers, industrialists and manufacturers to join the group which organised visits to Midlands industries and whose inaugural visit in 1931 was to the Kynoch Press.

Customers were attracted to the Kynoch Press from both the local and national branch of the DIA and included publishing houses, local and national industry and both private and public concerns. External customers were necessary to the Press so that it could minimise its dependency upon ICI. To attract outside work the Press embarked upon a series of publications which were produced as show-cases to advertise its printing abilities and typographic style. The most important of these publications were its type specimens and the popular series of Kynoch Press Notebook and Diaries.

Printers' type specimens, as books rather than sheets, first emerged in the mid-1920s when any printer with a mind to his reputation and an eye for quality regarded them as a necessity. The Kynoch Press and its closest competitors Lund Humphries and the Curwen Press all published their first specimen books in the 1920s—Kynoch Press in 1927, Curwen Press in 1928, and Lund Humphries during 1929. Shortly after Herbert Simon arrived in 1922, the Kynoch Press issued a type specimen in the form of a broadsheet (760 x 540 mm) which displayed with elegance, and to good effect, a modest range of hand- and machine-set types.

> This type sheet has been compiled with usefulness as its primary object—an assistance to you in the selection of a good typeface for every kind of printed matter. One of the essentials of good printing is the use of types which are at once pleasing to the eye and appropriate to the subject. Our aim is to set good type well. This coupled with the care and efficient workmanship in all departments, forms the highroads of good printing. [11]

It was a specimen which reverberated with classical elegance and set the Press apart from the archaic composing rooms which populated Birmingham.

Under Herbert Simon, the Kynoch Press underwent great typographic expansion and it wished to advertise this to its customers. It also had a new mechanical system of composition, Monotype, and it was essential for the Press to make the availability of this system known. The most effective way to do this was through the issuing of type specimen books which were particularly useful vehicles for self-publicity as they allowed the Press to display its skills in composition, press-work and binding as well as providing an inventory of typefaces at the Press. The type books also provided the technical information necessary for using the types to their best advantage both mechanically and artistically. The type specimen books were designed following the principles of good typography and contemporary design, displayed well-chosen founts and served as a prospectus for the Press.

In 1927 *The Kynoch Press Book of Type Specimens* was issued and was accompanied by a twelve-page leaflet describing the departments of the Press. It was the first major item of advertising which it had produced. A solid, unpretentious piece of printing, it gave a straightforward presentation of the Press, with no embellishment and no euphonious text. Its modesty of production reflected the quiet decency in management which so characterised the management of Herbert Simon. Cased with black cloth quarter-binding, its dimensions (242 x 178 mm) were such that it would easily sit on a general bookshelf. Divided into machine- and hand-set founts the typefaces were printed in red and black and shown as text settings from the smallest to the largest type sizes set solid and leaded. The publication included displays of borders and arabesques, and fifteen pages of sample settings demonstrated various arrangements of typefaces and ornaments. The *Supplement* to *The Kynoch Press Book of Type Specimens* was issued in 1930, but it was not until 1934 that the Press issued its second major type specimen book and with it revealed the extent of its typeface expansion.

When *A Specimen of Types in use at the Kynoch Press* was published in 1934 it came as a breath of fresh air whetting the appetite of the typographic connoisseur with types which had never been seen, in a way in which they had never before been displayed. The 1934 *Specimen* was designed by Harry Carter and produced to a convenient format of 222 x 138 mm and 160 pages, which, by the addition of two supplements, was increased to 178 pages which were decorated with small wood engravings by Eric Ravilious. The book was cloth-bound and, sunk deep into the cover, was Stevens Shanks' Elephant type, an innovative treatment of a rare face which allowed the letters to be felt as well as seen, giving the type a third dimension, emphasising its physical as well as visual characteristics. It was a wholly typographic cover produced by a printer which liked to regard itself as a typographer's press.

The well-known series of Kynoch Press Notebook and Diaries, designed by Harry Carter, were first issued in 1929, and published each Christmas for 34 years, with the exception of the austerity years of 1943 to 1946. They were made for the friends and customers of the Press and were charming and inexpensive annual goodwill gifts which became more than mere gratuities or a public relations exercise. Their format remained a constant and convenient 174 x 125 mm, small enough to be transportable but large enough to be serviceable. All the

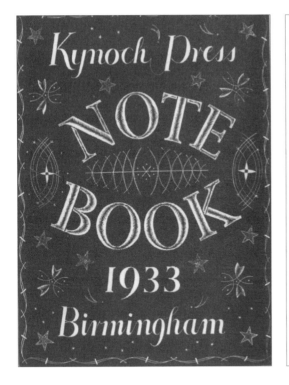

The Kynoch Press
Notebook and Diary took
on a fresh typographic
appearance when
Eric Ravilious designed the
diary for 1933. The former
bookish solutions for the
Diary were abandoned
when Ravilious designed a
bright and flamboyant
title-page depicting a fantasia
of star-bursts and flourishes
which were reversed out of
a vivid seasonal red.

Notebooks were in a hard-cased binding, covered with buckram or
paper and each received a fresh typographic and illustrative arrangement and was accompanied by an individually designed compliments
slip. The notebooks were a means by which the Press could display to
good effect their unique range of typefaces; they also allowed the Press
artistic patronage, and permitted an artistic detour which was not
always possible in its customary scientific and industrial environment.
Each Notebook was given to illustrators both known and unknown.
The first, issued in 1929 was designed and illustrated by Donald Ewart
Milner OBE, MA, ARCA, RWA, who was headmaster of the Aston
School of Arts and Crafts in Birmingham, with a reputation as a
painter, stained glass artist and book decorator and who also designed a
woodletter for the Press. The 1930 Notebook was designed and illustrated by Tom Poulton with scenes from a printing works, whilst J. B.
Fletcher illustrated the 1931 Notebook with masterpieces of English
craftsmanship. The following year electrotyped woodcuts from a typefounders' stock were used as decoration, but originality was restored
and the Notebook's reputation was really established when, in 1933,

Eric Ravilious produced 53 vignettes depicting scenes of rural and domestic life which the Press teamed-up with its newly acquired Ludlow Tempo typeface. But for all that, the Notebooks were primarily commercial publications made for a purpose, not limited editions printed on fine paper for the collector of precious ephemera. They were work-a-day products to be used, disposed of and replaced by a successor twelve months later. The Notebooks were produced under business conditions by a Press with a mercantile sense but despite this, they became eagerly awaited publications which have, latterly, become expensive collectors' items. The type specimen books and the Notebook and Diaries helped the Press attract some particularly prestigious accounts, foremost amongst which was Francis Meynell at the Nonesuch Press.

In 1923 the Kynoch Press produced its first book for the Nonesuch Press, *The Letters of George Meredith to Alice Meynell 1896–1907*. The Press printed a total of thirteen books for Francis Meynell and in 1923 alone it printed one-third of the books published by Meynell. The Nonesuch publications were a means by which the Press was able to display its

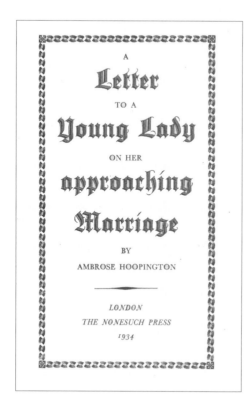

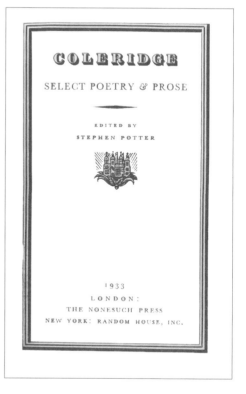

original collection of founders' types. Ancient Black was employed in 1923 on *Sermons* by John Donne; in 1928 Shaded Black was boldly displayed on the title-page of John Bunyan's *The Pilgrim's Progress* and ingeniously balanced with a frontispiece illustrated by Karl Michel; Shaded Black was used again, in 1934, on Ambrose Hoopington's *A Letter to a Young Lady on her approaching Marriage*; the delicacy of Union Pearl was accompanied by Bembo on *Astophel and Stella* in 1931; and Coleridge's *Selected Poetry* gave a modest first airing to Thorne Shaded in 1933. Meynell sought the services of the Press not merely for its extraordinary range of display types, but also for its up-to-date range of Monotype faces. He used Garamond for the earlier publications and Baskerville and Imprint for later ones. Two Nonesuch books provide a rare record of collaboration between the two Simon brothers. The text of the *Pilgrim's Progress* was composed and printed by the Kynoch Press from a photographic reproduction of the original first edition in the British Museum. The Caslon type and the inconsistencies in the author's spelling blended to produce an unique edition. The illustrations for the book were printed from the original wood-blocks and colour stencilled by the Curwen Press. So elegant was the book that the *Pilgrim's Progress* was displayed at the Annual Printing Exhibition in 1929. James Thomson's classic, *The Seasons*, was also composed and printed by the Kynoch Press but the illustrations were copper-plate engraved and water-coloured through stencils by the Curwen Press and this book too was included in the 1929 exhibition of modern books at the British Museum.

Through its association with the Nonesuch Press, the Kynoch Press produced books of high quality and the liaison helped to create its reputation as a press of stature. To have the Nonesuch Press as a regular client was a recognition of its quality, and Kynoch's work with the Nonesuch Press helped bring book production back to the Midlands and enabled the Press to attract work from other trade publishing houses both from London and elsewhere in the United Kingdom.[12] One of the earliest books it produced was Mr Perrault's *Tales of Times Past* which was published by Selwyn and Blount of London in 1922. It was a book for children, colourfully illustrated, capably printed and typeset in Caslon. The Press applied itself with skill to this class of work, producing books of sufficient quality to receive regular mention in the top Fifty Books of the Year.

But book production was only a small part of Kynoch Press output; in addition, the Press regularly worked for the Design and Industries Association (DIA) for whom it produced a number of the well-known

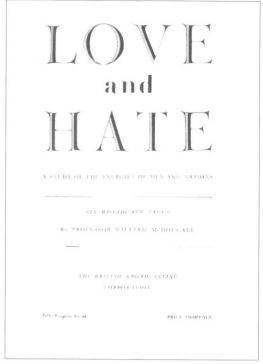

LEFT

The cover of *British Art*, a
pamphlet designed by
Eric Ravilious using hand
drawn letters, and printed
by the Kynoch Press for
the BBC in 1934.

RIGHT

The cover of *Love and Hate*,
a pamphlet produced by the
Kynoch Press for the BBC in
1931 and displaying to good
effect Stempel's Ratio Free
Initials and Stephenson
Blake's Fat Face.

series of *Cautionary Guides*. The Press also agreed to design, print and
fully finance *Design for Today*, the organ of the DIA which was published
by Weekend Publications and for two years was edited by Noel
Carrington, Frank Pick, Jack Pritchard and Gerald Barr. *Design for Today*
was a monthly magazine which commented on all aspects of design in
commercial and public life, a periodical aimed at promoting the ideals
and beliefs of the organisation. The publication measured 284 x 210
mm, had an average extent of 36 pages, was composed in Baskerville
and was printed monochrome with numerous half-tones. Characteristic
of all Kynoch Press work, the magazine was of a simple design, with
uncomplicated typography and functional in its presentation. *Design for
Today* was produced without profit by the Press which had allied itself
with the DIA cause, but it did give it involvement with a laudable and
prestigious, if not profitable project. *The Face of the Land*, the yearbook of
the DIA, published by George Allen and Unwin, edited by Harry Peach
and Noel Carrington, was also printed by the Press. The work brought
the Press prestige, if not great wealth, and was recognition by the DIA
of the Kynoch Press' printing ability.

Its association with these two publications brought the Press to the

Two leaflets produced in the
1930s by the Kynoch Press
for Barrow's Stores of
Birmingham.

attention of other DIA members, including the British Broadcasting
Corporation for whom it printed many pamphlets. These publications
were issued by the BBC in conjunction with a long-running series of
broadcast talks given on a range of subjects and by a variety of speakers
and which were arranged under the auspices of the Central Council for
Broadcast Education. The pamphlets contained a synopsis of each of
the talks, were photographically illustrated and sold for 6*d*. Measuring
215 x 136 mm they were produced to a standard layout with the text set
in Monotype Baskerville or, less frequently, in Monotype Imprint, with
the occasional use of some of the more exotic faces at the Press—Ratio,
Milner Initials or Delphian Titling, Ancient Black, Cloister and Fat
Face—on those texts which required typographic atmosphere.

Work also came from local members of the DIA such as Barrow's
Stores who were located in Corporation Street, Birmingham and were
regarded as the premier luxury foods store of the Midlands. The store
recognised the importance of well-designed and well-produced printed
material to the success of its business, and from the mid-1920s to the
1950s the Press produced a large and continuous supply of pamphlets,
post-cards, flyers and small posters for Barrow's, all of which were either

mailed directly to customers or were freely available to visitors to the shop. These items of ephemera not only provided the customers with information but acted as ambassadors for Barrow's, reflecting their standards and generating an impression of quality. Barrow's literature varied in format and function, but was united by a consistency of style, quality and interpretation. Each item was illustrated and was printed in three-, four- or five-colours and frequent use was made of some of the brighter types at the Press: Vesta was particularly popular and Fat Face, Thorne Shaded and Ratio were all used to great effect alongside the lively and entertaining illustrations which decorated each production. This work allowed the Press to give a rare demonstration of its talent for typographic exuberance which could rival that of even the Curwen Press.

The Dryad Press of Leicester, makers of cane furniture and publishers of books on handicrafts, was a member of the DIA and a regular book publishing client of the Press with whom it had personal links as Harold Peach, director of Dryad, was formerly at the Kynoch Press. One of the most popular of Dryad's publications was *Printing Explained,* printed by the Press—an elementary practical handbook for schools and amateurs on the process of printing written by Herbert Simon in collaboration with Harry Carter in 1931.

> This is a book about a process—not about a product. It is, I believe, the first book of its kind in England since Johnson's *Typographica,* published in 1824, from which I learnt to set type. In the last ten years there have been published tome after tome about the aesthetics of printing, the function of printing, the history of printing, collection after collection of examples of fine printing; but until this book, not a single book simply about printing—the process of combining types and taking impressions from them. [13]

Despite its prestigious and expanding external clientele the largest proportion of material produced by the Kynoch Press remained business printing for the ICI combine. In 1926 ICI set up its own publicity department to oversee the production of all company literature which was required in vast quantity and for which a budget of £65,000 was allocated in 1929 and which had risen to £94,930 by 1931. Most other businesses of the period issued printed material in a haphazard manner, but ICI were almost unique in having a professionally constituted publicity department staffed by a team of writers, editors, production supervisors and a small group of designers, illustrators and photographers, and ICI were also particularly fortunate to have an in-house printer capable of producing high-quality, high-volume printing. The two departments, Publicity and Press, worked in tandem to produce a range of professionally manufactured company material and ICI employees were privileged to be involved with a continuous supply of well-designed, well-printed, innovative publishing.

The work undertaken by the Press for ICI fell into two classes. First, there was that work which was produced for the Metals Division which represented one-fifth of the Press turnover and consisted of stationery, printed cartons and labels for ammunition and all the general printing needed to service a large manufacturing organisation. Secondly, there was the work for the rest of ICI: that placed by Central Publicity, which included books, booklets and brochures in various languages; and that placed by Central Purchasing which consisted mostly of stationery, but included some internal books and technical printing.

The material produced for ICI was diverse both in form and content, as well as quality and quantity, and consisted of material issued for both domestic and external consumption: house-magazines, annual reports and accounts, catalogues, manuals, technical documents, programmes and menus. The format of these publications was as varied as their function and included books and catalogues, pamphlets and leaflets, magazines, newspapers and an assortment of ephemera. Their production encompassed both the cheapest utilitarian monochrome leaflet and the most lavishly produced and highly illustrated prestige commemorative publication. The work undertaken by the Press for the main company gave it a workload as varied and stimulating as might have arisen from a whole assembly of clients.

The largest of all Kynoch Press clients was the *ICI Magazine*,[14] a staff-magazine which aimed to supply employees with information about the running of ICI and contained items both informative and entertaining relating to company performance and staff exploits. The *Magazine* promoted company pride by recounting ICI achievements at home and abroad whilst domestic news from all eleven divisions engendered camaraderie. Health and safety advice was dispensed to fulfil the company's paternal concern for social welfare and the entertainment pages occupied a worker's idle mind. The *Magazine* was intended to link workers located in widely separated units and employed in diverse manufacturing activities. It was produced at a time when house-organs were still something of a rarity and was so unusual an enterprise that when, in November 1926, the *Spectator* published an article on the organisation of ICI by Lord Melchett, its first chairman, the plans for a works magazine were cited as one of the five points of major interest.

The *Magazine* was a professional publication managed by full-time

AUGUST 1932

I.C.I. SAVINGS BANK

RECENT FINANCIAL DEVELOPMENTS, OF WHICH THE SCHEME FOR THE CONVERSION OF 5 PER CENT. WAR LOAN IS AN OUTSTANDING EXAMPLE, HAVE REQUIRED ALL IN CONTROL OF INVESTMENTS, SAVINGS BANKS AND SIMILAR FUNDS TO GIVE CLOSE ATTENTION TO THE CONDITIONS UNDER WHICH THEY ACCEPT DEPOSITS. THE PRESENT TENDENCY IS IN THE DIRECTION OF "CHEAP" MONEY. THAT IS, THE RATES OF INTEREST WHICH CAN BE EARNED ARE COMPARATIVELY LOW. THIS, WITH OTHER FACTORS, HAS BEEN CONSIDERED BY THE MANAGEMENT WHO, IN THE OFFICIAL NOTICE WHICH IS PRINTED BELOW, EXPLAIN THE CONDITIONS UNDER WHICH DEPOSITS WILL BE WELCOMED AS FROM 1ST SEPTEMBER, 1932.

CHANGES IN CONDITIONS

[OFFICIALLY COMMUNICATED BY THE MANAGEMENT]

THE I.C.I. Savings Bank was originally instituted in order to afford employees a simple and easy means of saving by small periodical deposits, and to encourage such saving interest was paid at the liberal rate of 5 per cent. per annum.

The scheme was made as easy and convenient as possible and everything possible was done to make it attractive.

THE PURPOSE OF A SAVINGS BANK

It was not intended, however, that employees should deposit in the I.C.I. Bank sums of money which, if there had been no I.C.I. Bank, would have been invested elsewhere for the purpose of earning an income. To use the bank for this purpose is contrary to the nature of Savings Banks which, as their name implies, afford a means of saving money for special purposes but are not intended for the investment of capital merely to earn an income. With this in view, and having regard to the fact that the terms offered by the Company are more generous to the depositor than could possibly be obtained were the bank run as a business proposition, the Directors now consider that a limit should be set to the total amount an employee may have to his credit in the I.C.I. Savings Bank and have decided to fix this limit at £500. Employees whose balances already exceed £500 are therefore notified that they will be expected to reduce their deposits with the Savings Bank to £500 before 1st September, 1932.

103

I.C.I. MAGAZINE

April 1933

FOR I.C.I. GIRLS

CONDUCTED BY "VERA"

WITH April here we feel that at last the long winter is over. Reluctantly, perhaps, we may put away our hockey sticks and skates, and our thick clothes, sighing for those invigorating days, those glorious games and warm, firelit evenings. But even so it is with a smile we take up tennis racquets instead, with the possible addition (alas!) of umbrellas!

This year will be a spring of strong, vivid colours. Everything is fresh and youthful, with bright reds and greens predominant. White has come into favour again, and you will see it on most hats and frocks.

If you have not completed your outfit, remember that coats, which are worn long, have shawl collars and unusually deep cuffs, while another style is the straightly cut dark coat, with no fur collar, and fitting snugly over a frock. Fashionable tennis coats are being made of heavy white jersey cloth.

Loose flowing draperies are being replaced by neat, well-fitting garments, with shorter sleeves; jackets, too, will be short. A useful costume, which would be very chic, is in grey, with a blouse of linen or shantung. Tuck-in blouses are still very good, but still newer is the tunic jumper worn outside the skirt and belted at the waist. Peter Pan collars of varying widths are in vogue once more.

It is a mistake to change too rapidly from winter wear, but little jumper suits and costumes are ideal for the changeable weather.

Field-grey and rose is a new colour combination, while a fresh green with orange and brown provides a delightful contrast. Striped skirts are being worn with short flannel coats, and bright, gay scarves should replace for collars. The popularity of the light jacket over a dark frock increases.

And now a word about hats. The whole charm of the modern hat lies in the way you put it on. It can be made expressive of your personality or a complete and utter failure. Hats are still worn off the forehead and moulded neatly to the shape of the head, with hair peeping out just a little.

I.C.I. GIRLS' GUIDE TO CHIC
SKIN CARE

"And, of course, she's got a lovely complexion!"

Well, that settles the matter, doesn't it?

If you have a really nice skin, you can't help looking attractive. A good complexion means charm, freshness and vitality; it means that almost any colour is becoming and it means that you always "look your best." But a dull skin or a rough neglected one cancels out all the charm of fine features or a good figure, and even a taste for clothes doesn't help you much because nothing seems to suit you.

Chic begins with a good complexion, and a good complexion isn't just a matter of make-up. It's not so much what you put on your skin that matters, but what you take off.

430

The *ICI Magazine* of 1932 (left) and 1933 (right). Although the treatment of the body of the text remained constant, the Press permitted itself some flexibility with the headlines.

editorial staff based at IC House, London. The first issue was published in January 1928 and was printed by the Kynoch Press for the next 54 years, with a gap between 1940 and 1946. Sold to staff for a nominal fee, the *Magazine* was published monthly. The original idea was for a 64-page issue, but the first edition ran to 104 pages. In the early years the *Magazine* was printed in monochrome with the occasional use of a single spot colour but after the second world war four-colour process printing was introduced. Typographically, the early issues of the *Magazine* were neatly composed in Monotype Baskerville but over the years the design changed to reflect the latest trends.

In addition to the *ICI Magazine*, the company communicated with its dispersed work-force through a relentless programme of Technical Circulars and Auxiliary Products Pamphlets. These documents were required in quantity and updated employees on new products manufactured by the company and described techniques for their application. Technical Circulars first appeared in the 1930s, but their format remained unchanged for two decades. All the pamphlets measured 215 x 155 mm, were printed two-colours, were self-covered, wire-stitched or thread-sewn and were hole-punched to facilitate filing in proprietory folders. The Auxiliary Products Pamphlets were similar. Both publications were neat, considered and typographically gratifying, and moreover, they were printed on a more than adequate stock. These publications were functional documents, for internal viewing only, but as much care and attention was taken over their production as would have been given to more prestigious external material and they also provided the Press with a constant flow of work which utilised both composing and press-room capacity.

With a steady stream of work from ICI and an ever-expanding external client list, the Press increasingly found its dual role as both commercial and captive printer a difficult one to resolve and this led to a crisis of identity. The relationship with ICI brought both advantages and disadvantages to the Press. On the one hand, being part of such a large organisation forced the Press to expand and raise its own standards of work and it gave it the opportunity to make contact with a large number of important clients from within the group. The Press was also forced to become financially sound and capable of producing a service of unsurpassable quality commensurate with all other company products. But its relationship with ICI was anomalous, for although the ICI

ICI leaflets from the 1930s. The leaflet on the right makes use of the Kynoch Press's newly acquired Prisma typeface.

account represented house-work to the Press, it was work which had to
be tendered for in open competition with outside printers and was not
guaranteed to the Press. ICI's printing requirements were not specialised and could therefore be bought from printers other than the
Kynoch Press, and as ICI was obliged to buy its printing from the cheapest source and its native printer was not always the most economic, other
printers were also employed. In addition, new members of the combine
brought with them established printing contacts to whom they often
remained loyal.

All ICI's printing requirements were handled by ICI Central
Publicity in London and the Press had to apply to this office for work.
By the 1930s it was responsible for printing 50 per cent of ICI's work;
much of this was for the Metals Group, for which the Press received
special preference. But if the Press won 50 per cent of ICI work then 50
per cent was lost, often because a large proportion of it was jobbing
work that was unsuitable for the Press or because its location made it
impossible to take on urgent work, or where close daily co-operation
with the consuming factory was required. But its biggest handicap was
its high estimates which were, on average, fifteen per cent above those
of its competitors on short-run and jobbing printing, although the Press
was competitive on large sheet work. Its charges were high because the
Press carried heavy overheads imposed by ICI (welfare, holidays, Staff
Grade Schemes, and general services) whereas its competitors did not
carry such a heavy burden. Central Publicity allowed the Press a minimum preference of ten per cent on company tenders, and this helped it
to secure a large proportion of the orders. Unfortunately, such prefer-
ences could not be extended to the Press by its external clients.

By 1929 the Press had reached crisis point as ICI complained about
the decline in quality of its service and over-pricing.[15] The crisis was a
result of the huge quantity of enquiries received by the Press for a class
of work which, for technical reasons, it was not suited. The Press had
reached a hiatus. It was working to full capacity, unable to commit itself
to a greater volume of work without expansion and unable to make
itself more competitive. Its fate hung in the balance. For it to survive,
expansion was imperative. For it to expand, further expenditure on the
Press was required from ICI. But before ICI were prepared to invest it
had to ascertain whether additional work for the Company could be
undertaken on a competitive basis. If not, the Press faced likely closure.
Even the *ICI Magazine*, the biggest client of the Press, was making
known its concern:

13 May 1929

To R. Lloyd Roberts, ICI Ltd

I have to draw your attention to the serious position now arising in connection with the printing and binding of the Magazine. In two important departments the Kynoch Press has had difficulty for several months in producing the necessary output in a given time—a factor which makes a reasonable magazine schedule an impossibility.

The equipment at the Press is already employed to its maximum capacity. For some months it has been obvious to me that this department of the plant has only kept pace with Magazine demands by working overtime. This month, an unexpected urgent order received by the Press has resulted in a breakdown of the Magazine schedule at a time when the Whitsuntide holiday made it specifically necessary to work to fine limits. The results of this breakdown are: loss of time and money by members of the Magazine staff at Witton; further demands for overtime and high pressure work by the Press and the Magazine staff in order to publish on the scheduled date.

I have pointed out in a previous note that the bindery at the Kynoch Press is inadequate for magazine purposes. At that time four-and-a-half to five-days were required for binding. The time now required, owing to increased circulation, is six days, and since our efforts to increase the sale at Billingham seem likely to be successful this may be extended to eight working days within a few months.

This, frankly, is ridiculous, and I should like to place on record my view that the present binding facilities are completely inadequate for a magazine of this size, and that it is impossible for me, as publisher of this magazine, to produce a first-class topical magazine under these conditions.

The proposal to remove the Kynoch Press to another site having been rejected, I understand that proposals have been placed before the Metal Group Management for extensions on the present site involving expenditure of £15,000.

May I draw your attention to the urgency of the position, which is becoming steadily worse, month by month. I understand that the alterations proposed, if approved, will not be completed in less than nine months. Long before that time it will have become my duty to advise you that a topical magazine containing up-to-date information can only be secured by printing it elsewhere until the Kynoch Press is reorganised.

Finally, two small points. The pressure on the staff of the Press is too much for continued efficient working, and if you knew the circumstances, I feel sure that you would not wish the Magazine to be responsible, however unwittingly, for the inevitable results of protracted overtime. Second, the little Magazine staff is extraordinarily keen, and has worked for months on Saturday afternoons and Sunday nights to save a few hours. For the last four months, at least, we have travelled to Birmingham on Sunday night to be in the works early Monday morning. It is disappointing to find, as we invariably do now, that the time thus saved merely balances out time lost simply because the Press cannot cope with the work.

The Management of the Press had, I know, raised the subject of extensions with his Management several times during the last year, and my view is that, considering the inadequacy of the plant, we get a far better service than might be expected. My reason for submitting this memorandum is that apparently no progress is being made towards a decision, and that I shall soon be compelled to advise you that the long period required for printing is setting a limit to the effectiveness of the Magazine.

H. R. Payne
Editor, ICI Magazine

In 1929, C. N. Shearer of ICI Purchasing Department, P. Frank of ICI Finance Department, and the Metal Group Delegate Board examined the role of the Press within ICI and assessed the financial efficacy of extending the Printing Department. All reports concluded that there were advantages to expanding and modernising the printing facilities: new methods and equipment would shorten production times and increase turn-around resulting in profits from the extra work from both ICI and outside. It was anticipated that the expansion would enable the Press to contract for an additional £5,000–£7,000 worth of orders from ICI, and that greater efficiency would bring commensurate financial savings. With additional Monotype machinery and printing presses, the Press would be able to attract more outside work which would provide it with an additional £3,000 of business in a year. Expanding the Press was seen by ICI to be of both practical advantage and economically sound, and it received a reprieve. But the report highlighted the fact that the fate of the Press was, and always would be, in the hands of ICI.

In 1933 Herbert Simon resigned from the Kynoch Press with great reluctance. His decision to leave was made as a result of the pressure exerted on him by Oliver Simon who wished to become a director of the Curwen Press and who required his brother's financial support. So Herbert Simon left the Kynoch Press to take up an active directorship with his brother at the Curwen Press, but he always maintained an affection and association with Birmingham, regularly returning for the Edgbaston Test Match and to lecture to the boys at the Birmingham School of Printing. His departure was greeted with sadness by those with whom he had worked.

With genuine regret we record the resignation of Mr Herbert Simon from his post of Manager of the Kynoch Press. In a comparatively short time Mr Simon has achieved for himself and ICI's Press an enviable reputation in a sphere where competition is keen and standards are high. Printing is one of the few industries where a high degree of craftsmanship and personal skill is still the deciding factor and under Mr Simon the Kynoch Press reached the stage where its products equalled the best . . . We say that he [Herbert Simon] has definitely lifted our printing to a very high standard—so high in fact that the Kynoch Press can now successfully compete with any book or commercial printing house in the country. His is the credit of creating constructive employment for those of outstanding ability or specialist knowledge or craftsmanship by means of go-ahead methods and foresight in bringing the plant up-to-date, to the advantage of the Kynoch Press and the trade generally. Indifferent binding, poor paper and sorry "letter" are anathema to Mr Simon. [16]

It was not an easy job that Simon had undertaken at the Kynoch Press. Attempting to establish contacts with an outside clientele while producing work of an unfaltering high standard for ICI was difficult. Simon made great efforts to extend business away from the main works, to establish an independent identity for the Kynoch Press and reduce its dependence upon ICI. Simon's achievements were great, he succeeded in advancing the external reputation of the Press and raising standards of production from the composing room through to the bindery. He established a well-equipped and busy Press with an enviable reputation both within and without the ICI group. His plans for expansion and quality were backed by sound business organisation which was necessary to the successful running of a printing house, making possible the work that others performed. He left the Press at the zenith of its reputation.

Chapter 5

1933–1938
H.V. DAVIS
the fall of the Kynoch Press

In 1933, H. V. Davis succeeded Herbert Simon as Manager of the Kynoch Press. He was an unfortunate and inept appointment for he lacked any feeling either for the craft of printing or the achievements of the Press. Davis brought the Kynoch Press into decline through his poor management and his concern for the account book in preference to the client.

Little is known of H. V. Davis.[1] Contemporary editorials reported him in dull and distant tones and photographs showed him to be an awkward, starched and uninspired individual who won neither the affection nor the respect of his staff. Herbert Simon was always going to be a hard act to follow, but the personal character of Davis, his standard of work, and attitude towards his profession and those who worked for him, could not have been further removed from those of his predecessor. Yet his *curriculum vitae* suggested he was particularly well qualified for the role of Press Manager.

Born in London and educated at Aylesbury Grammar School in Buckinghamshire, Davis followed his father into the printing trade after he left school. His practical experience of the printing industry was supplemented by his studies of printing business management, accountancy, costing, estimating and general printing at night-school where he gained first prize in the Stationers' Company costing examination, passed the City and Guilds examination in typography with distinction and won prizes from the Midlands Counties Union in various printing and allied subjects. His first job was with Messrs. Hazell, Watson and Viney of Aylesbury, a sizeable printing house which gave him experience of all areas of the trade. After leaving Hazell, Watson and Viney, Davis became assistant manager at the Athenaeum Printing Works in Redhill, Surrey where he worked for seven years before joining the

Kynoch Press in September 1931. Originally employed at the Press as a commercial manager in the costing department, he proved himself a diligent accountant and with his good academic background and sound commercial experience he appeared a reasonable choice for promotion to Press manager in 1933. However, all managerial appointments within ICI Metals Group were made by the directors of the local board, none of whom had any knowledge of the printing industry, and their decision to appoint Davis was made on his ability to control the accounts books rather than on his ability to manage a printing house. But financial acumen and good qualifications failed to make him a successful manager and under his direction the Press fell into decline. He was, as his successor, Michael Clapham, later wrote:

> a man who might have done well in other fields, but whose total ignorance of design, typography, or any of the arts of man-management caused the standards of the Press to go to hell.

Under Herbert Simon the press room had been greatly expanded, but Davis failed to maintain this development; all expansion was halted, no new equipment was bought and the printing plant remained entirely letterpress. Stagnation gripped the works. The composing room also became moribund as Davis failed to continue the imaginative expansion of the type racks which had been inspired by Simon, and nothing that was extraordinary was added although Harry Carter did persuade Davis to purchase a few useful founders' types. In the Monotype department not even the most popular and necessary of new faces were added to its range. The Press, which had once been ahead of typographic fashion, failed to keep up with even the most basic of typographic developments, and as a result its reputation began to wane.

This was reflected in the decline in the number of staff employed by the Kynoch Press which was around 170 when Davis took control of the Press, but by 1935 this had started to drop, and although the number of staff in the press room rose slightly from 22 men in 1934 to 24 men in 1938, the number of compositors fell during the same period from 37 to 31 men.[2] A number of key personnel also resigned, including Noel Carrington in 1935, followed by Harry Carter in 1936. Both had been loyal to Simon and his typographic principles which both men did their best to maintain, but with Herbert Simon's departure the reputation of the Press had declined beyond recognition and neither man could tolerate working under the new regime. Carter's job was taken by a young man named Denis Megaw who arrived at the Press fresh from his typographic training at the Leipzig School of Printing and who was full of optimism for his new role, as his letters to a German colleague show:

12 May 1937

24 Churston Mansions, Gray's Inn Road, London

Dear Stresow

. . . then after Easter I began to work at the Kynoch Press. And this is certainly a very good position, with great possibilities. Herbert Simon, brother of Oliver (now both at the Curwen Press) worked here four years ago. (Also Harry Carter, now Nonesuch). Now I am fortunate, and the work pleases me greatly, and I have enough time to do *something* on each piece . . .

Yours

Denis Megaw

But his delight very rapidly turned to frustration:

20 June 1937

140 Adelaide Road, London

Dear Stresow

. . . at Kynoch, naturally, everything is not as wonderful as I had initially thought. It really is incomprehensible how Herbert Simon came here; the current boss has no understanding for anything other than money . . .

with my best wishes

Denis Megaw

Davis had inherited a flourishing and busy Press. For the first twelve months of his tenure the Press workload remained high and it ran to capacity as Simon had left the Press with well-stocked order-books which it continued to process. The only production of any quality that the Press continued to produce was the Diary and Notebook which remained under the direction of Harry Carter who between 1933 and 1938 continued to produce original solutions for these publications using the talents of reputable artists such as Albert Rutherston, Edward Bawden, Agnes Miller-Parker, and Mary M. Kessell, combined with some of the most rare and extraordinary typefaces at the Press— Thorne Shaded, Elephant, Fat Face and Prisma.

But the Press could not survive on past achievements and the odd quality publication alone, and new work had to be got to maintain its reputation; but by 1934 the adverse effects of Davis's management were felt and the Press was unable to maintain or attract quality work. With the departure of Harry Carter the Press had no one to oversee the design of clients' work, and when Carrington resigned there was nobody in the sales office who had sufficient contacts to attract the

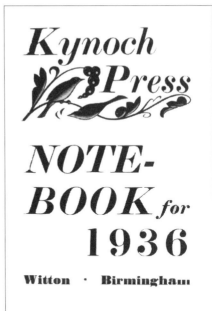

The Kynoch Press
Diary and Notebooks:
the 1934 Diary was
designed and illustrated
by Albert Rutherston,
and the Diary for 1936
was by Agnes Miller-Parker.

'right' clients and without Simon there was also a general deterioration in composing-room standards. Many customers took fright: Francis Meynell placed no work with the Press after 1933 and the Design and Industries Association discontinued their patronage when Davis refused to print further editions of *Design for Today* even though it had reached the point of self-sufficiency through its advertising revenue. With the loss of major clients from both the publishing and commercial sectors other customers also withdrew their patronage. Even the loyalty of ICI was tested and both ICI Central Publicity and the *ICI Magazine* expressed dissatisfaction, issuing warnings to the ICI board that unless standards were restored at the Press they would cease to use it as their printers.

H. V. Davis was a weak manager with little personality. To manage the Kynoch Press successfully, it required someone with the ability to both serve and stand up to the mighty ICI and to balance its commitment to the main company with its obligations to outside customers. It was a difficult tight-rope to negotiate and not one that Davis succeeded in walking and by 1938 he had brought the Press to the precipice of disaster. The future of the Kynoch Press hung in the balance, and its fate was once again wholly in the hands of ICI.

Chapter 6

1938–1945
MICHAEL CLAPHAM
resurrection of the Kynoch Press

By 1938, the reputation of the Kynoch Press had sunk very low. Neither the ICI Public Relations Department nor the *ICI Magazine* could tolerate its falling standards and asked the ICI Board for permission to take their work elsewhere. It was evident that Davis needed replacing and ICI were forced to consider the future of its ailing Press. The Secretary of ICI Metals Group, Captain W. E. Smith, was given four months to recruit a new Press manager but after two months he was still unsuccessful and so took advice from Walter Lewis at the Cambridge University Press. Lewis recommended that Michael Clapham, an ex-apprentice of his who was then working at Percy, Lund Humphries in Bradford, might be a possible candidate for the job. In May 1938 Clapham arrived at the Kynoch Press as Master Printer and General Manager.

Michael Clapham[1] was an academic turned artisan who had studied Classics at King's College Cambridge but who neglected his studies when he developed an interest in printing. His fascination began when he decided to send valentine cards to all those girls at Newnham College who had caught his eye. To have them printed professionally would have been prohibitively expensive; for Clapham to print them himself was something of an experiment. However, for 30*s.* he purchased a fount of Bruce Rogers's Centaur type from Walter Lewis at the Cambridge University Press (CUP), made a type bed from some hard wood, and an improvised printing press from a pair of shelves. From this rudimentary equipment Clapham managed to extract a series of attractive and competent valentine's cards. Flushed with his success as an amateur printer, he became increasingly intrigued by the process. Clapham graduated in 1933 and was fortunate to be able to turn his hobby into his profession when he was employed by Walter Lewis at the CUP as a master printer's apprentice for two years on 10*s.* a week. It was also at the CUP that Clapham came into contact with Stanley Morison. In 1935 he left Cambridge and moved to Bradford to work at Percy, Lund Humphries where Jan Tschichold was then employed and where Clapham worked as an assistant overseer in the composing room, rising to joint Works Manager. But in 1938, eighteen months before the outbreak of World War II, Clapham was approached by ICI:

> . . . I got back from work to find a letter waiting for me. It was postmarked Birmingham and bore the roundel of ICI . . . I knew little of it save that somewhere in that vast organisation there nestled one of the four or five most notable printing offices in the country, the Kynoch Press. And this letter was written by a Captain W. E. Smith: he was indicated to be the Secretary of the Metals Group of ICI, whose twenty-odd component companies littered an undistinguished letterhead.
>
> It was short and to the point. The writer had been in touch with Mr Walter Lewis who had indicated that I might be interested in applying for a position which would shortly become vacant, that of master printer and general manager of the Kynoch Press. Would I kindly indicate whether I were interested and if so send a *curriculum vitae*. . .
>
> Once again there was no doubt about the interest. Here was I, aged 26, beginning to think that I was reasonably on top of a works manager's job. There were in the United Kingdom only half a dozen printers who Francis Meynell of the Nonesuch Press trusted to print his books: and Kynoch, like Cambridge and Lund Humphries, was one of them. Of this group the Kynoch Press was the smallest, but ICI, which had unknowingly acquired it as a fraction of Kynoch Ltd, would no doubt be able to spare a bit of capital for expansion, for innovation. However small my chances, it must be worth a try.[2]

Clapham was offered the post which he accepted with a princely annual salary of £715 which included a ten per cent annual performance bonus. His mandate was to rejuvenate the Kynoch Press and rescue it from the mire into which it had descended. Clapham started work in Birmingham in the May of 1938:

> . . . let me take you to the Kynoch Press. It is a low, mainly single-storey building, but with two storeys in the front, and it stands in the forecourt of the main entrance to the Kynoch Works, besides the five storey red brick Edwardian office block which is the administrative headquarters of the Metals Group of ICI. The Press building was put up during the 1914–18 war to house the manufacture of percussion caps, but it was later thought imprudent to have that sensitive and dangerous explosive, mercury fulminate, in such a populous area, and the operation was moved to a remoter part of the mile-square factory site. Now the two-storey section at the front holds offices, the Monotype department, and the readers' room. The single-storey part runs back about two-hundred yards and contains the paper warehouse, the composing room, machinery room, foundry and bindery . . . [it was] mostly a good modern plant, installed under Bobby

Simon in the 1920s; but all the printing plant was letterpress . . . In the Monotype rooms and the composing room the equipment was pretty good again, though the acquisition of new types from the ever-increasing Monotype range ended with Simon's departure . . .

In the front of the building on the ground floor, is what is to be my office: a simple, square room painted in cream and with all the furniture, desk, table, chairs and bookcases made from pale oak by Gordon Russell of Broadway. At one end it adjoins a secretary's office, where my secretary, Miss Buck, an agreeable woman about ten years older than me, is installed. At the other end a door opens into the production assistant's office, where Clover, a decent commercial artist but no typographer, and his secretary Marion Cook, are installed. Crossing the passage which leads to the front door you come to the general office, where France, the office manager presides: as staff he has an assistant, Irving, who acts as estimating clerk, and four girl clerks, who look after the costing, invoicing, order processing and general office jobs. Behind that and adjoining the warehouse, is the office of the paper buyer, Notley. Beyond the paper warehouse you are in the works, light and airy with its north-light roof: first the bindery, then the work's managers' office, where Kennedy and his progress clerk, Stella Roberts are installed. Beyond them are the composing and machine rooms side by side. A staircase and a lift run up to the Monotype rooms and to the readers' room, on the first floor of the two-storey block. All is compact and well-arranged: but with not much room for expansion.[3]

There was much work for Clapham to do in order to gain the confidence of the Press employees, raise the standards of the Press and win back the loyalty of its clients. Through Clapham's obvious knowledge of the practicalities of the printing process, his kindly and respectful attitude to his staff and his ordinary and approachable character, he gained the trust of the Press members, and with their trust and respect he was able to start to raise the standards of the Press. To win back the lost faith of the clients, Clapham had to turn his attention to bringing the machine and composing room back up to date.

In 1938 the machine-room was all letterpress and Michael Clapham ordered new printing equipment to facilitate the smooth running of that department. In March 1939, the Kynoch Press committee started discussing the introduction of offset lithography:

> The general condition of the plant and the probable requirements of the next few years were discussed, with particular reference to the tendency of the Publicity Department to use lithography. The recent discussions with Mr Cheveley of Publicity Department had shown that the process was unimportant as long as the desired effect was obtained, and Mr Clapham had undertaken to carry out an experiment to show that the desired effect could be got printing letterpress on cartridge paper with the existing plant. It was agreed that the present

LEFT
The Kynoch Press
Monotype composing room
circa 1938.

RIGHT
The *ICI Magazine*
being 'finished' on a
Seybold trimmer in the
Kynoch Press bindery.

needs of ICI did not justify such a major step as the installation of litho plant, but that in view of the rapid technical improvement of the litho process it would be necessary to watch its developments closely. For the next two years it was agreed that the chief need was to eliminate certain bottle necks in the production departments, and in particular to overcome the virtual stoppage of general work caused by the Magazine, whose increased size was making the congestion more severe. This congestion was worst in the Bindery, where all other work had to be put to one side for 3 or 4 days every month, and it was agreed that the only way to overcome this would be to install a covering machine which would cut down the number of girls required on covering from 10 to 3, and would at the same time make for more continuous production. The replacements of plant that would be necessary during the next two years were also discussed, and a provisional programme of applications was drawn up. [4]

Clapham also set out to redeem the typographic reputation of the Press. Times New Roman was immediately ordered as Davis had failed to install the face when it had been released in 1932. Monotype Bodoni Heavy Italic was also bought as it was a fount regularly used by ICI. New matrices for several other faces and additional casters were also installed. Plans were also put in motion for the production of a new type specimen book, the first major specimen book since Herbert Simon's departure in 1933. Production of the new specimen began in 1938 and was produced to a design by Clapham; it was to be in two volumes and bound by the wire-o process and would use ICI rexine on the cover. One thousand copies of the book were to be printed at a cost of £300, distributed free to customers and prospective customers of the Press, but sold for five shillings to anyone else. Work on the specimen book was done during slack periods in the composing room, some headway was made on the project, but the composing room failed to complete the work before the outbreak of war twelve months later. At that time production of the specimen book ceased, but was resumed once again after the end of the war.

As well as re-designing the type specimen books, Michael Clapham also brought about the first major change to the design of the *ICI Magazine* when in 1938 Times New Roman replaced Baskerville as the body text and Cartoon was a surprising choice for titling. Clapham was at great pains to explain these changes to the readers of the *Magazine*:

> This month the *Magazine* is printed in a new type. Some cases in the Kynoch Press which for years had been filled with Baskerville, have been emptied into the melting pot and re-filled with Times New Roman, and the 500,000 or so separate letters of which this issue is composed have been cast from new matrices on the Monotype machine . . . The type in which this issue is printed is called Times New Roman, with a heavier version, Times Bold for the headings . . . In particular, the legibility of its smaller sizes and its increased boldness, make it more suitable than Baskerville, for a magazine like this, in which shiny paper is necessary to reproduce photographs, and there is a good deal of closely set text . . . and so this change has been made. Admirers of Baskerville—and patriotic citizens of Birmingham—may regret it. But the rule applies to this as to other periodicals, that those which fail to follow the modern trends in layout eventually look dull and uninviting besides their more up-to-date rivals. [5]

In the eighteen months between his arrival at the Press and the outbreak of World War II, Michael Clapham succeeded in going some way to restoring the confidence of the Press in itself, and with the re-enthusing of the staff came a gradual resumption of confidence from ICI and outside customers. The order books began to swell and the composing and machine rooms and the bindery were fully occupied and turnover on both ICI work and outside work started to show an increase. But in August 1939, with the anticipated declaration of war with Germany, there was a dramatic falling-off of work. Staff in the London office were either moved to Birmingham or sent home to await further instruction and by the end of September the presses were virtually at a standstill.

Of the printing produced during the war there is little comment to be made. The production of many regular publications was halted and there was little scope for anything other than the utilitarian and after the first year paper became scarce.

Despite the outbreak of war, the Kynoch Press continued to produce its Notebooks. The Notebook for 1939 was designed by Richard Beck for a fee of 35 guineas and used ICI leathercloth for the spine. In 1940 Gordon Cullen produced a Notebook with 71 illustrations tracing the rise and decline of classical influence in English architecture. The austerity measures imposed as a consequence of wartime conditions were made apparent in the 1941 Notebook which was illustrated by Robert Gibbings, where case-binding gave way to comb-binding and where a substrate of inferior quality was used. An explanation for the poverty of production was given at the end of the war:

> After four years of interruption by paper shortage the Kynoch Press resumes this year the publication of its Notebook and Diary. The war years have not seen great alteration in the Press, but two things should perhaps be mentioned here. First, we record with deep regret that two men who were partly concerned with this Notebook in the last five years of its publication, C. R. Hiles and B. Poore were killed on active service. Secondly, it may be of interest to admit more openly than was possible at the time that the 1941 Notebook, produced on a variety of types of coloured paper, owed its appearance to a bomb which fell in the Kynoch Press warehouse, causing no injury to our staff, but decimating our cherished paper stocks. [6]

Of the Notebook itself the Press gave the following comment:

> Some may expect an apology for the appearance of a Kynoch Press Diary at all in times of war and paper scarcity; others, for its strange format. But people still have appointments to keep, and printing has still its uses; so it was decided to produce a diary as usual, though halved in bulk. Its variety of colouring must be blamed on an undiscriminating bomb; from whose crater, not a hundred miles from here, most of the paper was dug in fragments too small for general use. The wood engravings by Robert Gibbings were meant originally to illustrate Kingslake's *Eothen*, whose text is used in the new Kynoch Press type book: but this has had to be put aside for a time, and meanwhile the engravings are too good to be hidden away for the war's duration. [7]

The only new publication of any note produced during the war was the scientific journal *Endeavour* [8] which started as a propaganda exercise for the promotion of British science but which became one of the world's leading scientific reviews. *Endeavour* was first produced in 1942 by the Kynoch Press and was the idea of Sidney Rogerson of ICI Central Publicity:

... before the days of the last war, ICI was not concerned to advertise itself ...
a small-scale public opinion poll held shortly after the outbreak of war disclosed
that the few people who were aware of ICI at all thought of it as some sinister
"merchant of death" manufacturing munitions of war for private gain. It would
never do to allow such an impression to continue to deepen during the war years
and accordingly I obtained permission to spend some money on advertising the
nature of ICI and the objects for which it was formed. That I was allowed to do
this was largely because I was able to plead national necessity: that the German
propaganda offensive was particularly successful in the scientific field; and that
no one better than ICI could be found to combat it. The enemy boast that
Germany led the world in science and that Britain's inventiveness "died giving
birth to the steam engine" could be shown up for the lie it was by listing the
achievements of British scientists since 1900. There was no need to concentrate
on ICI or do any special pleading for the company—ICI would profit automati-
cally because it was the biggest unit and the most successful in the British chemical industry. [9]

Although it was published by ICI it was not a house-journal. ICI
approved and financed *Endeavour* whose circulation was facilitated by the
British Council, the Central Office of Information and the Foreign
Office. Paper was especially allocated for the project and the production
was directed by an editorial board. War in Europe meant that Britain
was subject to restrictions on the export of commodities, but intangible
assets, concepts and beliefs could still be promoted. *Endeavour* was published to ensure British scientific achievements were kept in the minds of
those abroad. The journal served those European scientists who were
isolated by war, and was the only source of reference for scientific
research performed during the conflict. *Endeavour* provided a cultural
life-line for the sequestered scientific community abroad and was sent to
individual senior scientists, to libraries of scientific laboratories, hospitals
where research was undertaken, a few of the larger city reference
libraries and press attachés abroad. Over 98 per cent of the copies published were for overseas consumption, with only a few hundred available
for distribution in the United Kingdom (to the divisions of ICI, university
and industrial research laboratories and scientific libraries). It was the
only British scientific journal to be published in a foreign language, with
the early issues published in English, French, German and Spanish. In
1943, a Russian edition was printed, but this was discontinued in 1946
due to the difficulties in setting, the expense of the special paper on
which it was printed and doubts as to whether the publication reached
its intended recipients. An Italian edition was started in 1948.

Endeavour continued to be printed by the Kynoch Press until the late

The title page of *Endeavour* magazine issued in 1943. The typographic arrangement of *Endeavour*, which had been designed by Michael Clapham, remained unchanged until 1963.

ENDEAVOUR

A quarterly review designed to record the progress
of the sciences in the service of mankind

VOLUME II · 1943

1970s when it was sold to the Pergamon Press. It was originally issued quarterly, but later came out three times annually and had a circulation of 25,000 in 1942 which increased to 35,000 by 1955 which was a distribution regarded as considerable for a publication with such a high-level content.

Responsibility for the typography lay with Michael Clapham who created a neat and simple two-column design using Monotype Baskerville, a design which was used, with no amendments, for all foreign editions. But the most important feature of its production was the inclusion of full-colour illustrations and half-tones, a novelty for scientific publishing and an expense that most journals were not able to afford, but *Endeavour* encouraged contributors to use colour wherever necessary.

Endeavour was not the only ICI production which was introduced as a direct result of the war. With German propaganda berating British technical achievements, ICI rose to the offensive in 1941 when it began placing advertisements in the British and overseas press. Each advert was issued as part of a series and each series was based on a single theme. The first, 'Aspects of an Industry', was designed to show that the chemical industry was the most essential of all industries to the country. This was followed by 'Services of an Industry' which revealed the effects of the chemical industry's products on all members of the community. 'Personnel of an Industry' was a particularly successful series, which showed ICI employees (captured on canvas by eminent artists) at their work, as a celebration of their contribution to the war effort. 'Equipment of an Industry' showed the apparatus used by industry and was intended to bridge the gap between laboratory test tubes and full-scale machinery. 'Ancestors of an Industry' reinforced what the world owed to British contributions to the sciences by individual men. 'Achievements of an Industry' recorded the scientific discoveries of ICI. 'Elements of an Industry' described the elements found in nature and how important they were to the chemical industry. These adverts proved immensely successful, and have become collectors' pieces. As a measure of the success of the campaign, the company was inundated with requests to publish the advertisements and after the war each series was bound into book form and distributed to schools or other interested institutions. The books were impressive productions, large in format. Some, like 'Elements of an Industry', were direct reproductions of the advertisements, whilst others, such as 'Equipment of an Industry', were given a new setting in which to display themselves, with expansive margins and well-leaded type. Others were treated more conventionally in book form. After 1945, these series of advertisements gave rise to other popular publishing projects on the same theme: 'Background to Discovery' and 'Advancing the Techniques of an Industry'. They were picture books on a grand scale, in which the image dominated the printed word. They made great use of quality photography, which was reproduced by the Press to a high standard, and displayed effectively using space and a minimum of description. The advertisements and the ensuing books not only helped ICI gain the goodwill of a well-informed public, but they also helped to forge a relationship between art, industry, science and the world of printing — and particularly with the Kynoch Press.

Between 1939 and 1945, Clapham was seconded to alternative duties on the Witton site and the day-to-day management of the Press was relinquished to John Kennedy who deputised for Michael Clapham throughout the war. But the 'alternative duties' of Clapham during the war form another story altogether, and tell of the remarkable part a printer played in the development of the Allies' greatest deterrent:

. . . my initial work during the war was living on the top of the control tower at the centre of Kynoch Works, from which the movement of ambulances and fire appliances was directed in our heavily (and not unjustifiably) bombed munitions works. Later in the war, when I had been asked to do an impossible job by a photo-engraving process, which failed, I thought of another way to produce metal perforated with many of thousands of tiny holes of a few microns diameter, and suddenly got directed to the so-called Tube Alloys Project, a code name for the atomic bomb team, where I was told to make millions of barriers for diffusing uranium hexafloride, a problem which at that point was holding up the project. My process used some equipment which was used in the litho process, but Kynoch had not got this yet and I had Lund Humphries and Sun Engraving as my main contractors, while I worked from a small office cum lab in the Kynoch Press.[10]

ICI foresaw that the end of the war would give them huge personnel problems. Many staff of pensionable age had stayed on during the war, but with the outbreak of peace they would take their right to retirement. With a different pattern of life and working practices emerging in the post-war world, ICI would have to embark on a huge programme of retraining and recruiting. To which end they decided that each Division should have on its board a Personnel Director and Michael Clapham was appointed as Personnel Director of ICI Metals. Clapham resigned as Manager of the Press on 1 January 1946 but continued to maintain an interest in the development of the Press. His place was taken by his deputy, John Kennedy, whose task it would be to adapt the Press to the new post-war trading environments.

Chapter 7

1946–1959
JOHN KENNEDY
modernisation of the Kynoch Press

The Kynoch Press emerged from the war with its reputation revived and intact. But the commercial, technical and social environment of the printing industry had begun to change and the challenge to the Press was how to adapt to the new conditions. Technological advances in both pre-press and printing techniques meant that the Press had to modernise and re-equip its plant and recruit new employees who had knowledge of contemporary working methods. The new techniques engendered new services which forced the Press to re-structure itself and to establish specialised departments for graphic reproduction, design and proof-reading. In the years following the war, the Press had to navigate its way through a technological revolution and its passage was steered by three Scottish expatriates: firstly by John (Jock) Kennedy assisted by David Hopewell and then Wallis Heath.[1]

Jock Kennedy came from a publishing background; his first job was with Messrs. William Collins and Sons of Glasgow where he was employed as an assistant works manager, and he then took a job with Messrs. Wells, Gardner and Darton who were London publishers, followed by work in the books department of the *Daily Express*. In 1934, Kennedy got a post in the costing and estimating department of the Kynoch Press and in 1936 he became works superintendent, deputising for Michael Clapham between 1939 and 1945. In 1946 he became Manager of the Kynoch Press. David Hopewell was also from a publishing background and was a member of the Holmes family of educational publishers of Glasgow, and it was with Andrew Holmes and Company that he was apprenticed as a young master printer. After demobilisation from the Army in 1946, Hopewell rejected an offer of work from the printing office at Cadbury's of Bournville in favour of a job as works manager at the Kynoch Press. Kennedy, with the assistance of David Hopewell, was responsible for modernising the Kynoch Press and equipping it with the personnel and machinery which would allow it to trade in the post-war world.

The first step taken by Kennedy and Hopewell was to strengthen the composing room management. Hopewell wanted to find a composing room overseer who was capable of directing his staff to produce the complicated settings which were required of the Press:

> One of the best ways of finding where good people in those days was you had travelling all over the country, and throughout the whole of the printing industry, reps for ink and paper and for Monotype Corporation and Linotype Corporation and people like that. So I wrote a specification of the kind of man I wanted to head-up the Composing Department. I passed it out to one or two of these people and back came the news that there was this very competent chap who was not terribly happy, having come back from the RAF . . . That was Bert Pace. I saw Bert Pace and offered him the job—and he came. That was the first really good step. Bert Pace really was a first-class man and comp. He had an encyclopedic knowledge of arithmetical and mathematical composition—having spent his life on railway timetables, which had tremendous problems of justification. So that was that. [2]

Bert Pace started his printing career on the *Crewe Chronicle* where he was apprenticed for seven years as a Linotype operator; this was followed by time at J. C. Hammond and Co. Ltd in Moor Street Birmingham which was equipped only with Monotype machines and where Pace had to learn his apprenticeship all over again. After demobilisation from the RAF, he worked briefly for W. J. Rodway's in Birmingham and F. W. Pendenbury in Oakengates in Shropshire from where he took the job of composing-room overseer at the Kynoch Press. One of the first jobs Pace had to do was to move the composing-room and plan its layout, which was necessary to make room for the offset litho department:

> When the time came for Hopewell to really get down to studying the new composing-room he gave me the job of planning it out. I used the works study that I had been taught. I produced a plan and that was accepted. We had to move it in one weekend. The plan was to centralise all the ancillary equipment. In the old composing room there was so many mitring machines, so many lead cutters things like that. What I did was centralise all of them so that everybody could get to them quite easily and there was no hassle. That was the main thing, it was to get everything centralised and also to flow. The proof presses—for taking proofs off galleys—that was easily reached by the two proof-hands. In the old composing room, they were way down the middle of the room and the imposing stone was somewhere else. It was a hotchpotch of various things! In the new composing room it was all centralised. What pleased me more than anything else was

> that PA—Personnel Administration—came in to do works study, and when they
> went to the composing room, the only thing that they could add was some 'v'
> lines on the cases to make sure they went back into the right place. So I got my
> status from doing that job.[3]

Bert Pace eventually took over Hopewell's role as Works Manager and
was responsible for the introduction of computer-assisted typesetting.

After the war, the Kynoch Press developed its machine room in a
way that allowed it to continue to produce the quality work with which
it had always been involved, to which end the Press was equipped with
colour offset lithography. Before the war the Press had already begun to
realise that there was no real future for either letterpress printing or the
associated process of photo-engraving, but the war delayed any plans it
might have had for its installation. Post-war, the lack of lithographic
experience at the Press meant it had to recruit staff to help it to set up
and run the new department. Bill Jones from Walsall Litho was recruited as the first litho foreman at the Kynoch Press with control over a
machine-room of 31 men and a say in the structuring of the litho
department. Hopewell recruited Jones, as he had done with Pace, by
word of mouth:

> I wanted to find who was the best litho printer in the Midlands. I used an ink
> traveller, a man called Bob Bettles, and he said there was a chap called Bill Jones
> who worked for Walsall Litho. He was the first litho foreman and he stayed about
> twelve years. Then he met someone and went off and set up on their own . . . Bill
> Jones served his apprenticeship with Walsall Litho, who were very good lithogra-
> phers. When he'd been called up for service during the war, he'd gone into the
> Royal Engineers Ordnance Survey Unit as a printer because they had ten ton
> trucks with two-colour Crabtree presses in them which followed the army where
> ever they went. He'd risen to the rank of Sergeant. He had leadership qualities,
> so he was recruited even before the first machines arrived, and he was given
> complete freedom as to the kind of layout he wanted. [4]

In 1952, the Kynoch Press added three offset machines to its outdated
range of Miehle colour letterpress machines; the new presses included
one two-colour and two single-colour Crabtree quad-demy presses, one
of which had a specially cut cylinder so that it would take board one-
eighth of an inch thick to print the wads that went into the ends of cartridges. The plant was later expanded with a Countess MK 4A press, a
Crabtree Countess machine, a Rotary offset press, and two Rapida
four-colour presses.

Setting-up the offset litho department meant a big reorganisation of
accommodation at the Press, and some re-investment in the letterpress

department which continued to run in conjunction with the litho department for several years:

> The main reason for installing litho at this stage was the fact that carton printing was printed mostly on this Miehle colour press. It was printed from electros— stereos could not stand up to the wear on the carton board—so it had to be electros and these were quite costly. The two-colour was pretty ancient and pretty slow so they put up a case for bringing in litho machines. Now, to make room for the litho machines, the composing-room had to move. Above the works office and bindery area there was an area used by ICI Central Literature Store, they were asked if they would get out. They moved and a building was found for them somewhere. Then it was a case of planning the new composing room. As well as starting the litho department, it was decided that the letterpress should be re-equipped with large Miehles. That was one of the biggest mistakes we ever made because litho was coming along and I don't think anyone foresaw how the quality of litho could improve so dramatically in, say, ten years. But the installation of three quad-demy Miehles was a big mistake. The litho department then consisted of three double-demy machines. I think there was one two-colour and two single-colours, and of course they took over all this work for cartons. Then Hopewell decided he wanted a bigger one, so we had a Quad-demy Crabtree Monarch installed, and that was the next mistake. The old two-colour letterpress machine was taken away and the Crabtree Monarch was put in its place. That was a monstrous machine. It would have been a very good machine but unfortunately the man who erected it at Witton, he boobed! He was trying to put board through, and he allowed too many through together. That machine couldn't quite take the quantity of boards that was going through and somehow or other it did something to one of the cylinders and it was never right after that! But we didn't find out what had happened for two or three years. It was only after the cylinders were taken out to be re-ground that this defect was found. What nobody thought at that time was that four-colour printing would be so much superior. [5]

The offset machines took over the work of the outdated Miehle colour letterpress machines which were no longer adequate for their task of printing cartons. But as the process evolved, and the Press established its own reproduction department, the nature of the litho work changed to include lucrative full-colour illustrated publicity work, advertising booklets and brochures. Offset lithography brought with it improvements in quality, versatility, speed and cost and the Press could faithfully reproduce detail in fine-screen half-tones which meant it could attract the high-class colour work it was so keen to produce. The rubber blanket, used in the offset process to transfer ink from plate to paper, adapted itself to most printing surfaces and allowed the Press to experiment with printing on a variety of substrates and using mixed make-ups. What is more, litho plates could be made very quickly and the rotary principle used in offset lithography made it a faster process than letter-press. This led to increased capacity which the Press desperately needed and shorter production times.

Offset lithography enhanced the quality of the colour work pro-duced by the Press but this could not have been achieved without good graphic reproduction, and the Press understood the advantages that were to be gained by starting an in-house lithographic studio. Most of the reproduction work needed by the Press was done by Siviter-Smith letterpress blockmakers of Ludgate Hill, Birmingham who had a photo-litho off-shoot called Bentley Photo-Litho based in Oldbury in the West Midlands. It was from here that Hopewell recruited the exper-tise which allowed the Press to develop its own lithographic studio:

> One day I was talking with a very knowledgeable ink rep called Bob Mair who was another ex-pat Scot. He was a very senior—I think he was *the* senior—sales-man with Manders Printing Inks. He said: I know exactly the chap you want. He's working for the people who do your platemaking, Bentley Photo-Litho, and his name is Kilminster. He got an external degree whilst he was a prisoner of war. He did it by correspondence. Kilminster was so valuable that he was never allowed to contemplate escaping himself. He was Warrant Officer in the Royal Airforce, he was a navigator. That is the first clue to the way the man's mind works. I mean, if you can take a quarter-of-a-million pounds worth of aeroplane and fly it to a dot in the middle of the continent and bring it back again, you must be a very numerate person indeed. Whilst he was a prisoner of war he built a printing press, he used the tiled plates from lavatories, polished the surface off them, made them into litho plates and printed maps. He forged documents, did all sorts of wonderful things. There is a whole book about him. He came back from the war and said to Oscar Bentley: I've studied this, and I have got this degree, external through the Red Cross. Oscar Bentley's reply was: You're a cameraman, get on with it! So we sent for Kilminster. The scientific fraternity in ICI general and in the Metals Division said: What, one of us in Kynoch Press, how marvellous! And they welcomed him with open arms. And it became a colour laboratory, which is where our reputation for colour came from. [6]

The Press had already started a small lithographic studio with a staff of four who were responsible for drawing work, negative spotting and cam-era operations. Roy Kilminster was recruited as department manager for litho colour reproduction in order that he might develop the exper-tise of the department. When he arrived at the Press, Kilminster found:

> . . . a small department with some quite good equipment, but there was nobody really technically competent in the specialist areas required to get it off the ground. There were a couple of young girls who did a bit of drawing work, and perhaps a bit of negative spotting and things like that. One was particularly

good at drawing. They had probably both been to art school. They produced simple artwork for reproduction . . . however, they had not had any training in colour reproduction work. There was also an experienced camera operator and another young man on the litho reproduction side, but he wasn't really technically competent to run the place, he hadn't the experience to set the department up for high quality colour reproduction. They needed somebody with more technical knowledge. The main bit of equipment on the repro side was the camera which was the best you could get at the time. Far better, in fact, than was necessary for the work they were doing in the early stages. The camera was made by Klimsch in Germany. Quite an expensive job and no doubt it was bought with an eye to future developments at the Press. [7]

Kilminster turned the studio into a sophisticated colour laboratory which had a scientific and measurable approach to graphic reproduction, an attitude which was fundamental to the success of the post-war Press. Kilminster experimented with two processes which allowed the Press to produce high-quality colour work: a means by which colour proofs could be simulated by optical methods and a colour masking system for use in photo-mechanical reproduction processes.[8]

Colour proofs in offset lithography were needed both for approval by the customer and as a guide to colour retouching. In retouching a number of progressive proofs were normally required; this was costly and time-consuming and prompted Kilminster to look at other methods of colour proofing. Retouching was usually done by artists using subjective methods which produced uncertain results and Kilminster recognised there was a need for a more reliable preliminary proofing method to check and analyse the reproduction before the final colour-proofing stage. Several methods of preliminary proofing were available, but they were time-consuming and expensive, but Kilminster was attracted by an American optical device which comprised three projectors which demonstrate additive colour synthesis with three film separation positives and which was used for checking colour work for newspapers. The equipment had the advantages of speed and cheapness of use and allowed the retoucher to check his separations as often as was necessary. Kilminster constructed his own apparatus using this projection principle. It was a highly successful aid to retouching for it was possible to allow for ink spread and the effect that the paper used for printing the job would have. The great advantage was that a retoucher could check the separations quickly and as many times as desired and the only expense was the capital cost of the equipment. Kilminster also looked into the problems of colour masking. Masking was necessary to correct deficiencies in printing inks used in reproducing originals. Without colour correction, colour printing would not correctly reproduce the original image. If colour masking was successful it eliminated the need to retouch by hand. There were many masking systems in use, but not one that could be used universally, so Kilminster applied himself to the subject and developed a system that produced improvements in quality and savings in retouching and camera time and also in materials.

The advanced capabilities of the lithographic studio brought the Press to the forefront of contemporary printing techniques, enabling it to produce award-winning excellence in colour reproduction. But the Kynoch Press was not alone in taking a scientific approach to graphic reproduction. John Jarrold's of Norwich realised it had to be in the forefront of technology and set up an experimental team which investigated the problems of colour masking and scanning techniques. Hazell, Watson and Viney of Aylesbury had its own research department and Lund Humphries of Bradford also took a laboratory approach to graphic reproduction.

One of the first jobs that the Press produced using offset litho and the skills of Kilminster was:

> . . . *Hexagon Digest* [published by ICI Dyestuffs Division] which was a book on colour which was certainly quarterly, might even have been monthly, and they were printing all the qualities of colour work and its fade properties and all its colour characteristics. There were charts within this magazine which then was 10 by 8 inches, before it went up to A4. It would have a particular blue dye and testing its fade qualities for a month hour by hour and we used to have to represent the diminishing quality or intensity of the blue. Absolutely phenomenal work. That was all hand re-touching, transparencies were given, but Roy [Kilminster] would separate them then they would work on them by the hour, reducing the size of the magenta within it and increasing the cyan and so on—amazing really. That really led to a lot of the work that happened with Paints Division. People were not now decorating for decorating's sake, they were beginning to decorate their homes to make a different sort of home. So they would buy old furniture and paint it. Paints Division were running a colour advisory service from Slough saying: You can buy this rubbishy furniture from round the corner, this is what you can do with it! And the colour had to be spot-on accurate. *Colourful Homes* the book was called and we did it for three or four years and that was a phenomenal run. I think it was probably the biggest initial litho colour job Kynoch Press had ever handled we were talking about millions. Phenomenal job. [9]

The lithographic studio was not the only department at the Press which produced award-winning work. After the war, British manufacturing became increasingly design-conscious and alert to the necessity for styling all manufactured goods, including printed literature. Well-produced publicity material aided successful sales, and a greater proportion of industry was demanding high-quality printed literature. The importance of well-designed publicity material had been highlighted at exhibitions at the London Design Centre which educated people to the significance and application of design to print; discussions on design for print were conducted at the British Federation of Master Printers Congress, and reinforced by an exhibition arranged by the Federation in co-operation with the Council for Industrial Design. The expansion of international trade also helped to change rigid attitudes towards design and helped the public and the industry to see it was a necessity. The social status of the designer had also improved; the majority of post-war designers received formal training and were highly professional in their work. Typographic design was viewed as a specialised and marketable skill which the printing industry could utilise to its advantage. Industrial demands and changing social attitudes led some British printers including the Kynoch Press, the Curwen Press, Cowells and Lund Humphries to introduce design policies, and offer a graphic service as integral, rather than subsidiary, to business.

In 1956, as a response to changing attitudes, the London design studio relocated to Birmingham because the Press believed it was necessary for designers to be a part of the manufacturing process so they could oversee the production of their work. The Press realised that the designer-printer had an advantage over others because it had a complete vision of its product and total control over the process which contributed to its success and profitability. 'Designed at the Kynoch Press' started to appear on material in the mid-1950s when the Press realised it had a separate and specialised service to offer in the field of typography and graphic communication. Acknowledging design as an individual and measurable service was also part of a broader plan for the Press to present a new, structured and coherent image of itself to the public. The studio was run by Roger Denning who was a graduate of the University of Reading. The studio provided an individual and marketable service which produced work more distinctive than that of most printers. Denning spent twelve months working in all departments of the Press, experiencing every aspect of the trade in order to obtain a full understanding of the printing process so that a studio might be established which was run by designers who were used to printers and printers who understood designers. The design studio was seen as a professional consultancy with wide experience of all printed matter; it was not, as Denning pointed out at the time:

> . . . a printer's layout service, a soling and heeling department to ease production complications, a slick commercial studio producing tarty visuals having no relation to the final product. The group is a design consultancy, experienced in both the whole gamut of printed matter and also in pure and applied graphic design . . . The designer must make a choice of typeface and letterform, the nature and manner of illustration and illustrator, choice of paper and binding materials, method of binding and finishing operations. The designer is therefore constructing the anatomy, physiology and clothing of the printed job . . . The important fact is that the designer still remains responsible for the final decisions which have to be made. [10]

The studio had an holistic, coherent and analytical approach to design and it consciously based its solutions on its knowledge of the client and their requirements. The studio tried to anticipate design trends in order to offer an advanced rather than subservient design service; it had its eyes on international markets and produced work which rejected national design concepts. It was a far-reaching service which was more than an mere accompaniment to print, for it was a useful selling point for the Press and a chargeable and measurable part of its service. The studio also investigated avenues of design beyond the print-based environment and had the perspicacity to realise that design for print might not be the only area of design that might be explored. It extended its work to exhibitions, vehicle liveries, price ticketing for supermarkets, exterior directional and mandatory signs, railway rolling-stock decoration, packaging design, shop fascias and filmstrips. The Press handled most of the material which needed designing, but some work was placed with external agencies and freelance designers when the studio became overloaded, or deadlines were expedited, or because it had a lack of sympathy for the project. Midlands-based freelancers, agencies and illustrators that had been groomed to the ways of the Press were preferred, but there was a limited supply of creative Midlands photographers and those that did exist were geared up to the motor trade or were very industrial in nature. The studio offered a service which was provided by few other printers and brought acclaim to the Press on an international scale.

When Roger Denning resigned in August 1968, Bob Gill,[11] a heavyweight graphic designer from the London agency Fletcher | Forbes | Gill, was brought in to spearhead the Graphic Design Unit. He brought a fresh permissiveness to the studio, but one which was often discordant with the attitudes of ICI and as a result his association was short-lived, as a Kynoch Press designer Len Harvey remembers:

> He did a few mailing shots for us which were good. Posters. One of them which I remember was good was *We Print in any Flavour:* there was a lot of ice-cream, repetition, good Pentagram, Fletcher|Forbes|Gill style, repetition, all different flavours of ice-cream. There were several. Then we did a book for him, *Bob Gill's Portfolio,* on a silver cover with Coca-Cola across the front in red. A hell of a game to print on this metallic stuff. He didn't care, and didn't know anyway! He brought a breath of fresh air for the short time he was there. He didn't care about print, because printers were there to do what you wanted them to do. Fair enough if you're a designer, but not so good if you're a printer! So I afterwards got away with one or two things we wouldn't normally have done because he'd broken the ground. Kynoch Press was straight up and down, and the management were that way. Bob Gill came to a sticky end at Kynoch Press because he'd decided to do a Christmas card. At that time we were doing double blacks and grey and black to get extra depth to them. We were experimenting with Roy Kilminster, who was bloody good, head of litho, experimenting on this double black. You know the technique, you have a black and a grey and the grey's a bit off so it looks a bit better. The chappie who was with me, went down to work with him on this card. It was a brick wall which he did in black. It had got 'Blacks Go Home' scrawled across the wall in chalk. Then you opened it up and 'Blacks Go Home' had been crossed out and it had got something like 'Goodwill to All Men'. Brilliant idea I thought. Forget the racism, 'Goodwill to All Men'. Brilliant. It was a bit dubious when they did it. Anyway they did it and that got the storm going. It was in *The Times* and the Chairman of ICI was on the phone to Wallis Heath! ICI top brass were up in arms because it was in *The Times* and Kynoch Press was part of ICI. It was picked up in the *Birmingham Mail* because it was in *The Times.* Abusive letter came to Kynoch Press from coloured nurses. I mean they missed the point. It was a dodgy thing to do, but if you were a graphics man, or a copy writer, you could see it. I don't know. It caused hell! I can't remember what happened to him (Gill) after that, but he didn't do much more with us! So where he was creative, he didn't know where to stop. He didn't know the market, that was the other thing. It might be a good idea, but there are things you've got to pull back on. You've got to stop somewhere and I don't think he quite knew. [12]

The reputation of the Press depended in no small part upon the efficiency of its reading department which was the unquestioned protector of standards at the Press, winning for it a reputation for almost error-free work. The reading room was an independent department located in an office adjacent to the composing room. In addition, a reading box was built in the machine room for the readers responsible for passing the final proofs on press. The reading room had its own head of department, Eric Bastow, who implemented the tough rules of composition and was assisted in his task by seven other professional readers, including Alex King, who remembers:

> . . . Eric Bastow, the head reader, struck me as being rather eccentric and a little fuddy-duddy, but he turned out to be very much a kindred spirit, and he took to me like a father and I took to him like one. And for the first week I worked in the main reading room with the other men—I think there was seven of them, I'm almost sure there were seven, Eric Bastow made eight, and I made the ninth. And for the first week I worked in the main-room, with the other men. It struck me, right away on the first day, how impressive the work was. It was like I had never seen before, the standard and quality of it. Then one day, on the Tuesday or Wednesday, he took me down into this little cubby-hole, at the far end of the machine room, it was an ordinary paint store. At the far end of this paint store, right at the very back they'd got a proof-readers desk, very primitive, very dirty and filthy. He said, when you've settled in, I want you to come and work down here doing all the commercial work and passing the final proofs for press. He said, what we'll do is, we'll have a little office built for you. Money is no object for the ICI, whatever you want they will do. So after about ten days, the joiners were called in and they built this magnificent little office, minus the roof, and this desk was transferred into it, and they put a telephone in and everything, and a bell so they could reach me, because I had to go out and check the litho films in the photo room and if I was in there and the red light was on it meant I couldn't get back, so I had to be contacted by bells all over the place and it made me feel rather important. Anyway, I settled in quite happily, down below, and they said if you need any help (a copyholder) just phone up and we'll send a boy down or a girl. I found I could do all the stuff on my own. I was very, very busy. It was obvious to me it was like nowhere else I'd ever been before. The quality of work was unbelievable. And the attitude of the staff and the men and the bosses, it was just like going from a shanty to Buckingham Palace. I didn't have very much dealing with the main-room upstairs. I'm not really very sure what they did in that room, because I never really went into it. All I did was the passing of the proofs downstairs and the commercial work. [13]

The proof-reading department had to identify the mistakes made by the writer or the printer; the work demanded an exact knowledge of perfect printing so that unacceptable errors of composition could be spotted and corrected. The proof-readers had high standards of general knowledge and their erudition and exactitude was of paramount importance as they checked all material for its veracity as well as total literary content and consistency of the manuscript. Copy that entered the Press was prepared for production by the proof-readers, each of whom had their own subject specialisation. Each proof stage was checked and corrected for typographic inconsistencies, literals and page make-up. Every stage of the galley was read several times before going to press and also during printing:

Material to be read reaches the proof-reader either as 'galley-proofs' or as 'page-proofs'. Each time the reader follows the same drill. First, he 'rules the copy' by running a rule one line at a time down the printed matter. At this stage he is looking for what he calls literals—mistakes in the printing, grammar or style. Then, as a double check, the original material is read aloud to him while he concentrates again on the printed matter. In this way he can be certain that nothing has been accidentally omitted, added or misplaced. [14]

Mr Bastow, he showed me a tip whilst he was there. He said never trust anybody. Always check yourself and double check. Never take anybody's word for it. And he had a hat pin, a big, long hat pin that his wife had given him, with a little silver knob on the end. He said I'll show you what I do with my proof. I punch a little code in the bottom right hand corner. And in this fountain pen I have six different colours of ink, I don't let anyone use it, and they can't be copied. At the Kynoch Press they had rubber stamps, and my number was four, and you rotated them like a date stamp, and it would have on it 'first revised' or 'second revised' or 'final proof' and it was really quite open to abuse if anybody got it, because it was a stamp, and there was no proof that it wasn't you that had done it. So he said, always sign it in pen and ink and punch little holes in it. Leave a little code in it so nobody can copy, only you know where the code is. And never, ever take anyone's word for it. Always look it up in a reference book. Check and double-check. [15]

Proof-reading followed the rules issued to all compositors and readers at the Press. The instructions were devised in order to generate a recognisable house-style, a uniformity of approach which was adhered to in all jobbing, periodical and bookwork. Proof-reading, like design, was a separate and chargeable production cost.

The influences of the new departments could be seen on many of the publications issued by the Press in the 1950s. Full-colour offset lithography had an impact on the work the Press was able to undertake and the design solutions it was capable of producing. Accompanying the modern processes was a greater range of substrates including toned and textured stocks of various weights which were used in unfamiliar sizes, and bound and folded in novel ways. Advances in technology brought about unaccustomed printing surfaces such as plastics, fabrics like Terylene and various metals. In addition, the Press composing-room bought a fresh selection of continental sans serif types which overtook the established founts of the Press and also altered the appearance of its work. Changing technologies altered the work that the Press was able to undertake.

Alongside this new work the Press still continued to produce its established titles, but with a new emphasis. The Notebook and Diary continued to be published by the Press after the war, but its appearance changed in 1952 to reflect the new process of offset litho. The covers demonstrated the four-colour process with their use of cyan, magenta, yellow and black geometric shapes and an increased amount of colour was used on the text pages which were printed on stock of high-white wove and which favoured the use of the new continental sans faces. In 1952 the *ICI Magazine* was printed by offset lithography and offered its readers large and dramatic half-tone reproductions of excellent quality which brought a boldness and excitement to the pages of the *Magazine*. The new process also gave the Press the opportunity to restructure both the *Magazine* and the working practices behind its production:

> The *ICI Magazine* before the war was a most fuddy-duddy sort of thing. It really was terrible! . . . It was about this thick and every division went into all their intimate domestic details and local gossip and everything else. There followed a whole lot of meetings and finally we came up with the idea that we'd produce a very high-quality magazine running to seventy-two perhaps ninety-six pages. For each division within the company there would be produced an inset—and there were about twelve divisions. Metals Division inset ran to 25,000 copies, but the Paints Division inset might run to 2,000 copies. You had to think of paper rationing . . . the then management of the Press said we can't do it, it can't be done, it'll have to go elsewhere. To which my answer was rubbish! We'd work shifts! . . . they only thought in terms of running machines for eight hours a day. So we started to run them sixteen hours a day, and at peak periods we ran them twenty-four hours a day. [16]

The capabilities of the composing and reading rooms were tested by the complex material the Press produced for scientific and learned societies. The largest of these productions was the *International Tables for X-ray Crystallography*, a book aimed at scientists and students of crystallography. Published by the Press on behalf of the International Union of Crystallography, it was jointly edited by Dame Kathleen Lonsdale and Norman F. M. Henry who were assisted by an international editorial committee. [17]

> One of the marvellous experiences I had in the mathematical field, was becoming very closely associated with the famous Professor, Dame Kathleen Lonsdale, who was very much involved with the development of the atom bomb and was so disgusted with it she became a Quaker. She was a fascinating woman. We subsequently published about five separate volumes of *X-ray Crystallography*. Every crystal of anything had specific angles and numbers and they were immutable. You can have a thousand crystals of iron and the angles and numbers and everything will be constant, but the equations to express that would sometimes run to ten quarto pages. [18]

It was generously funded by both UNESCO and the US National

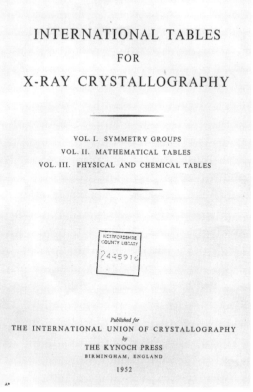

Cover of the 1959
Kynoch Press Diary,
printed in cyan,
magenta, yellow and
black to demonstrate
four-colour process
printing.

The title page of the
*International Tables
for X-ray Crystallography.*

Research Council and published during 1952 in three volumes. The publication had an authoritative appearance and was composed in Monotype Times to a format of 275 x 200 mm and an extent of 570 pages. The *Tables* represented a substantial achievement for the Press who displayed and printed the difficult material with elegance and efficiency and produced a result which was both pleasing to the eye and convenient in use.

With the recruitment of a number of key staff and the establishment of offset litho, a lithographic studio, design and a reading department, Kennedy and Hopewell had successfully equipped the Kynoch Press for work in the post-war world. What the Press still needed to establish for itself was a niche market, but this task was to be left to Kennedy and Hopewell's successors. John Kennedy resigned from the Press on grounds of ill-health in 1959 and his place was taken by Wallis Heath.

Chapter 8

1959–1976
WALLIS HEATH
finding a niche market

After the war, manufacturing industry in the UK became increasingly competitive and business-like. With the advent of many new technologies British companies started to produce a huge range of products in volume, and consumers with their new wealth could buy more commodities from a wider range of suppliers. Businesses could no longer just produce and sell those items required by the customers, goods had to be advertised to establish their competitive advantage over many rivals. Marketing became an important function of business. A major part of marketing was promotional literature, and this was a class of work the Press was interested in securing.

The Press needed advice on how to capture a greater percentage of the industrial publishing market. A survey conducted for the Press by Personnel Administration [PA], management consultants, highlighted the fact that the Press had no cohesive image, that it failed to project itself beyond ICI upon whom it had become too dependent, and that the Press was too isolated from the world. This situation was not acceptable in a world where self-sufficiency in the open market was essential. General manufacturing had become large and anonymous and the Press could no longer depend upon personal contacts to attract business. The old allegiance of ICI to the Press was fading and it could not be relied upon to entrust the Press with its vast amount of printed material. The Press was in a vulnerable position with no guarantee of work from ICI, little sales representation, and few marketing skills to attract external work. To address the problem PA advised that changes were needed at the Press, and the first of these changes was the recruitment of a new Press Manager.[1]

Wallis Heath left school during the depression of 1933 with no qualifications and, at a loss as to what to follow as a career, he started work at Valentines, greetings card printers, in Edinburgh where his father was a director. He was employed as an apprentice publisher of greetings and postcards and ultimately rose to become works manager, but by the late 1950s, having studied business management, he became frustrated with his job and was keen to test his skills at another firm. Heath had been given training in the theory of work study by PA who also approached him with an offer of a job as Manager of the Kynoch Press:

Personnel Administration [PA] were engaged by ICI to find somebody for the Kynoch Press because Jock Kennedy, the Manager, sorry to say it, was an alcoholic, and they wanted to retire him. PA were retained by ICI to find somebody, they advertised as well, but fundamentally they were doing head-hunting. They approached me, all very secretive, because in those days, 1959, if companies learned that any of their staff were sniffing the outside air you got sacked . . . So I went down for interview. There was a Monday spring holiday in Scotland, I went down on the Sunday night to meet the ICI people on the Monday and then I went back and nobody knew I had been. They offered me the job and I reckoned joining ICI was an offer too good to miss. So that was really how I got into the Kynoch Press. [2]

Although the Press had a full order book when Wallis Heath arrived there in 1959, it was one which was too dependent upon ICI. The task that lay before Heath was to establish and maintain a wide and stable external client base, but to do so he had to find a niche market by which to serve industrial clients in a changing environment and to publicise the skills of the Press to the world beyond ICI. The survival of the Press was dependent upon Heath's ability to bring about these changes:

It was a well stocked sales list when I arrived and it lasted quite well for quite sometime, and then the cold winds came whistling in, and there was considerable curtailment, and in the end all the calendars were disappearing. The ICI Divisions stopped them, they were saving money and they left very big holes. I can't give you dates and times, but it was borne in on me in discussions with Tom Haig [a Kynoch Press sales representative] and others, that a press of this size was in a peculiarly vulnerable position. If you were a jobbing printer in a town or village or city you were alright, or if you were a big combine doing contract work publications, it was probably tough going, but at least you had big power and scope. But if you were in the middle you had to face the fact that essentially you were offering a service to people and this was extremely difficult to define, and it was borne in on us that very successful people in the printing industry who built big businesses, did so by sensing and isolating some kind of product. [3]

The quantity of work available from both inside and outside the combine was substantial, but competition was increasing and many other printers were better represented and often more experienced in the open market. To secure its share of the work the Press set up a sales department through whom it tried to build upon its tradition for quality, to achieve a soundly based contemporary reputation, advance itself in the world of printing and attract the sort of clients who would make and maintain profits. Sales representatives were recruited in London and Birmingham to make personal contact with customers, create immediate sales, maintain contacts, and secure repeat orders by explanation and demonstration of the Press services. The sales representatives were ambassadors for the company, chief amongst whom was Tom Haig (another Scot), John Slee-Smith and Brian Emmerson. The sales force started to evolve competitive marketing strategies which were implemented by a client liaison department at the Press; the marketing plans included advertising, sales promotions and public relations events. Promotional literature advertised the services of the Press to clients, and public relations events educated customers by means of lectures, exhibitions, symposia and week-end seminars in Britain and in Europe.

The sales team moved its focus towards more consumer-centred strategies and researched its markets to establish what it was the customer required. The Press saw that industry was moving into a different environment when, in 1964, Britain was preparing to enter into the European Common Market's outer group of seven, which made trade with the Continent a necessity. The international scene had also changed with increased literacy in the third-world and growing consumerism in both the Arab states and the Far East. Consequently, to

An advertising brochure produced by the Kynoch Press in 1963 in which it sang its own praises by describing the cups and awards it had won for design and printing. This brochure forms the second in a series.

succeed abroad British industry needed printed literature in a diversity of languages and advice on how to market its goods. Industry was slowly waking up to the advantages of printed literature and the Kynoch Press research concluded that clients needed assistance with the preparation and distribution of material for export, but few British printers were either able or willing to offer printing services to exporters. Some offered foreign language setting, including Stephen Austin of Hertford, Lund Humphries in Bradford and Williams Lea in London, but the Weather Oak Press in the Midlands was one of the few printers offering a complete export service.

The Press saw that there was a move towards international trade and that few printers in Britain were able to supply this market. Research done by the Press found that buyers of print for export had problems purchasing translation services and that they believed to attract foreign sales, export literature needed to be attractively designed and well-printed. Having identified what it saw to be an under-served growth area, the Press assessed its ability to fill the gap. The Press was fortunate to be a part of ICI which was a massive and astute international trader with whom the Press had nearly a century of experience in producing material for export. The Press was able to offer its experience of export-ing to those sectors of British industry which were willing to take advantage of its services.

The Press believed it had found a niche market and in 1966 it responded by starting Kynoch International Print [KIP] which offered a complete printing service for exporters. KIP provided clients with specialised knowledge of the export business, an international outlook and the ability to provide foreign-language composition, translation, design, printing, documentation, shipping and forwarding. It was con-cerned with all the creative stages of planning, print production and distribution, saving customers both time and money through their need to liaise with only one organisation. KIP tried to sell its radical approach to potential customers by holding a series of meetings in Amsterdam and Rotterdam for executives of major British exporting companies. The purpose of the meetings was to tell industry about KIP's services, to persuade it to think on an international wave-length, and to allow the Press and its clients to make personal contact:

> . . . we produced a kind of teach-in, and we collected all the principal buyers from ICI and other customers and took them all to Amsterdam. It was just a jamboree and we made this presentation to them stressing all the things we could do with translation, language printing, language setting. The object being

that we could sell them the idea that going into Europe, (we were about to join Europe) that we were the people in the van ready to produce their stuff for Europe. It was just a sort of symposium, it didn't exist as an organisation, it was simply an idea that was enclosed in a teaching symposium we gave a copy of the KIP newspaper to them all . . . We all got up . . . It was a presentation really. I [Wallis Heath] had to lead-off giving a broad outline. Then Bert [Pace] would talk about computer typesetting, information retrieval, manipulation. Roger [Denning] would talk about design. Tom [Haig] would talk about selling. The language facilities and so on. [4]

The Netherlands was the chosen venue because KIP felt that the symposium should be conducted in an international atmosphere. The Press also issued broad-sheet newspapers explaining its services, which it distributed at the London 'Export Services Exhibitions' and a KIP handbook was issued to explain international printing terminology to exporters including DIN international paper sizes, business languages and metric measurements.

Kynoch International Print provided clients with technically qualified native translators, resident in the country of the language, who not only specialised in technical language but also possessed literary ability. KIP stressed the importance of a good translation service because export literature was often the solitary salesman for British companies in non-English speaking markets. The foreign languages could be composed by the Press in a range of non-Latin founts including Arabic, Chinese, Esperanto, Greek and Russian and it had a library of 18,587 characters which were outside the normal English alphabet, making an average of 1,500 non-Latin characters for each of its twelve most popular typefaces. Through its proof-reading department, KIP was able to ensure that spelling, technical abbreviations and the splitting of words was correct in the language concerned. KIP Design steered clients through the problems of designing for several languages. It provided tables calculating the difference in extent between copies of a multitude of languages, advised on financial savings if the use of reversed-out line blocks was avoided and recommended clients adopt the DIN international paper sizes for export material as these were taken more seriously abroad than at home, brought economies and implied modernity. KIP could distribute direct from Birmingham to any destination around the world through a comprehensive shipping and forwarding service which routed, forwarded, documented and financially insured all export traffic. It was run by staff fully conversant with the problems of export literature and it released clients from the added expense of outside forwarding agents.

KIP gave British business the opportunity to surrender all its export problems and charged a reasonable price for its troubles, yet the venture had only limited success and the Press was unsure why, despite ample publicity by KIP, and large export budgets in industry, its new venture failed fully to develop. In retrospect it can be seen that Europe was a new prospect for the UK, and much of British industry was sceptical and slow to see the advantages of business with the Continent and in the 1960s only eighteen per cent of the UK's print buying budget was spent on foreign-language work and only twenty per cent of export literature was designed specifically for overseas distribution. An insufficient proportion of British business was willing to see the advantages of well-designed and well-prepared literature in the promotion of its products overseas. Wallis Heath later commented:

> Well, I think it didn't succeed to the extent we hoped it would. It did get some business. But it was early days in Europe and British industry weren't really jumping to it. I don't think British industry really jumped to the gun until about 1980. It took the recession of the late 1970s to make them jump to it, these were terribly difficult years. I don't think we were ever actually in the red in the Kynoch Press, but we must have been perilously close to it at times, and we never declared anybody redundant, in my time. I think it took the cold wind of recession to sharpen up British industry and make them really go into Europe. We were terrible at languages and things in this country, we still are, we're all spoilt because everybody speaks English on the Continent. [5]

At the same time as it established KIP, the Kynoch Press also repackaged itself in order that it might present a more professional and co-ordinated image to those who were producing for the home market and it started to offer a complete printing service to consumers who were more accustomed to buying printing services in a fragmentary fashion. The new operation, Kynoch Communications (KC), provided several services: KC Analysis Package, KC Service, KC Foreign, KC Writing, KC Graphics and KC Printing.

KC Analysis Package offered clients an assessment of their existing and projected publicity needs in terms of writing, graphic design and printing. KC Service dealt with distribution and export and had offices in London to serve clients in the south, and Birmingham for clients in the midlands and north, and it could distribute material anywhere abroad taking advantage of IMI representatives and its shipping facilities across the world. KC Foreign helped those companies who needed to describe and sell their products abroad and translators could either originate material in a language of the customer's choosing, or translate current literature into the necessary language. The service was backed by a composing room capable of typesetting complex material in any language. KC Writing was staffed by a full-time Editorial Director with experience of producing journals and technical literature, feature writing and fiction and who advised on literary acceptability in a wide range of disciplines. KC Graphics was an award-winning graphic design group specialising in techno-commercial literature which provided high standard presentation graphic solutions, typographically marked-up copy and layouts in preparation for typesetting, and which advised on the stock to be used in production. Specialised artwork and photography would be commissioned by the design group, then sized in preparation for block- or plate-making. Finally all proofs would be checked by the group and printed at the Press.

The advantages of using the integrated services of Kynoch Communications were those of cost, quality and efficiency. Its flexibility allowed the customer to purchase only those services which were necessary, which made Kynoch Communications a process for the cost-efficient production of the commercial word. And yet, this venture too only had a limited success because print buyers were not accustomed to buying a complete service, preferring the sub-divided purchasing processes; furthermore, the Press was expensive in comparison with its competitors and often lost work on price, and at the same time customers remained suspicious that ICI would always receive preferential treatment from the Press.

As well as making a change of identity for itself, the Kynoch Press also brought about great changes in the composing room when, in the late 1960s, it began to abandon its traditional methods of composition in favour of a process whereby computer-based information was integrated with traditional printing. The transition began in 1968 when Elsevier in Amsterdam asked the Press to collaborate in developing a computer typesetting system. The system was to handle the large quantity of abstracts produced by Elsevier, material which required both the manipulative ability of a computer and the quality output of a photosetter. It was hoped that the Press, through ICI, would have a similar quantity of work, but after consideration the Press decided it did not produce enough work to justify the liaison. However, the Press began a successful association with Professor C. J. Duncan, director of the Department of Photography at the University of Newcastle and Nigel Cox, an internationally renowned expert in the field of data manipulation for computer typesetting from the computer laboratory at

Newcastle and Managing Director of Oriel Computer Services.[6] Together the two men were researching computer applications in printing. The alliance between Newcastle and the Press was successful and on 26 August 1969 it was announced that they had begun exploiting a new and sophisticated printing technique which integrated the fast manipulative ability of a computer with the high typographic standards for which the Press was already renowned.

The system linked a computer program capable of handling extensive records with a photo-composition program tailor-made to suit the requirements of each client. The client data was fed into a computer and a program manipulated the material to produce the necessary headings and cross-references and sorted and grouped the original data into any number of sequences. Proofs were supplied either as a computer print-out or run on a photo-composing machine. The manipulated data was stored on a master punched paper tape which was coded by the composition program with typographic instructions which were in a form capable of being read by a photo-composer. The photo-composer programmed the type and generated the film ready for conventional lithographic printing. Initially, the data processing was handled by a KDF 9 computer at the University of Newcastle and the punched paper-tape was put on an aircraft to Elsevier in Amsterdam where photo-composition was undertaken on a Digiset. The printing process was done at the Press in Birmingham from film supplied by Elsevier. By 1973, the data processing was handled by the main-frame computer at IMI in Birmingham, film was generated by a high-speed Fototronic cathode-ray-tube device at a trade-typesetters in London and the Press continued to print from the resultant film.

The Press was unusual among printers at the time because it regarded its printing works as a peripheral device to the computer which allowed it to secure new work such as directories, stock maintenance records, subscribers' mailing lists, research data abstracts, indexes, gazetteers and concordances, which required manipulated data to be output in normal printers' typefaces to a high quality and at great speed.[7]

The first application of the system was the July 1969 issue of the *British Technology Index* which was a monthly publication issued by the Library Association which comprised 122 pages and a million-and-a-quarter characters of intricate listings. The schedule was fast and it took just ten days from the submission of the finalised text to time of delivery. It had previously been the case that complex data was produced by using computer print-outs for reproduction; these had little typographic flexibility and were wasteful of space. Computer photo-typesetting had greater legibility and was more economic on space as the typefaces were compact, which helped to keep down the cost of printing, paper and distribution. It also meant that data, accurately committed to a computer by the customer, could be reproduced without the need for intermediate keyboarding and its attendant transcription errors, or the need for vigilant proof-reading. In the 1960s computer-assisted typesetting was viewed with suspicion by many potential clients, but it did give the Press experience of what the future of typesetting was to be and prepared the way for its own photo-typesetting installation.

In 1975, the Press made an analysis of its future based on its current equipment. To update its existing plant would give limited improvement in productivity and no potential for growth. To develop, the Press had to invest in a computer-photo-setting installation and it spent twelve months evaluating over 25 second- and third-generation photosetting systems. Second-generation machines would have provided quality and productivity improvements but little increase in capacity; third-generation photo-setters would provide better quality, increased productivity, greater capacity and the flexibility to improve the system by expanding the potential of the equipment with bolt-on modules as the computer typesetting market developed. The decision as to what to purchase lay with Dick Hurst, the composing room overseer.

> In the 1970s, I put up a proposal that we had to go into photo-typesetting, particularly as we were already in this volume typesetting which was being done through Bert [Pace]. We'd got to get up in the same line in the conventional work. So I put up a case, over a period of time, to buy a Linotron 303 system. The Linotron 303 was a high-speed photo-typesetting machine. It was tape controlled, by paper tape, although it could be controlled by magnetic tape. It was being used by newspapers, but it had never been used in the commercial field. So I had to put up a case that we would take it. The case I put up was that we would have one Linotron and, I think, eight keyboards with VDUs and we produced a paper tape. That was the case I put up, and it was purchased. [8]

So in 1976, the Press became the first printer in the UK to install a Linotron 303 photo-setter. The 303 was a high-definition system which scanned the type characters at a resolution of 1,300 lines per inch ensuring needle-sharp clarity of the type image at production speeds of 3,500 characters per minute. The installation comprised seven non-justifying keyboards, an ASR teletypewriter and a Linoscreen visual display terminal, disc storage, a magnetic-tape drive, proofing and pagination routines as it changed from off-line to on-line operations. The system

The Linotron 303 photo-setter which was installed at the Kynoch Press in 1976; this was the first time the machine had been used by a commercial printer in the United Kingdom.

could receive input from a computer, a keyboard, video display terminal or OCR reader and output in the form of punched paper-tape, magnetic-tape, cassette or direct by wire to the photo-setter. It was the speed of production, clarity of output and expansion potential that persuaded the Press to invest in the Linotron. The Press understood the need for a system which integrated the main-frame computer with the photo-setter and the ability to input directly from a computer by bolting-on a package was imperative. The information processing was done on the IMI main-frame computer and the punched paper tape was fed into the Linotron, the type-matter was corrected on a video display unit, a new photo-typesetting punched paper tape was fed into the 303 and clean photographic paper galleys were produced for pasting-up and then turned into film-negatives for making printing plates. Four typefaces were available: Baskerville, Times, Plantin (roman, italic, bold), Helvetica (light, medium, bold, extra bold), fractions, mathematical Greek, and signs and symbols for technical and mathematical setting. All the characters could be reproduced in half-point sizes from four- to 72 point to a maximum measure of 64 picas. With the Linotron's ability electronically to condense or expand a typeface, the choice of characters could be increased and because 30 per cent of Kynoch's typesetting was in a foreign language, the system had hyphenation programmes for English, French, German, Spanish, Swedish and Italian which together covered 95 per cent of its foreign languages.

The Linotron 303 greatly augmented the Press's output and reduced its dependence upon CRT photo-setters outside the group. The heavy investment brought £0.5 million worth of business to the Press as it captured a large share of the information market and within a month, one-half to two-thirds of the Press work was set on the new equipment, including the IMI annual report and accounts. The system was not, however, installed without some consultation between the composing room journeymen and Dick Hurst:

> We had a lot of discussion about this, of course. We didn't just put it straight in. They were sceptical, having to move over. The keyboard operators were on more or less the same, they didn't have to change. Had to close all the casting department down, but that was near the retirement age of the two-man set up, so there weren't any real problems there. The keyboard operators adapted to the new system because it was, for them, better anyway, being used to Monotype machines. Now they'd got VDUs with marching displays so they could see what they were doing. So that part of it went very well. The composing room was then geared up with light-tables and what have you. I can't remember the details of what we did at the time but, it all went in very smoothly. I must say, to me, it was a relief really. We did put a lot of research into it. I had a young chap, Robert Davis, who was a graduate from one of the printing colleges, he was given the exercise of looking at everything, of doing the leg work for me. So it went in quite smoothly. So we got rid of the old typesetting machines and went over, virtually overnight, to photosetting. And the decision to do that was on my shoulders . . . The decision was taken. The decision was that we would produce right-reading positives, not use film, use paper and assemble by paper. Now that's quite a significant decision. If you have got a page to assemble, you can either assemble film or you can assemble paper. In practical terms it was decided that it would be better if they stuck paper on rather than stuck film on because the comps had been used, if they'd been used to anything, to handling paper. They'd never been used to handling film. There were also lines of demarcation with the unions as to who should handle what. So it was decided to do that, and then, when the whole assembly was made up, to re-photograph it and strip the pictures in. From that point, once the type was assembled, then it went to the litho art department to do their side of it. It left as a patchwork page. The patch-work assembly was photographed by the litho department and they dropped in the pictures. [9]

Initially, the Linotron complemented the existing hot-metal composition, but photo-typesetting rapidly became the only typesetting system at the Press. Although the Press claimed that the transition to photosetting was smooth, its output declined in quality as the compositors failed to bring consistency of resolution to their typesetting. With the arrival of new machinery and processes at the Press, the old equipment and materials were in need of disposal and Colin Baines, the Press engineer, oversaw the removal of the redundant machinery and the metal type:

When the film setting came in, it befell me to get rid of all the hot-metal. That was another job I'd never been involved in. They wanted the best price for the metal. Most of Kynoch Press type was sold to a German firm. It was trans-shipped to Germany. We were getting a better price for the metal in Germany than we were in this country . . . they weren't after the type, it was all being melted, it was all being dissed. It was put into bins. It was my job to have it weighed and to see it off the premises. Being on the IMI site, which was a metal bashing site, its main business being non-ferrous metals, they had a whole department called Metal Procurement. Metal Procurement was the metal market, the futures market. At a certain time of day—if I remember rightly, between eleven and twelve o'clock—the prices of all the different metals, precious metals as well, copper, antimony, zinc, everything, is sorted out on the London Metal Exchange. Firms like IMI had to decide whether they were going to invoice orders to IMI customers, or whether a buyer was going to buy. Because this was the first time that there was a large quantity of the type of metals we had coming up —tin, antimony, lead—the Metal Procurement people were involved. I walked into a meeting where the doors were sealed and it looked like the Tokyo Stock Market with every one waving their hands and shouting deciding whether to buy or sell. I got shoved out quickly! But where else would a printer get advice on the metal prices? We used to hold it until they told us right, get rid of it. Because Monotype and founders type has a different analysis, we had to segregate the type. We had to analyse each batch, and this was done on site in the metal labs and they would tell me the average of the batch I was doing. For that we were getting a better price. A normal printer would just get in a metal dealer and say they'd got so many tons of metal, and if the dealer said it was such and such an analysis the printer would just have to accept it. But Kynoch Press didn't. We had it analysed on site and it was sold off in different batches of that analysis. We had more back-up than what the metal merchants had! [10]

In November 1969, Wallis Heath began offering the typesetting services of the Press to American publishing companies specialising in high-quality, complex academic work or foreign language books:

The *Birmingham Post* said it was my idea! I suddenly thought that . . . American labour was very expensive, and we had this facility for driving photosetting, and it seemed to me that it would be quite simple to get a manuscript, get their ideas about design, set up a specimen page, airmail that across the Atlantic—that could be done in a week—get the OK, proceed to set the whole book, send it all out in film (because they were printing photo-litho, anyway). Our setting costs, and producing film for them, were much cheaper than they could do in America. So that's what we did. [11]

The Press undertook the composition, editing and designing of the manuscripts which would be sent from the United States to the Press, who would set-up a specimen page and air-mail the specimen back to the USA. On its approval, the whole book would be composed, and either paper or film would be produced and air-mailed back to America where the books were printed by photo-lithography. Several American publishing houses participated in the scheme: Aldine Publishing, Chicago; Appleton-Century-Crofts, New York; and American Elsevier Publishing, New York. For a year to eighteen months in the early 1970s the American connection thrived as between one-third and one-half of Kynoch's typesetting capacity was given over to the US market for which the Press produced over 40 books in twelve months:

> And we did quite well for perhaps a year, eighteen months and then it slowly died as they could do it themselves . . . That was the time when the exchange rate was nearly a dollar a pound. Then gradually when it came up it actually reached a point when it was two to three dollars to a pound. That was no good. I think the exchange rate of the dollar, and having got the idea and seen it working, they all thought why do we need to send it to Britain anyway? [12]

The scheme prospered for as long as British typesetting costs were cheaper than in America, while the exchange rates favoured the dollar over the pound. With changes in the exchange rates the Americans ceased to use Kynoch's services.

The sort of work that the Press was producing during the 1960s and 1970s made full use of all the new technology in which it had invested, and much of the work can be described as industrial publishing which came from major manufacturing industries and techno-scientific organisations. The customers were all large companies who had great economic power and who were willing to apportion a significant part of their budget to the production of printed publicity. Post-war industry had become increasingly aware of the advantages of well-designed and well-produced printed material and was prepared to commission printed publicity in ever greater quantities. They were the sorts of clients who helped raise the Press profile and gave it access to high-quality material:

> The advantage of Kynoch Press designers over other printers was the clients we had and the money they would spend. And, initially, that's what I liked about it having come from a company where someone would say: Well its a single-colour or two-colour job. At Kynoch Press it was four- or five-colours—eight-colours on a calendar. So the clients were good. ICI Plastics Division, ICI themselves, Agricultural Division, Explosives Division they were ours. They all had budgets. They were not professional buyers, not like today. If they'd got £10,000 to spend they wouldn't tell. If it cost £5,000 to produce they wouldn't say can we do it cheaper. If they liked it they'd have it. This was great. When Roger [Denning]

did a lot of stuff on Terylene we did four, five, six workings on the cover, not in process, but in different colours and he'd superimpose stuff to give plus colours as we used to call it. But other people weren't doing it outside as they hadn't got that link with clients with money. And you're only as good as your clients, and if your client's got money, and he likes what you do, you can do what you like. [13]

The introduction of full-colour offset lithography at the Press had an impact on the services the Press could offer, the work it was able to undertake and the design solutions it was capable of producing. Accompanying the modern processes was a greater range of substrates which were toned and textured and of various weights and which were used in unfamiliar sizes, and bound and folded in novel ways. Advances in technology brought about unaccustomed printing surfaces such as plastics, fabrics like Terylene and various metals. In addition the Press introduced a fresh selection of types into its composing room, particularly sans serif types which were imported from the Continent. As Roger Denning remembers:

There was a great deal of care lavished on the choice of paper: whether it was coated, or matt, or textured, or whatever, a great deal of time was spent on choosing the right material and weight of material and so on for any particular requirement. We were very experimental, using a lot of mixed make-ups on books—putting a matt-art with an antique paper, this sort of thing: by using various forms of binding, like wire-o, all these sort of things—so from a business rationale, stock holding rationale and an end effect we were very experimental. In the 1960s, there was a lot of experimental work with paper. Most designers were putting their feet in the water for the first time with tinted stock and different textured stock and so on. It was very much part of the sixties typo movement. With all of this came a much greater range of typefaces. The Press had always had a good range. There was some Ravilious initials that were actually cut for the Press. But they had the majority of regular book faces, and then came in things like Annonce Grotesque, Grot 215, 216, 126 and we were one of the early people to put these in because there was a demand for them and we wanted to use them as well. [14]

The early 1960s marked the beginning of the typographic change at the Press and in this period, the appearance of the Press's own printed material was changing. In 1963 the Kynoch Press brought the Notebook and Diary to a close. A product conceived during the 1920s, it was no longer considered to be sufficiently flexible to display the new graphic advances that were being made and was published too infrequently for the Press to demonstrate contemporary developments:

As with the vanishing waterways—our theme this year—so, after many years,

The Kynoch Press Notebook and Diary is to vanish. For this is a time of change: change in our craft, and change in the industries and the world which our craft serves. It is a time, moreover, of exciting changes in the field of graphic design. Though many, we know, look forward to the Notebook and will miss it, we need to have a means of showing these new design developments more freely and more often. So in place of the Notebook we shall be publishing every quarter an essay in graphic design which will display the work of representative designers of today and, we believe, of tomorrow. We are sure you will find these stimulating and valuable. We are discarding nothing from the past that is good: craftsmanship will, as ever, be everything. [15]

A section from the first 'Design Essay' published by the Kynoch Press. Entitled *Bill Boards*, it was designed by Tom Wolsey in conjunction with the photographer William Klein and showed images of typographic street art taken from around the world.

Under the direction of Roger Denning, the Kynoch Press started a highly original publicity campaign of 'design essays' which attempted to provide a visual commentary on new approaches to design which were arising out of the new techniques. The publications demonstrated contemporary printing techniques, with the medium itself being the message. The 'essays' showed what results could be achieved when good design was combined with good printing. They were advertisements for the Press, intended to establish its reputation in the vanguard of post-war printing developments, showing it to be a printer daring enough to support and court controversy in design. The 'design essays' were also an exercise in publicity-for-publicity; they demonstrated that such material was an indispensable sales tool for any commercial venture. The 'essays' coincided with the launch of the annual and influential Design and Art Direction Exhibition and were printed and

A page from
Bob Gill's New York,
part of the
'Design Essay' series.
It was a highly personal
reflection upon
New York City shown
through the nib and brush
of the illustrator.

published by the Press in conjunction with the Art Directors' Association of London. Each 'essay' was handed over either to award winners at the D&AD exhibition or to other carefully selected designers. The designers were not constrained by any brief, and were given a free platform to express their views on any subject about which they felt something should be said. Any medium could be used and normal commercial considerations were disregarded. Only two constraints were imposed by the Press: a page format of A4 and top limit of production cost. Those selected to produce the 'design essays' included: Tom Wolsey, art editor of *Town* and art director of Jaeger, with experience of the American advertising industry; John Donegau, art director; Anthony Froshaug, typographer; Terence Donovan, fashion photogra-

pher; Bob Gill, an American graphic designer who was working in London; Derek Birdsall, BDMW Associates; and the advertising agency of Richard Williams Associates.

The 'design essays' were published quarterly and a complimentary copy was given to customers, and prospective customers, who took an interest in design for printing. Additional copies were available at 6*s*. each, or one guinea for the four issues of 1963–64.

Anthony Froshaug designed *Typographic Norms*, an original and experimental argument for the advantages of 'standardisation' in printing. Froshaug attempted to identify norms for line-spacing material and showed the relative width of spacing material in sizes ranging from 5 to 72 point by means of tabular matter which was then re-displayed as visual analogues. Where spacing material of one size coincided in width with spacing material of another size it was printed in red (for example, when a 5 point em space was equal to a 10 point thick space). It was an essay which demanded much and explained little and readers were left to fathom the theory and surmise the value for themselves. Most of them must have been baffled, as were many at the Press:

> There was one created by Anthony Froshaug. To this day I can't understand what he was trying to do. But it was something to do with the 12pt unit and he'd got this twisted thing on his mind about this 12pt unit and you'd open the book and there were 12pt dots getting bigger and bigger. I couldn't read it and I couldn't explain it to anybody. I don't know what it was about. It was typography

gone wrong for me. None of the clients understood it, almost without exception I'd say. I couldn't explain it. The let out was, well, we didn't design it! This is what it is and if you want to read it I'm sure it'll make sense! But I didn't really understand it. It was black with a few red units and a fold out that got bigger and bigger. It's all to do with the norm and the 12pt. Totally unsuitable for a mailing shot to anybody other than an academic typographer who's done nothing else all his life. You know, we didn't say we wouldn't do it and that's what he came up with so we did it. [16]

Women throooo the Eyes of Smudger Terence Donovan was a photographic 'essay' which included seventeen small monochrome halftones and a ribbon of continuous verse. The photographs showed women in a way which freed them from the role of angel in the kitchen or glamourous icon; instead they focused on the ordinary to capture the extraordinary and in doing so showed images which caused something of a stir at the Press, forcing the Union to lodge an objection and prohibiting the women in the bindery from handling the material:

> One of the shots was a woman [the model, Celia Hamilton] on the toilet. Now why they do these things I don't know, but there it was. There was this woman on the toilet and it was about this big on a whole page. It was a gimmick. He had a whole page of white with a little picture in the middle and a line of copy down the bottom, and the copy ran all along the bottom in all this strange cockney-ism. When Slee-Smith brought this up from London the production controller's assistant was straight down the general managers! They managed to pacify her and it didn't do anything, it didn't create any stirs. [17]

It was also an essay in photographic techniques. Donovan showed how images could be enhanced when photographed out of focus, or in soft focus, the drama that could be got from flare or burn-out in the developing process, and the atmosphere that could be added by over- or under-developing a film. He showed what could be achieved when 'bad' photography, handled skillfully, could become 'good' practice. *Women throooo the Eyes of Smudger Terence Donovan* was an attempt to educate the purchasers of photography, by expanding their expectations.

The 'essays' served as an experimental and controversial catwalk for design at the Press. The approaches to design they presented were not necessarily the ones industrial clients would adopt outright, but they were the inspiration behind more pedestrian solutions. They represented a showcase by which the Press had revealed itself to the world of design and printing.

ICI's own literature including the prime publications of *Endeavour, Plastics Today, Outlook on Agriculture* and the *ICI Magazine* were given a

The title-page from the re-designed magazine *Endeavour*, 1963.

ENDEAVOUR

A review of the progress of science, published in five languages

design overhaul as they ceased to display the friendly intimacy that was evident before the war, and they became increasingly functional and simplified as the information being displayed became more complex. The varied typefaces used on the earlier publications were substituted by the more uniform and solid sans serif types such as Monotype's Grotesque 215, 216, Univers, Helvetica and Amsterdam's Annonce Grotesque, all of which gave a more international flavour than could have been achieved with the previously favoured range of English types. It was not only the typefaces but also the page layouts that changed. Formats were standardised to the DIN series of page sizes and new elongated formats became popular. Publications with bookish margins were substituted by solutions which turned typographic tradition upside-down. As the range of substrates altered the designs became more experimental, although this was not without its problems, as Bert Pace recalls:

> We used to do a lot of work for Fibres Division. I went to Paris, to a printing exhibition in Paris. Fibres asked us to consider producing, for the fashion industry, a lot of little folders showing the various designs made out of crimplene and things like that . . . And did I tell you about trying to print on plastic? I can't remember quite why it was but I had a certain number of sheets of polythene for doing something or other, maybe producing the books for either the Forth or

Severn Road Bridge. I asked the manager in the letterpress machine room, to print on the polythene and I was amazed at the result we were getting — really beautiful. Of course, I showed one or two of these around, and we played around with one or two inks and things like that and Les Hardy tried to formulate inks for me. Then Plastics Division. EuroPlastics Exhibition was going to be held in Paris on 31 May 1965. P. I. Smith was head of publicity, and he said: What I'd like for the exhibition is to see something printed on plastic, do you think you can do it? I said we'd tried it and there was no reason why we shouldn't try it again. Then he, unfortunately, retired and another chap took over. He still wanted this thing done. He got so very late with all his copy and proofs and we'd got about ten days to do the job in the end. We'd had the plastic produced by then, it was all there, it was all ready for us to start printing. Six days before EuroPlastics exhibition opened we tried to print on this plastic. It was just hopeless! We worked all weekend trying to get it done, but couldn't do it at all. I rang the bloke up and said we are having trouble printing on this plastic and he said: You said you could do it, EuroPlastics opens on Thursday and they have got to be there on Thursday. Tuesday I rang him again and said we are getting no results at all—can't make it. But then the overseer in the machine room decided he was going to put some normal ink on—just normal letterpress ink. And believe me it worked! After all these formulations that we'd been trying for days. I rang him back and said: We've won, we can do it. He said: What you have got to do is send them by air to Paris and tell me the flight number and everything and send me a telex. We did everything like that, the job went by air to Paris and we sent him a telex and I sat back thinking this is great. Then a call came through saying: You've let me down again. I'm going to have a word with your Directors and get you sacked! What had happened, there was a strike at Paris and the telex never got through to him. So 31 May 1965 is engrained on my memory. [18]

Changing technologies coupled with improved services and increased budgets altered the nature of the work that the Press undertook for external customers, which was increasingly four-colour lithographic printing for advertising literature, calendars and publicity material for large industrial concerns. Such work won it many distinctions in national printing competitions. Annual reports and accounts for industry formed another lucrative branch of work for the Press, and technical literature utilised its ability to handle complex composition. Commemorative literature was also a burgeoning area of post-war industrial publishing as companies, established in the previous century, celebrated their anniversaries. In addition, as Britain began to re-build its towns and cities, commemorative literature was required to mark the opening of new construction projects. The change in typographic style is clearly seen in the work produced by the Press for Coventry Cathedral.

The construction of a new Cathedral for Coventry was one of the most significant and symbolic post-war architectural achievements in Britain. The building of the Cathedral, to the design of Sir Basil Spence, was an attempt to express the spirit of a new age, to place Christianity in a modern context rather than in the past. To fulfil the vision, Basil Spence used contemporary artists to decorate the fabric of the Cathedral, including Ralph Beyer, Graham Sutherland and Einar Forseth. To celebrate the consecration, a month-long arts festival was held in Coventry and included performers such as Benjamin Britten, Michael Tippett, Malcom Sargent, Georg Solti, Frederick Ashton, Peggy Ashcroft and Yehudi Menuhin. It was a festival of both national and international significance and the Kynoch Press was chosen to print the literature for the new Cathedral and arts festival. Its remit was to produce a printed image for Coventry Cathedral which would establish a new approach to graphic design for the Church and which was as contemporary as the Cathedral itself.

It was the most substantial and significant of all commissions undertaken by the Press during the 1960s and involved the production of books, pamphlets, leaflets and posters, most of which were ecclesiastical in content. The project included eight separate Orders of Service, programmes for 127 individual performances, posters for each event and text sheets for all music concerts. The remit required the design to be contemporary but also timeless, functional but bright and attractive and with none of the trappings of traditional and archaic ecclesiastical symbolism. It also had to be easily adaptable across many formats. A whole new corporate identity for the Cathedral was developed which overturned many of the principles of ecclesiastical literature. Set in Monotype Bembo and Monotype Grotesque, it was a mixture of symmetry and asymmetry which used a photograph of Jacob Epstein's St Michael to symbolise the magnanimous nature of the Church. The result was a bold attempt to combine the best principles of modern graphic design with the needs of the Church and it was significant that the responsibility for supervising the design as well as the production was given to a designer-printer.

With all the post-war changes at the Press, its relationship with ICI became increasingly tenuous. The Press frequently complained that it was not getting enough work from ICI, which, on the other hand, was unwilling to give the Press preference and treated it like any other commercial printer. The Press was convinced that it was not getting an equitable proportion of ICI work and believed its capabilities were not fully recognised and that jobs which were within its scope were being allocated

A selection of brochures produced by the Kynoch Press for ICI during the 1970s.

elsewhere. In 1965 an internal enquiry was conducted by D. G. Haffenden, General Manager of ICI External Relations, to examine the position of the Press at ICI. The report showed that the Press was financially stable with a turnover of £765,000, but despite this, the Press only returned a profit of £32,000, because its proportion of Group overheads amounted to £44,000 which meant that its prices continued to be in excess of its competitors by around five per cent.

Haffenden canvassed the Publicity Managers of all the Divisions for their opinions of the Press and found that although the Press was praised for the high standards of its finished products, it was criticised for a lack of appreciation of urgency; therefore jobs which were needed in a hurry were often lost despite being within its capabilities. Insufficient representation coupled with the lack of access to those individuals responsible for the job within the factory was a problem. The report concluded that the Press should seek to improve its image with ICI by developing outside representation supplemented by visits to 'clients' by senior members of the Press staff. ICI also needed to be made aware of the capabilities of the Press. But the Press found itself with the same conundrum that it always faced: how to secure a greater share of the ICI account while forced to carry its percentage of the prohibitive and unavoidable overheads imposed by ICI. In August 1972 a report examining the relevance of the Press to ICI was issued. The report was the work of A. L. Sumner, Head of ICI Publicity Services, and Wallis Heath, General Manager of the Press and it recommended that the Press should be transferred from IMI to ICI with the intention of increasing the profitability of the Press, reducing the necessity of the ICI Divisions to spend capital on in-plant printing facilities and to provide rationalised facilities. The Press wished to develop communications between itself and the publicity departments of the ICI Divisions whose additional work would allow it to be developed more effectively. The main purpose of the transfer was to give priority to ICI's printing requirements, although the Press wished to retain its separate identity, since it felt that loss of independence would jeopardise relations with its external customers.

The delicate balance between sustaining an independent identity whilst giving priority to ICI's requirements was hazardous. The Press had attempted this fine balancing act for 70 years and had failed to achieve harmony. ICI abandoned the proposal, but just five years later, a new plan was being pursued which was to unbalance the Press once and for all.

Chapter 9

1976–1981
HARRY WAINWRIGHT
sale and closure

Wallis Heath was joined at the Kynoch Press by Harry Wainwright from ICI Education. Wainwright was brought in to work with Heath to produce a report on the future of the Press, and they concluded that if ICI were not able to make any further investment in its printing department then it would be better to sell the Press as a going concern. Wallis Heath retired in 1976 and the task of negotiating a sale for the Press was left in the hands of Wainwright.[1]

From time to time approaches had been made by other printers to merge with, or acquire, the Kynoch Press. The talks had always floundered either because a merger was unacceptable to IMI, or because prospective buyers could not comply with the vendor's demands. IMI would not contemplate a sale unless the buyer could maintain the terms and conditions of employment enjoyed by all Press staff, secure the good-will of all the employees, and find suitable accommodation locally. In the autumn of 1979 an approach was made by a printing company that was able to agree to all IMI demands.

There were several reasons why IMI wished to sell the Kynoch Press. By the late 1970s, the position of the Press within the main company had grown increasingly difficult. IMI was fundamentally a metal manufacturing company which had unintentionally become the proprietor of a printing office. It was a peculiar inheritance, and IMI did not understand the needs of the Press which were so significantly different from other units on the site as to appear irrelevant; at the same time the Press was providing a domestic service, the need for which was diminishing

The recession of the 1970s affected even giants like ICI and IMI. The printing industry had undergone an expensive technological revolution, and the conflict between the need for expensive new equipment and the financial cutbacks imposed by the main company was to the

detriment of the Press. The Press had to compete with the metal-work-
ing sections of the group for limited IMI resources and IMI was neither
willing nor able to apportion adequate funds to modernise its printing
office. IMI could not reconcile the level of investment needed for the
Press with the mainstream investment demands. The recession also saw
redundancies at IMI with over 1,000 Ely Ammunition and Lightning
Fasteners workers losing their jobs at Witton. Selling the Press helped
IMI raise money to offset redundancy payments.

The Press began to struggle to get work as it had to absorb its proportion of IMI overheads, rendering it more expensive than its competitors. If the Press was not able to offer a service which was cheaper,
better, or different from external printers, IMI had no reason to maintain it as part of the Group.

The Press employees were members of a different range of trade
unions to other employees at Witton. Press salaries and employment conditions were largely determined by national agreements between the
British Printing Industries Federation [BPIF], and the print unions. As a
result, employees at the Press were paid higher rates than staff at similar
levels elsewhere on the site, which produced resentment at Witton, as
Roy Kilminster recalls:

> Well I think IMI had got a bit fed up with the Press during the latter years. The
> trade unions created quite a bit of trouble at the time. They were creating a lot of
> trouble and IMI were not prepared to tolerate it, the Press's work was so far
> removed from their main line of business. One problem was that, when IMI did
> sanction new presses, the unions would refuse to work them until they got wages
> upgraded. The presses lay idle for a week or a month or whatever. The unions
> argued that the company was going to get more profit out of new equipment and
> they wanted their cut. At that time, in the 1960s and 1970s, the trade unions were
> calling the tune, not the managers. Some of the tales I could tell you about the
> trade unions would make your hair stand on end. I was a trade unionist myself,
> had to be, because it was a closed shop. I mean, let's face it, quite a lot of things
> the trade unions did were good, and the things they stood for were good, but of
> course, they got taken over by the left wing [they had succumbed to the militant
> left-wing ideology rampant at the time]. They weren't interested in the prosperity
> of the country, they thought the money was there for the taking, and their job was
> to grab as much of it as they could without giving a thought as to what they gave
> in return. That's what happened throughout industry, like the car industry.

By the late 1970s, lack of investment by the main company had
caused the Press to become run-down: equipment was decaying and
employees were not replaced. IMI acknowledged that if the Press was
to survive it would require sustained and significant investment in its

plant. In 1978 an appraisal of the Press concluded that if capital was not available the Press should be sold as a going concern.

In 1979, an approach was made to purchase the Press by the Gilmour and Dean Group[2] based in Hamilton near Glasgow. Gilmour and Dean felt the Kynoch Press would complement its existing business by providing a base from which to expand its market share in the Midlands and the Home Counties, improve its profitability, widen its client base, provide access to the lucrative ICI account and equip it with the design capacity that was lacking from the rest of the Gilmour and Dean Group. In return, the Kynoch Press would benefit from being controlled by a printing company from whom investment and development was more likely, where more modern and appropriate accommodation would be provided, and new machinery was a certainty. But the majority of the Press staff wanted to stay with IMI as it offered job security, good pay, and a level of facilities and benefits they could not hope to have from another employer. However, there was also a growing sense of insecurity at the Press and the majority of its staff felt their future with IMI was uncertain and that a sale had to be contemplated; but the agreement of the staff and their unions was not to be obtained without a fight.

The Litho Chapel opposed the transfer as it was sceptical that employment terms and conditions could be maintained and concerned that not all Gilmour and Dean's past takeovers had been successful. The Composing Room Chapel was divided between the older and longer-serving members who were concerned at losing their employee benefits and the younger and shorter-serving members who were optimistic about transferring to a printing group. The Letterpress Chapel supported the transfer, anticipating investment in offset machinery and the re-training of letterpress machine men to operate litho presses, a proposition which was more realistic under the direction of a printing company. Ultimately, after much pressure, all staff recognised the inevitability of the transfer, hoping it would improve conditions and prospects for all.

IMI was attracted to the Gilmour and Dean offer because it gave guarantees for the continuation of full employment under conditions equal to those offered by IMI and provided the Press with a better chance of investment. Dick Hurst recalls the sale period:

> In 1978 the Press was put up for sale and in 1979 Gilmour and Dean made a firm offer. There had been others. We had previously set a number of jobs for Robert Maxwell's Pergamon Press and he approached IMI as a possible buyer

but they refused (thank God). At one stage a merger with Nuffield Press seemed on the cards but this eventually fell through. I don't know how they got to know about it, it was never advertised as far as I was aware. Eventually Gilmour and Dean started negotiations. Gilmour and Dean was a company, quite a small company really, that had acquired other companies like Chorley and Pickersgill. It was a Scottish company, mainly involved in carton printing. They took over Chorley and Pickersgill which was running successfully, they also took over another company, and they'd not had that too long when they had to close it down. So it was a bit of a gamble to come in for Kynoch Press almost two years later. Anyway, they came in and had a look at it, and negotiations went on between their principals and our people who consisted of Harry Wainwright, Roger Almond who was Deputy Company Secretary of IMI and R. Tennant, MD of the Ammunition Division. They were the three principal people doing the negotiations. There came a point at one of the meetings when Harry Wainwright and their principal fell out at a meeting and I think it was in danger of collapse. I believe they fell out over the way they thought the new company should be run. Gilmour and Dean wanted to put their man in as boss-man and Harry Wainwright wanted to put me in as Chief Executive. So when the next meeting came, they had to rake me in. I had to go into the negotiation because Harry Wainwright couldn't take part, he was there but he couldn't take part because the friction was so great, it would have collapsed. That meeting took place in Yorkshire, Monk Fryston, in a hotel. Negotiations took place that night. It was fairly easy going, there was no friction whatsoever that night. It broke up, and subsequently Gilmour and Dean made an offer which was accepted by IMI. When it was decided that Gilmour and Dean would take over, David Nunn, who was Sales Director at Chorley and Pickersgill, was made Managing Director and I was made Assistant Managing Director. Brian Emerson, who was Sales Manager at the time, was expected to be Sales Director, but in the period before the change-over he fell out with David Nunn. So Brian Emerson packed his bags and left. So they had to appoint another Sales Director, he also came from the Group, but he had no experience in the type of work we were dealing in. They also brought in a Financial Director and he came from Hovis McDougal, he'd not been part of their Group so he was a stranger to it. When it was decided that it was going to happen, then the unions were brought in, and we did quite an extensive publicity exercise, getting the information down through the ranks, and they also had the opportunity to discuss it and so on, and they could have vetoed it. I was a firm believer that it was right to go over. I thought it had to go, because there was no way we were going to get any investment and it seemed sensible.

On 1 October 1979 the Press was sold to Gilmour and Dean for an undisclosed sum. Re-named Kynoch Press Limited, it was once again in Scottish hands. The Press was moved just 200 yards away from its Witton site, to the F. A. Power building on Holford Road, a modern single-storied and well-equipped factory. Immediate investment was made

The press-room and graphic reproduction unit in the new Kynoch Press Ltd.

in a Roland Rekord four-colour press, with the promise that Gilmour and Dean would identify the equipment needs of the Press and make further purchases as necessary. Roy Kilminster was happy with the investments the new owners made on the litho side of the business:

> Gilmour and Dean started off by buying a new four-colour press, which is something we had needed for a long time. Certainly this new press gave us an up-lift in quality. There was also investment in the camera department. They would have been prepared, I think, to carry on investing in new equipment, but of course it wasn't long after they took it over that the recession hit, and of course the orders dropped off, particularly from ICI. The Press was hard hit due to the fact that much of its work came from that source. There remained some of the older presses, if things had gone all right they would probably have replaced those. No reason to suppose they wouldn't have done because they were more of a printer, a technical printer, who knew what they were doing. Whereas the old management at Kynoch Press was basically from the typesetting side, the letterpress side, and didn't really appreciate the technologies of litho, which was evolving very rapidly at the time.

Kynoch Press Limited was not destined for longevity. The promised investment in the Press failed to materialise as the recession forced Gilmour and Dean to renege on many of the promises it had made at the time of purchase. Despite every effort there remained insufficient work to occupy the presses and the financial situation at the Press became problematic, as Roy Kilminster recalls:

> Gilmour and Dean started off with great promises and great hopes and they

Printing at the new
Kynoch Press Ltd.

gradually had to whittle things down. They started off by giving us a canteen and
then they had to cut that out. Eventually, towards the end, I had my suppliers, like
Kodak's, refusing to supply me with materials as Gilmour and Dean hadn't paid
the bills. It came as a nasty shock to me when I wanted a packet of film to do a
particular job and they said no we can't supply it you haven't paid your last bill.
Nasty shock! It was a sad demise really for what had started with such high
expectations. Gilmour and Dean didn't keep us in the full financial picture. I
mean we knew it was going down the nick because of things that were happening and the things which weren't happening—no more equipment for instance.
But they didn't tell us what was actually happening, but we knew it was bad
because we couldn't get any new equipment because no one was going to put
new equipment into a place that was going down! Gilmour and Dean were very
unfortunate with the table of events, I am afraid. They had a very good set-up in
Scotland. In fact they took me to show me their factory, in the early days when
things looked rosy. Nobody anticipated the severity of the recession, or the
effects on the Kynoch Press order-book with its dependency on ICI and IMI
work. Gilmour and Dean were no doubt impressed with the illustrious name
that Kynoch Press achieved without realising the flaws in the situation. The
recession greatly increased the competition for work, and with the severance of
'family ties' ICI and IMI were not likely to feel any obligation to support the
Press through the crisis.

Ultimately the demise of the Press was a result of circumstances. For
many years it had been dependent upon the production of soda cartons
for ICI, but the EEC had ruled that soda crystals must be packaged by
methods and with equipment not used by the Press. As a result the

packaging contract was lost. A two-week strike by NGA members impacted on the production of the *ICI Magazine*, and the Press lost ICI's house-organ after 50 years of production. Having been sold to an out-side group, the links between the Press and ICI had been severed. ICI had no obligation to support the new owners of the Press and with the recession of the early 1980s, the Press failed to win sufficient work to make good the shortfall left by ICI and IMI.

It was obvious that the Press was spiralling downward and that the situation was not going to improve. A management buy-out of the company was proposed, with the intention of contracting the work-force by half and surrendering 50 per cent of its building. Although Gilmour and Dean were willing to sell to the management in order to rid itself of its liability, the local unions placed impossible demands upon both vendor and purchasers and the deal foundered, as Dick Hurst, one of the four directors, recalls:

> What was decided was, unless there was an improvement, they would close. There was no improvement, so it was decided to close. The directors—David Nunn, myself, Gavin Menzies and Andrew Purcell —got together and we decided that we'd make an offer for the Press. We were working fairly well together, so we made an offer to Gilmour and Dean. The offer was accepted. It meant that we would shut-down half the Press, reduce its size by half, instead of occupying all the factory we could divide it and take half, and we'd pay for half the lease. We set all the customers up, and it looked on the cards. It looked acceptable, viable. On paper it looked viable and from our point of view, and particularly from my point of view, it looked very good. We could have done it entirely from our own finances, because Gilmour and Dean wanted to get the whole thing off their hands. So, the proposition was put to the unions. The NGA decided, in their wisdom, that they would not accept the deal. The deal was for about half the staff to be made redundant and half retained. We were employing about 140 to 150 at the time. So there were about 80 going to be employed, I think, the rest were to be made redundant—right across the board, not just the NGA staff but SOGAT as well. At the time Gilmour and Dean were prepared to pay the redundancy moneys to the men, and we would just start off with a blank sheet. We'd still got customers, still doing work, and all those customers were still available. After negotiations—well, it wasn't really negotiations—after a number of confrontations between Gilmour and Dean and the unions, the NGA, supported by SOGAT, decided that the Press either made everybody redundant and then re-employ them, or else there was no deal. Well, Gilmour and Dean weren't going to stand for that. They said there was no way that they would do that. Either they (the unions) accept the terms as they were—and they were generous terms, they were over double the normal redundancy terms—they said unless you accept those terms we shall close it down completely. The unions were given

a deadline, and the deadline came and Gilmour and Dean wouldn't budge and the unions wouldn't budge, so the decision was taken to close the Press. Every customer was notified that it had been closed. At no time was the London or Bedford Headquarters of the NGA involved. But immediately after the decision was taken they came in to try and recover the situation. But it was too late.

So the Press was lost. Gilmour and Dean gave everybody redundancy notices, and everyone was given different times. It was a phased closure. It was phased-out so that no customer's job was not completed. It never went bankrupt, or into receivership. The men left over a period of time. The MD, the Sales Director and the Financial Director left immediately, and I had the unsavoury task of running down the Press. I then advertised the plant for sale, and I used to have a sale each weekend. I sold anything anybody wanted. If they were payroll or staff, it was sold to them at a nominal fee. And the rest of the stuff I sold over a period of time, mostly on private deals. The dealers took what was left and the rest went for scrap. On the weekend sales, we used to sell a hell of a lot. The last of the people left and we paid them off—that wasn't a very pleasant task. On 24 December, 1981 I shut the factory for the last time, and that was the end of the Press. It went down fighting. Its reputation remained, still remains to some extent. Kynoch Press was the envy of many printers in town.

The Kynoch Press met its demise in 1981 after just over 100 years of successful trading. Its ultimate failure was due, in part, to the same element that had made it a success: its relationship with the parent company. The Press owed its very existence to another industry which created, sustained and expanded it, but as a mere department within another industry the Press was always dependent upon that business for its own success. For as long as the main company flourished and the Press was seen to be a useful adjunct to the main business, it would survive, but the perilous state of this position became evident when the financial and industrial health of the main company became less than buoyant and when the Press ceased to serve any obvious and unique usefulness. When this happened, its sale and ultimate closure became inevitable.

Chapter 10

1920–1979
TYPEFACES
novelties and necessities at the Kynoch Press

The Kynoch Press had a reputation as a printer for the typographic connoisseur. It was generally regarded as a curiously undocumented but typographically lively outfit which had very few rivals in terms of typefaces, typographic design and general printing. Three methods of type composition existed simultaneously at the Press from the 1920s through to the mid-1970s, and several type sources were used to satisfy these three methods. For hand-setting, the Press employed the founts issued by the typefounders of Britain, America and Europe; for semi-mechanical composition, the Press used the Ludlow Typograph Corporation of Chicago, America; and for mechanical composition, there was the Monotype Corporation at Redhill, Surrey, England.

During the twentieth century, the Kynoch Press performed several startling typographic gyrations which placed it apart from its contemporaries and competitors. The first revolution came in 1901 with the appointment of Donald Hope and the adoption of Caslon Old Face; the second revolution was brought about by Herbert Simon between 1922 and 1933 when the composing room was reconstructed, reconstituted and re-shaped beyond all recognition; this was followed by a period of war-time typographic stagnation and decline. The war represented a great natural divide, and inertia was followed by typographic resurrection and adaptation to the new post-1945 climate. Interwoven through all these phases was the perpetual battle between mechanical- and hand-composition, between necessities and novelties.

When Donald Hope assumed responsibility for the Kynoch Press in 1901 he inherited a composing room equipped with a bewildering and eclectic selection of nineteenth-century types which ranged from the exotic through to the monstrous. A selection of types for text setting including Cheltenham, Caledonian and Windsor and a collection of display types from Miller and Richard and Caslon such as Milanese, Monumental and Floral Letters. There was also a range of sans serif types. Typefaces of this kind were common currency in composing rooms the length and breadth of Britain, but ones which Hope rapidly banished from the Press and replaced with the clean and classical lines of Stephenson Blake's Caslon Old Face, a revival from the eighteenth century which had been resurrected in the 1840s by the Chiswick Press but whose use amongst ordinary printers in 1901 was not extensive. When Donald Hope introduced Caslon into the composing room at the beginning of the twentieth century, the Press was the first printer in Birmingham to re-introduce the face into its racks.

Caslon was advertised in the Press specimen books from 1901 until 1981 when the Press ceased trading. Yet despite its longevity, Caslon had an unsettled existence with the Press who advertised three different versions of the face, Stephenson Blake, Ludlow and Monotype, with each version sliding in and out of the specimen books over the decades. But it was a face which was to prove its popularity and establish a repu-tation for the Press, placing it in the vanguard of the typographic move-ment in the early years of the twentieth century. With Caslon Old Face, Hope had inadvertently laid the foundation stones for Press's passion for type revival. The presence of the resurrected Caslon in the compos-ing room initiated a trend for the re-adoption of those faces which Hope had removed from his racks. It is doubtful if he could have pre-dicted that, 30 years later, the once abhorred nineteenth-century types would be both reinstated and esteemed by the very Press from which they had been so early banished.

1922 to 1933 was a period of startling typographic growth at the Kynoch Press, putting it in the forefront of the printing renaissance that was taking place at that time. The emphasis was on providing choice from a wealth of new typographic material available from rich and var-ied sources. It was also an era which saw new techniques of production, and the Press demonstrated that modern techniques could produce high quality printing at competitive rates. In attempting to provide a wide choice of typefaces produced by various techniques, the Press was to be viewed as a pioneer.

In 1922 the Kynoch Press had a composing room equipped with decent type for text composition. In addition to Caslon, there were American Typefounders' Garamond and Fry's Baskerville, which were supplemented by a range of Cheltenham, but there were few, if any, faces suitable for display. Herbert Simon wanted a composing room equipped with types suitable for general printing as well as the book work for which Hope had already catered. His types were carefully chosen to produce a distinctive and original house-style which was spearheaded by an original collection of nineteenth-century English revival display types, and their corresponding twentieth-century derivatives. These types distinguished the Press as a pioneer in reviving genuine nineteenth-century English founts. It is ironic that Kynoch's early abandonment of its Victorian types which established its typographic reputation in 1901 was directly mirrored by Simon's bold decision in the late 1920s to re-adopt a carefully selected collection of these jettisoned faces and thus enhance its typographic reputation still further. The types Simon chose to re-adopt were made with the erudition of an academic typographic historian and his understanding of type led to a fount list so startling that the Press could not have failed to attract the attention of the pre-war typographic connoisseur.

The typefaces were acquired in their historical sequence. Following Stephenson Blake's Caslon Old Face, Simon bought a range of authentic nineteenth-century types of modern face construction and some of their twentieth-century derivatives. His acquisitions started with modern faces and fat faces which were followed by elephants, compressed and elongated faces right the way through to decorated founts.

Herbert Simon bought True-Cut Bodoni Ludlow series 3–TC in 1927, and Bodoni Bold Ludlow series 3–B in 1930. The Ludlow face

Ludlow's True-Cut Bodoni

ABCDEFGHIJKLM
NOPQRSTUVWXY
Z abcdefghijklmnop
qrstuvwxyz 123456
7890

was selected in preference to the more popular ATF Bodoni, because it closely resembled the original face and it was a 'type which has the elegance and polish of the Modern face, but is friendlier to the eye because the round letters have curved instead of vertical shading.' Bodoni started Simon's interest in nineteenth-century type and by 1929 he had bought 'Fat Face 1' and 'Fat Face Italic 1', also known as 'French Canon' or 'Fry's Canon'. The 48 point type came from Stephenson Blake and was dated 1820; it was one of the rarest of all the Press type faces. Regarded by Simon as particularly handsome it was one of the earliest known fat faces and was originally manufactured by Fry and Steel as 'French Canon No. 2'. The type was re-cast for the Kynoch Press from the original matrices which were, by the 1920s, in the possession of Stephenson Blake. It was not made generally available, nor was it ever completed in other sizes. Fat Face 1 was the first Victorian revival to be re-cast from the original matrices in England in the twentieth century but the Press did little to publicise its find.

Although Fat Face 1 was initially cast for the exclusive use of the Press, it did later appear in the specimen books of the Curwen Press. The impetus behind its purchase undoubtedly lies squarely with Herbert Simon, rather than his brother Oliver at the Curwen Press, for three reasons. Firstly, from the time he bought it, Herbert Simon continued to expand the Kynoch Press list along a nineteenth-century English revival route, while the Curwen Press type list developed in Continental directions. The type fitted well, therefore, into a planned policy of type development at the Kynoch Press while it was but an interesting appendage to the general development at Curwen. Secondly, Oliver's very different nature suggested that if Fat Face had been his discovery, the typographic public would most certainly have been informed of this fact. Herbert, a more reserved and modest character, would have maintained an anonymous association with the discovery—and much anonymity surrounds the acquisition of this type. Thirdly, the most compelling evidence that it was Herbert, rather than Oliver, who discovered Fat Face lies in the fact that though it appears at the Kynoch Press by the end of the 1920s, it is not advertised by the Curwen Press until the late 1930s. By this time Herbert had taken up his directorship at Curwen and had purchased a second casting of the face for use at the Curwen Press.

Stephenson Blake's Fat Face 1 was augmented by 1933 with 'Fat Face 2' and 'Fat Face Italic 2', from Stevens Shanks. This face also dated from around 1820 and was uniquely available from the Kynoch Press.

Stevens Shanks Fat Face (above) and Stephenson Blake's Fat Face (below). The specimen of the 30pt Fat Face shows how delicate the type was as the blobbed finials which should appear on the lower case italic 'f' and 'j' are missing, presumably damaged.

FAT FACE

(TYPEFOUNDER'S)

These are two unrelated types, both dating from about 1820. The larger is particularly handsome.

30 ABCDEFGHIJKLM
ABCDEFGHIKLM
abcdefghijkl 123456
abcdefghijklmnopqrs

48 ABCDEFG
ABCDEF
abcdef 123
abcdefghijkl

Manufactured in 30 point, it was an experimental re-cast by Stevens Shanks of Figgins 'Fat Face two-line English', but the matrices of the other sizes were discovered to be defective and the project came to an end. The Stephenson Blake and Stevens Shanks types were the only authentic fat faces of this kind available in England in the early 1930s and they paved the way for the Press to purchase other new display types.

Between 1930 and 1933 the Press bought a fount of 60 point Elephant and Elephant Italic from Stevens Shanks; re-cast from the original matrices for Figgins Elephant, it was 'much pleasanter in its curves than those of the twentieth-century Bodoni extra-bolds' and it was found in few composing rooms beyond the Kynoch Press in the 1930s.

Stevens Shanks
Elephant typeface.

ELEPHANT

A genuine 19th-century face. Note how much pleasanter its curves are than those of the 20th-century Bodoni extra-bolds.

60

ABDE

FGKL

abcdef

himlno

12345

135

Stephenson Blake's typeface
Union Pearl.

A B C D E F F G G I

P Q R S T T U V W

a b b c d d e f g h h i j k l l m n o

A series of expedien

the height of existi

In 1930 or 1931, Herbert Simon bought a fount of Stephenson Blake's Union Pearl, the first known English decorated type from the seventeenth century which came into the possession of Stephenson Blake in 1905. Union Pearl was only available in 22 point and was first used by the Press on the Nonesuch edition of Philip Sidney's *Astophel and Stella*, in 1931; whether the face was acquired at the behest of Francis Meynell, or under the inspiration of Herbert Simon is unclear, but it fitted comfortably into the Press's English Revival mode. It was a type that was never advertised by the Press in its specimen books, nor was it used in the Notebook and Diary, traditionally its method of exploiting new type acquisitions. It was not a face generally advertised in 1931 and Stephenson Blake did not revive it until 1948.

Union Pearl was quickly followed in 1933 by the shadow letter, Thorne Shaded, from Stephenson Blake. The first use of Thorne Shaded by the Press was in 1933 for the Nonesuch Press production of Coleridge's *Selected Poetry and Prose*—again, whether at Meynell's request or on Simon's advice is not known. Thorne Shaded had great curiosity value and much success. Set on an 18 point body, it was a small fount cast from matrices dating from around 1806, showing 'honourable scars' from their 127-year history. This small fount was produced as a

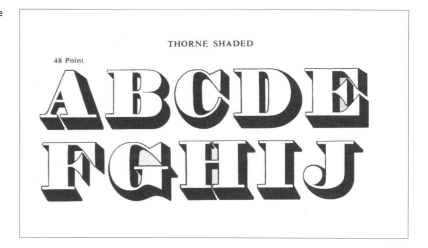

trial specifically for the Press and as a result of its success it was placed on general release by Stephenson Blake in 1936.

Thorne Shaded was the last of the English Revival types bought by the Press. With these types Simon was ahead of typographic trends, he had struck out independently of fashion and equipped the Press with something that was highly original. In doing so he had provided an antidote to the hungry purchasing of Continental founts by rival printers and had educated clients to the fact that display faces could be home-grown. Simon may have equipped the Kynoch Press composing room in collaboration with his brother at the Curwen Press, with the intention that between the two they could offer a unique and desirable, but not overlapping, range of faces. There may also have been some rivalry between the two brothers which prompted Herbert to tread his own, unique, path. However, by re-establishing the most elegant and interesting nineteenth-century faces Simon raised their profile, gave them gravitas and respectability, and elevated them from their jobbing roots and placed them in a contemporary setting.

From the early 1920s to late 1930s the better-quality printers were scouring Europe for unusual and original display faces because Britain was producing too few inspired native type designers, and British printers were doing little to encourage the development of distinctive English display types; foreign imports became fashionable merely on account of their foreignness. At the Kynoch Press, however, Herbert Simon tried to address the situation when he introduced two decorative types designed by English artists: Milner Initials and Ravilious Initials.

Milner Initials was an in-line titling of robust and solid appearance, a woodletter which was produced in 48 and 72 point. The designer of this face was Donald Ewart Milner OBE, MA, ARCA, RWA, headmaster of the Aston School of Arts and Crafts in Birmingham in the 1920s, who had a reputation as a painter, stained glass artist and book decorator. Eric Ravilious designed a set of initials for the Press between 1927–29; they were rather curious characters, strong and irregularly proportioned, with a decorative floral in-lay. A woodletter cut in 48 point, it was a face as exotic and as bizarre as any foreign import. Ravilious initials were accompanied by a series of six continuous strips designed for the Press by Tirzah Garwood, which in design and flavour bore more than a passing resemblance to her husband's type design.

Although Herbert Simon developed a unique range of English faces, he did not altogether reject those Continental types which had such an appeal for the British printer and so he bought a small, but select, range of German types. Typically, Simon bought what was rare rather than fashionable. Simon first chose two Gothic or Black Letters: Ancient Black from the foundry of Bauersche Giesserei was bought by the Press

The rather bizarre Ravilious Initials and the very popular Milner Initials.

RAVILIOUS INITIALS

Designed and cut for the Kynoch Press by Eric Ravilious.

A B C D E

F G H I J

K L M N O

P Q R S T

U V W Y

MILNER INITIALS

FORTY-EIGHT-POINT

A B C D E

F G H I J

K L M N O

P Q R S T

U V W Y

BLACK LETTER

12 A B C D E F G H J K L M N O P Q R S T U W X Y Z   abcdefghijklmnopqrstuvwxyz   fi fl ff ffi ffl
A B C D E F G H J K L M N O P Q R

18 S T U W X Y Z   abcdefghijklmnopqr stuvwxyz   fi fl ff ffi ffl

TWELVE-POINT BLACK LETTER

And J, even J, Artaxerxes the king, do make a decree
to all the treasurers which are beyond the river, that
whatsoever Ezra the priest, the scribe of the law of
the God of heaven, shall require of you, it be done
139

EIGHTEEN-POINT BLACK LETTER

The first press in North America was
set up by Stephen Day in Harvard
College, Massachusetts. There he
printed "The Psalms in Metre, faithfully translated for the use, edification
139

SHADED BLACK

An ornamental German letter designed by Prof. Rudolf Koch.
Occasionally useful for titles.

14 A B C D E F G H J J K L M N O P Q R S T U V W X Y Z   abcdefghijklmnopqrstuvwxyz !?&
1234567890

36 A B C D E F G H I J
K L M N O P Q R
abcdefghijklmnopq
rstuvwxyz 123456

48 A B C D E F G
abcdefghi 1234
138

Black Letter (otherwise
known as Ancient Black)
from the Bauersche
Giesserei foundry, and
Shaded Black designed by
Rudolf Koch.

in 1924 and Shaded Black, designed by Professor Rudolf Koch, a
rather fine three- dimensional character with horizontal inner shading,
was bought in 1927. Vesta Titling, designed by Albert Augsperg for
Berthold in 1926, swiftly found its way into the Press. This was a decorative, three-dimensional character with extreme contrasts in weight
and characteristic blobbed finials and although it was of contemporary
German design, it owed much to the nineteenth-century fat faces. It is
curious to find that while the Press possessed Vesta Titling in five sizes
between 12 and 30 point, the Curwen Press had also bought Vesta in all
the intervening sizes. No coincidence, but perhaps a result of filial typographic collaboration. Ratio Free Initials, designed by Professor F. W.
Kleukens for Stempel in around 1928 were available through Stempel's
agents, H. W. Caslon and Co., under the name 'Hiawatha', a spirited
type available at the Press in three sizes. The last German face bought
by Simon was Prisma, designed by Rudolf Koch for the Klingspor

VESTA TITLING
(TYPEFOUNDER'S)

12 ABCDEFGHIJKLMNOPQRSTUVWXYZ
ÆŒ 1234567890&!?

14 ABCDEFGHIJKLMNOPQRSTUV
WXYZÆŒ 1234567890&!?

18 ABCDEFGHIJKLMNOPQRS
TUVWXYZÆŒ 1234567890!?

24 ABCDEFGHIJKLMNO
PQRSTUVWXYZ ÆŒ
1234567890!?

30 ABCDEFGHIJKL
MNOPQRSTUVW
1234567890!?

RATIO INITIALS
FORTY-EIGHT-POINT

A B C D E
F G H I J
K L M N
O P Q R S
T U V W Z

146

Berthold's Vesta Titling, and Stempel's Ratio Initials, a typeface which was very frequently used on ICI publicity material.

foundry. An in-line type based on the sans serif Kable, it was the only type selected by Simon which was of wholly contemporary design. It was Simon's single departure into the realms of contemporary European type design, for it was the last of the display types he purchased before he moved to the Curwen Press in 1933. Had he stayed, it may have opened another typographic chapter, an embarkation into the world of modernity.

Herbert Simon introduced nine sans serif typefaces into the Kynoch Press. Despite the rash of sans types of modern design emanating from Continental Europe, the types that Simon chose were all of nineteenth-century English design, were primarily for use on the Ludlow and were for display setting only. Record Gothic, Square Gothic and Condensed Gothic were all designed by R. H. Middleton, and inspired by the English grotesques of the nineteenth century, with square endings and regularity in the width of capitals. Stephenson Blake's Granby

GRANBY CONDENSED

8   A B C D E F G H I J K L M N O P Q R S T U V W X Y Z   abcdefghijklmnopqrstuvwxyz £ &
1234567890

10   A B C D E F G H I J K L M N O P Q R S T U V W X Y Z   abcdefghijklmnopqrstu
vwxyz £ &   1234567890

12   A B C D E F G H I J K L M N O P Q R S T U V W X Y Z   abcdefghijklmnopqrs
tuvwxyz £ &   1234567890

14   A B C D E F G H I J K L M N O P Q R S T U V W X Y Z   abcdefghijklm
nopqrstuvwxyz £ &   1234567890

18   A B C D E F G H I J K L M N O P Q R S T U V W X Y Z
abcdefghijklmnopqrstuvwxyz £ &   1234567890

24   ABCDEFGHIJKLMNOPQRST
UVWXYZ abcdefghijklmnopqrs
tuvwxyz £ &   1234567890

30   ABCDEFGHIJKLMNOP
abcdefghijklmn   123456

116

36   ABCDEFGHIJKL
MNOPQRSTUV

42   ABCDEFGHIJ
KLMNOPQRS

48   ABCDEFGHI
JKLMNOPQ

60   ABCD 123

72   ABC123

124

Stephenson Blake's Granby
Condensed, and Ludlow's
Tempo.

Condensed for display, and Monotype Gill Sans for text composition, were also bought. The exception to these grotesque sans faces was Ludlow's Tempo, which was the only pre-war sans serif at the Press of contemporary European design with tapered endings and variable width capitals.

Under the direction of Herbert Simon, the Press had a range of typefaces which were wholly original, and decidedly English; mainly retrospective, but occasionally contemporary, they were types which spiced-up the composing room. The Press never dispensed with any of its types, and once they were advertised they remained in its specimen books until it ceased trading in 1981. The exceptions were both Milner and Ravilious initials which were withdrawn from the specimen books, but not the composing room.

The Kynoch Press first equipped its composing room with Monotype casters and keyboards on 8 April 1920. Monotype provided the Press composing room with typefaces for text composition, the typographic work-horses which were printers' necessities. Seldom did the Press turn to Monotype for its display founts. In the 1920s the Kynoch Press purchased a range of Monotype text faces which were selected from the classical revival range of founts introduced by Stanley Morison, rather than from the dated range of Clarendons and Cheltenhams which characterised Monotype's early output. The Press chose not to equip itself for machine composition until 1920, some years after its nearest rivals. Having dispensed with its archaic range of founders' text faces and having entered the twentieth century with a typographically advanced plant with Caslon, Garamond and Baskerville, the Press was not going to commit itself to a mechanical composition system which was only manufacturing those founts it had so recently jettisoned. It was only when Monotype introduced its classical revival range of typefaces that the Press committed itself to machine composition and when it did it bought Baskerville, Garamond and Bold Face. The range was further expanded by Herbert Simon with Bembo, Caslon, Cloister, Cloister Bold, Gill Sans, Imprint and Imprint Open.

The Press's choice of Monotype faces was based upon those founders' text faces which were already popular with customers. They were familiar faces by which the smooth transition from hand- to machine-set types could be facilitated. The transition was neither immediate nor total and founders' versions of these faces continued to be advertised alongside their Monotype equivalents. Baskerville was available both as a Stephenson Blake face and Monotype. Caslon came from Stephenson Blake and Ludlow as well as Monotype. Cloister was simultaneously available from Monotype and American Typefounders, as was Garamond. This concurrent advertising of faces may have indicated a reluctance by some clients fully to accept the new system, or perhaps a preference for the cut of the founders' type. Alternatively, economy may have dictated that whilst there was life in the old types they should be retained, and the Press seldom disposed of type. But the rising popularity of Monotype text faces eventually brought the demise of some of the foundry text types. The smaller sizes of founders' type were jettisoned so that customers could be encouraged towards Monotype, but display sizes remained the preserve of the type founders.

While the Kynoch Press was developing its composing room with native types, its competitors were developing in very different directions. Herbert Simon's brother Oliver at the Curwen Press travelled to the European foundries of Klingspor, Enschedé and Berthold, bringing back types such as Koch Kursive, Maximilian and Flamme, experimental faces which had freedom of movement and artistic flourish. Curwen types had a gaiety to them while Kynoch Press types were characterised by their restraint and intellect.

During the 1930s, Percy, Lund Humphries, rival to the Kynoch Press, was still operating a composing room equipped with nineteenth-century faces. It was not until the 1930s that Lund Humphries began to develop its composing room and when it did it took on a different complexion altogether. Neither retrospective like the Kynoch types, nor decorative like those of Curwen, the types selected by Lund Humphries were modernistic and functional and were mainly sans serif types of continental design—Kable, Erbar, Phosphor. In addition there were the 'new' Egyptians with five founts of Bauersche's Beton; a further two German faces, Holla and Gillies Gothic, were representative of the growing number of continental script types; and Corvinus and Locarno supplied the need for roman display faces. Lund Humphries developed a fount list which was as revolutionary as, although wholly different from, that presented at the Kynoch Press. Whereas the Kynoch Press was undoubtedly English and revivalist, Lund Humphries was European and contemporary in its outlook. Whilst Kynoch was selecting the rare and the intellectual, Lund Humphries chose to present the commercial.

The revolution in the Kynoch Press composing room ceased in 1933 with the arrival of the new manager, H. V. Davis. Under the unsympathetic direction of Davis, typeface development was all but discontinued. Against the odds, efforts were made by Harry Carter to maintain the programme of typeface acquisition at the Press and the spirit of Simon's revival list was reflected with the addition of two Victorian revivals, Elongated Roman and Playbill. Both typefaces were from Stephenson Blake and although they sat comfortably within the established nineteenth-century revival list of the Press, they were types which were populist rather than unique and which many printers were quick to install. The Continental list was supplemented by three faces from Bauersche Giesserei: Beton, one of the first of the popularly revived Egyptians, was bought in 1934; Cartoon, a commercially marketed type of freely drawn capitals and figures was bought in 1935, as was Corvinus. This was an attempt to introduce into the composing room a range of select, but commercially marketable, Continental faces. They were meant to redress the balance with the English faces which dominated the Press display list. When Herbert Simon vacated his post at the

TWENTY-FOUR POINT ELONGATED ROMAN

METHLEY RECOVERED ALMOST SUDDENLY, AND

THIRTY POINT ELONGATED ROMAN

WE DETERMINED THAT WE WOULD GO

THIRTY-SIX POINT ELONGATED ROMAN

THROUGH THE TROAD TOGETHER.

FORTY-EIGHT POINT ELONGATED ROMAN

¶ MY COMRADE WAS A

SIXTY POINT ELONGATED ROMAN

CAPITAL GRECIAN;

SEVENTY-TWO POINT ELONGATED ROMAN

ALTHOUGH HIS SINGULAR MIND

SEVENTY-TWO POINT PLAYBILL

when he gallantly drifted out at the head of the fleet. If Nicolou failed to

SEVENTY-TWO POINT PLAYBILL TITLING

CONTROL THE MANŒUVRES THERE WOULD

Stephenson Blake's Elongated Roman and Playbill were added to the Kynoch Press composing room in about 1935 as a contemporary supplement to the nineteenth-century English revival list.

Kynoch Press in 1933, there was as marked a demise in its Monotype purchases as there had been in its range of foundry types. Between 1933 and 1938, only Gill Sans Bold was added to the Monotype room; the Press fell woefully behind typographic trends and customers were complaining of declining standards. But lack of encouragement, if not outright prohibition, by H. V. Davis ensured that this development was limited and effectively all type purchasing ceased at the Press between 1933 and 1938. They were six typographically lost years, during which time the composing room fell so far behind as to have been almost without hope of resurrection. Whilst Lund Humphries and Curwen Press continued to explore the Continent for typographic novelties, the Kynoch Press became typographically moribund.

There was a glimmer of light in May 1938 when Michael Clapham arrived at the Press and attempted to resuscitate its dormant type list. Times New Roman, Times Bold, Bodoni and three weights of

Rockwell were immediately added to the Monotype room, and this went some way to restoring the floundering reputation of the Press. The light provided by Michael Clapham was quickly extinguished in 1939, when the outbreak of war halted all typeface development, but between 1942 and 1943 Plantin and Plantin Light were bought to be used with Plantin Russian on the war-time magazine, *Endeavour*. From the cessation of war in 1945 to the close of the decade, no new Monotype faces were bought. Any purchasing was confined to a few re-orderings of replacement matrices. After the war Monotype purchasing at the Press was, generally, a matter of maintenance, and involved the replacement of worn matrix cases for the long-established and well-used faces, such as Baskerville, and the expansion of the range of sizes and weights for popular faces such as Bembo, Garamond, Gill Sans and Plantin.

The Kynoch Press entered the post-war world on the same typographical footing that it had departed the pre-1939 era. During the war,

LEFT
Monotype's
Russian Plantin Light
bought specifically
for use on the war-time
magazine *Endeavour*.

RIGHT
Annonce Grotesque from
Lettergieterij Amsterdam.

THIRTY POINT RUSSIAN PLANTIN LIGHT

помощью карт большего масштаба, на которых местности нанесены более детально. ¶Британские карты не были начерчены *для пользования ими указанным образом, но уже до возникновения теперешней*

THIRTY-SIX POINT RUSSIAN PLANTIN LIGHT

войны предполагалось внести в них нужные изменения, и такие улучшения будут, несомненно, *сделаны с наступлением мирного времени. Одним из этих улуч*

TWENTY-FOUR POINT ANNONCE GROTESQUE

"There is nothing in all Damascus," said the good man, "half so well worth seeing as our cellars;" and forthwith he invited me to

THIRTY POINT ANNONCE GROTESQUE

go, see, and admire the range of treasure that he and his brethren laid up for them-

THIRTY-SIX POINT ANNONCE GROTESQUE

selves on this earth. These, I soon realised, were not as the other printers had rid themselves of the remainder of their archaic nineteenth-century types and those pre-1939 continental display faces that had ceased to be popular. The 1948 Kynoch Press type list was unchanged from 1939 and throughout the 1950s and 1960s the Press built upon this list. The 1950s saw a popular revival of Grotesques in Britain and the sans types purchased by the Press before 1939 enjoyed a new and fashionable lease of life. The Press supplemented its sans serif range with Stephenson Blake's Grotesque No. 9 and Monotype's Grotesque 215, 216 and 126 which, with the newly added italics, enjoyed a revived popularity. Meanwhile, the European type founders were producing a plethora of sans serif types but few found their way into the composing room of the Press or many other British printers. The Press purchased Lettergieterij Amsterdam's Annonce Grotesque, an extra-wide sans which was in stark contrast to the preponderance of condensed sans faces in the composing room and it belatedly bought Erbar and its companion face Phosphor, which was already 40 years old. But the Press had not indulged in the first wave of Continental sans faces, and the gap in the specimen books was bridged by the inclusion of Erbar. The decade, however, was dominated by Monotype Univers in all its variations. Univers was not purchased by the Press until its release by the Monotype Corporation in 1961. The arrival of Univers marked the beginning of the end for Monotype at the Press, for it was the last indispensable Monotype face that it was to purchase; by the dawn of the 1970s, the Press had dispensed with all metal composition, making a complete commitment to photo-typesetting. For the remaining Continental sans faces, the Press showed little interest. Helvetica was not released by the Monotype Corporation until 1970, too late for the Press who by then had moved wholly over to Linotronic photo-composition. The advent of computer-assisted typesetting in the early 1970s initially brought a more limited range of types to the Press: Helvetica, Times, Plantin and Baskerville represented the earliest founts available on the Linotronic phototypesetting system. These were followed by a range of Clarendon and Bodoni. For more exotic types, the Press was dependent upon the range available from Letraset.

Appendix 1

Typeface tables

The typeface tables in this Appendix help to establish a typographic profile for the Kynoch Press. They catalogue, from the 1920s through to the 1970s, the typefaces held by the Press, showing what machine- and hand-composition types were available in any given size, in any given decade, and from which foundry and the date these types were purchased.

Several sources have been used in the composition of the charts. They include: type specimen books and lists issued by the Kynoch Press; *Sales Ledgers* of the Monotype Corporation Ltd; and samples of Kynoch Press printing. Sources used for background comments on the typeface charts include: *Matrix Sales Records* of the Monotype Corporation Ltd; *Numerical Index of Monotype Faces;* and *The Encyclopedia of Typefaces* by Berry, Johnson & Jaspert, 3rd edition, 1962.

The specimen books, broadsheets and lists issued by the Kynoch Press were the primary source for ascertaining its foundry typefaces and confirming its machine faces. Specimen books for the Kynoch Press are readily available in sufficient quantites to be able to produce an accurate picture, decade by decade, of the hand-composition founts, and to verify the availability of Monotype founts. The available specimen books are:

1924 *Printing Types at the Kynoch Press* (broadsheet)
1927 *The Kynoch Press Book of Type Specimens*
1930 A Supplement to *The Kynoch Press Book of Type Specimens*
1931 Typefaces in use at the Kynoch Press (listed in the 1931 Diary)
1934 *Specimens of Type in use at the Kynoch Press*
1934 Supplement No. 1. Supplementary pages for *The Kynoch Press Type Specimen Book* showing types added during 1934
1935 Supplement No. 2. Supplementary pages for *The Kynoch Press Type Specimen Book* showing types added during 1935

1939   *A Bulletin on Types*
1948   Typefaces in use at The Kynoch Press (listed in the 1948 Diary)
1952   Typefaces in use at The Kynoch Press (listed in the1952 Diary)
1953   Typefaces in use at The Kynoch Press (listed in the1953 Diary)
1953   *Specimens of Typefaces at The Kynoch Press*
1962   Typefaces in use at The Kynoch Press (listed in the1962 Diary)
1963   Typefaces in use at The Kynoch Press (listed in the1963 Diary)
1966   *The Kynoch Press / Kynoch International Print Book*

The 1927, 1934 and 1953 samples are the only major specimen books produced by the Kynoch Press; all other items are either broadsheets, small leaflets or booklets, or they take the form of lists that appear within other publications. All the above items can be found either at St Bride Printing Library, Birmingham Reference Library, or within private collections.

Using the type specimen books, in conjunction with the Monotype records and printed examples, I have catalogued what typefaces were available at the Press from the 1920s to 1970s. I have viewed the typefaces decade by decade for two main reasons:

1] the production of type specimen books is a costly and time consuming process, and for this reason it is rare, especially after the 1940s, for more than one major specimen book to be published by a printer in any one decade.

2] coincidentally, the management of the Kynoch Press changed approximately with the decades, and its history can be viewed in terms of ten-year periods.

The information used to compile the 'Tables of Typefaces held by the Kynoch Press' is a composite of detail extracted from the printer's own type specimen books and type lists, information derived from the Monotype *Sales Ledgers*, and from the evidence of printed material. The availability of both founders' and Monotype founts from each printer decade by decade is shown in alphabetical order. The tables indicate: the date when each fount was purchased; the name of the fount as is was termed by each printer; the manufacturer; the full range of sizes available in a given decade and which of those sizes were hand-set and which were machine-set. When a typeface is new to a decade, the name of the face is shown in bold. When a size is new to a decade, the size alone is shown in bold.

DATING It is not always possible to provide an exact date of purchase for all founts because of the great lapse of time between the issuing of type specimen books. It is always possible to state that a fount was purchased either before or after a certain date, or that it was purchased between two particular dates. The Kynoch Press, for example, issued its first specimen sheet in 1924; all types displayed on this sheet were, therefore, purchased prior to 1924 (their purchase dates are listed on the table as 'pre 1924'). The second Kynoch Press type specimen was issued in 1927, and any faces new to that book must have been purchased in the two or three years between 1924 and 1927 (the purchase dates are listed as 1924–27). New types which appear in a specimen book issued in the first year of a new decade must have been purchased in the preceding decade and are thus entered on to the list of the earlier decade. Where there was a great lapse between the issue of specimen books, or lists, dating becomes more difficult. Dating can be narrowed down if a sample of printed work can be found in which a particular face has been used, or if the manufacture date of a particular face is known.

TYPEFACE NAMES The typefaces are listed according to the name by which they were known and advertised by the printers themselves. If this name differs from that by which it was known by the manufacturer, any such discrepancy is shown in the footnotes to the table. If the printers themselves changed the name by which they advertised a face from one year to the next, the new name has been adopted from the time it first occurs and highlighted the change in the footnotes.

MACHINE- AND HAND-SET TYPE SIZES The type sizes are entered under the headings 'Machine Set' and 'Hand Set'. All foundry types are, by their nature, hand-set. The Monotype faces are generally machine-set up to and including 12 or 14 point (and also Didot). Sizes larger than this were generally hand set. I have followed the printers own admissions as to which sizes were hand- and which were machine-set, although there are inconsistencies with certain faces over the decades (as to which sizes were hand- and which were machine-set).

INTEGRATING MONOTYPE RECORDS WITH THE PRINTERS' OWN INFORMATION When comparing the information supplied by the Monotype Corporation with what the printers themselves admitted to possessing, there is a satisfying degree of concord between the two. This indicates that a good degree of reliability can be placed on the Monotype *Sales Ledger*. There are however, some discrepancies and they fall into four distinct categories:

1] there are occasions when Monotype have recorded a purchase of a fount for which there is no corresponding mention in the printer's publications. This happens comparatively infrequently, and tends to be when only a single size of a fount has been purchased. This may have been an entry error on the part of the Monotype sales clerk, or it may be that the purchase was made for a particular client, or for a particular job, and not available to all customers, and therefore not advertised by the printer. When such a discrepancy occurs they have been entered onto the table in italics.

2] on occasions the printers' specimens advertise the availability of a Monotype fount in a full range of sizes, even though Monotype have no record of such a sale. A discrepancy of this nature may have been as a result of error on the part of Monotype, but a failure to record a large-scale purchase is unlikely. It is more likely that these 'extra' Monotype founts were purchased at auctions or from a printer who had ceased trading.

3] there are occasional discrepancies between the date on which Monotype record the first purchase of a matrix and the printer's first advertising of the fount, and such discrepancies are footnoted.

4] similarly, there are occasional differences between the sizes Monotype noted that they sold and the sizes which the printers advertise as possessing. If Monotype have recorded a size which does not appear in the printer's specimen books, then this size has been entered on the table in italics.

I have also included a second set of tables which show, at a glance, the availability, longevity and mobility of typefaces across six decades from the 1920s to the 1970s both for the Kynoch Press and, by way of comparison, the Curwen Press and Percy, Lund Humphires.

These table have been extracted from the appendix to my thesis on the Kynoch Press. The full appendix contains detailed typeface tables for a further twelve UK and European printing houses of the same period and additional tables comparing the holdings of the various printing houses.

Typefaces held by the Kynoch Press in the 1920s

DATE	TYPEFACES	MANUFACTURER	MACHINE SET	HAND SET
pre 1923	Ancient Black [1]	Bauersche Giesserei		12, 18
1920-24	Baskerville [2]	Monotype	8, 10, 11, 12, 14	
1920-24	Baskerville Italic [3]	Monotype	8, 10, 11, 12, 14	
1927-29	Baskerville	Stephenson Blake		18, Paragon on 18, 24, 30, 36, 48, 60, 72
1920-24	Bold Face [4]	Monotype	6, 8, 10, 11, 12, 14, 18	36
1927-29	Bodoni True Cut [5]	Ludlow		12, 14, 18, 24, 36, 48
1927-29	Caslon [6]	Monotype	8, 10, 12	
1927-29	Caslon Italic	Monotype	8, 10, 12	
1900	Caslon Old Face [7] [8]	Stephenson Blake		8, 10, 12, 14, 18, 24, 30, 36, 48, 60, 72
1900	Caslon Old Face Italic [8]	Stephenson Blake		8, 10, 12, 14, 18, 24, 30, 36, 48
1927-29	Caslon Heavy	Ludlow		12, 14, 18, 24
1927-29	Cloister [8]	Monotype	6, 8, 10, 12	
1927-29	Cloister Italic	Monotype	6, 8, 10, 12	
1927-29	Cloister Bold [8]	Monotype	6, 8, 10, 12	
1927-29	Cloister Bold Italic	Monotype	6, 8, 10, 12	
1903–13?	Cloister [9]	American Type Founders		8, 10, 12, 14, 18, 24, 30, 36, 48, 60
1903–13?	Cloister Italic	American Type Founders		8, 10, 12, 14, 18, 24, 36, 48, 60
1903-13?	Cloister Bold	American Type Founders		6, 8, 10, 12, 14, 18, 24, 30, 36, 48
1927-29	Cloister Bold Italic	American Type Founders		6, 8, 10, 12
1927-29	Delphian Titling [10] [8]	Ludlow		24, 36, 48
1927-29	Fat Face 2 [11]	Stephenson Blake		48
1927-29	Fat Face Italic 2	Stephenson Blake		48
1920-24	Garamond [12]	Monotype	8, 10, 12, 14	
1920-24	Garamond Italic	Monotype	8, 10, 12, 14	
pre 1927	Garamond [13]	American Type Founders		18, 24, 30, 36, 48, 60, 72
pre 1927	Garamond Italic	American Type Founders		18, 24
1927-29	Gill Sans Medium [14]	Monotype	6, 8, 10, 12	14, 18, 24, 30, 36, 42, 48, 60
1927-29	Gill Sans Titling [15]	Monotype	6 (3 sizes)	
pre 1927	Imprint [16]	Monotype	6, 8, 10, 11, 12, 14	18, 24, 30, 36
pre 1927	Imprint Italic	Monotype	6, 8, 10, 11, 12, 14	
pre 1927	Imprint Open [17]	Monotype		18, 24, 30, 36
1924–27	Milner Initials [18]	Bespoke		48, 72
pre 1923	Open Titling [19]	Stephenson Blake		12, 18, 24, 30
1927-29	Ratio Free Initials [20]	Stempel		48, 72
1927-29	Ravilious Initials [21]	Bespoke		48
1927-29	Record Gothic [22]	Ludlow		6, 8, 10, 12
1927-29	Shaded Black [23]	Klingspor		14, 36, 48
1927-29	Square Gothic [24]	Ludlow		6, 12, 14
1920-24	Typewriter [25]	Monotype	12	
1927-29	Vesta Titling [26]	Berthold		12, 14, 18, 24, 30
pre 1925	Type Founders Initials [27] [28]	Various		

Typefaces held by the Kynoch Press in the 1930s

DATE	TYPEFACES	MANUFACTURER	MACHINE SET	HAND SET
	Baskerville [1]	Monotype	**6,** 8, **9,** 10, 11, 12, 14	**18, 24, 30, 36**
	Baskerville Italic	Monotype	**6,** 8, **9,** 10, 11, 12, 14	**18, 24, 30, 36**
	Baskerville	Stephenson Blake		18, Paragon on 18, 24, 36, 48, 60, 72
1930–33	**Bembo** [2]	Monotype	6, 8, 10, 11, 12	16, 30, 36
1930–33	**Bembo Italic**	Monotype	10, 1	
1938	**Bembo Bold** [3]	Monotype	6, 8, 10, 11, 12	
1934	**Beton Light** [4]	Bauersche Giesserei		10, 12, 14, 18, 24, 36
1934	**Beton Medium**	Bauersche Giesserei		10, 12, 14, 18, 24, 36
1934	**Beton Bold**	Bauersche Giesserei		10, 12, 14, 18, 24, 36
	Black Letter [5]	Bauersche Giesserei		12, 18
	Bodoni True Cut	Ludlow		12, 14, 18, 24, 36, 48
1930–33	**Bodoni Bold** [6]	Ludlow		8, 10, 12, 14, 18, 24, 30
	Bold Face [7]	Monotype	6, 8, 10, 11, 12, 14, 18	
1935–38	**Cartoon Light** [8]	Bauersche Giesserei		8, 10, 12, 24, 36
1935–38	**Cartoon Bold**	Bauersche Giesserei		8, 10, 12, 24, 36
	Caslon [9]	Monotype	8, 10, 12	
	Caslon Italic	Monotype	8, 10, 12	
1930-33	**Caslon**	Ludlow		8, 10, 12, 14, 18, 24
1930-33	**Caslon Italic** [10]	Ludlow		8, 10, 12, 14, 18, 24
	Caslon Heavy	Ludlow		12, 14, 18, 24, **30**
	Caslon Old Face Italic [11]	Stephenson Blake		24, 30, 36, 48
1930–33	**Caslon Poster Type**	Stephenson Blake		6, 8, 10, 12, 14, 16, 18 line
	Cloister [12]	Monotype	6, 8, 10, 12	
	Cloister Italic	Monotype	6, 8, 10, 12	
	Cloister Bold	Monotype	6, 8, 10, 12	
	Cloister Bold Italic	Monotype	6, 8, 10, 12	
	Cloister [12]	American Type Founders		14, 18, 24, 30, 36, 48, 60
	Cloister Italic	American Type Founders		14, 18, 24, 36, 48, 60
	Cloister Bold	American Type Founders		14, 18, 24, 30, 36, 48
1930–33	**Condensed Gothic** [13]	Ludlow		6, 8, 10
1935–38	**Corvinus Medium** [14]	Bauersche Giesserei		12, 18, 24, 36, 48
1935–38	**Corvinus Medium Italic**	Bauersche Giesserei		12, 18, 24, 36, 48
1935–38	**Corvinus Bold**	Bauersche Giesserei		12, 18, 24, 36, 48
1930–33	**Elephant** [15]	Stevens Shanks		60
1930–33	**Elephant Italic**	Stevens Shanks		60
1935–39	**Elongated Roman** [16]	Stephenson Blake		12, 16, 24, 30, 36, 48, 60, 72
1930–33	**Falstaff** [17]	Monotype	8, 12	16, 18
1930–33	**Fat Face 1** [18]	Stevens Shanks		30
1930–33	**Fat Face Italic 1**	Stevens Shanks		30
	Fat Face 2	Stephenson Blake		48
	Fat Face Italic 2	Stephenson Blake		48
	Garamond [19]	Monotype	8, 10, 12, 14	
	Garamond Italic	Monotype	8, 10, 12, 14	
	Garamond [19]	American Type Founders		18, 24, 30, 36, 48, 60, 72

DATE	TYPEFACES	MANUFACTURER	MACHINE SET	HAND SET
	Garamond Italic	American Type Founders		18, 24
1930–33	**Gill Sans Light** [20]	Monotype	6, 8, 10, 12,	14, 18, 24, 30, 36
	Gill Sans Medium	Monotype	6, 8, 10, 12, 14	18, 24, 30, 36, 42, 48, 60
1934	**Gill Sans Medium Italic**	Monotype	10	18
1930–33	**Gill Sans Bold** [21]	Monotype		6, 8, 10, 12, 14, 18, 24
1930–33	**Gill Sans Bold Condensed** [22]	Monotype		14
	Gill Sans Titling	Monotype	6 *(3 sizes)*	
1930–33	**Gill Poster Type** [23]	Stephenson Blake		6, 8, 10, 12, 14, 16, 18 line
1930–33	**Granby Condensed** [24]	Stephenson Blake		8, 10, 12, 14, 18, 24, 30
1930–33	**Greek: New Hellenic** [25]	Monotype		9, 11
1930–33	**Greek: Porson** [26]	Monotype		8, 12
	Imprint [27]	Monotype	6, 8, 10, 11, 12, 14	18, 24, 30, 36
	Imprint Italic	Monotype	6, 8, 10, 11, 12, 14	
	Imprint Shadow [28]	Monotype		**14**, 18, 24, 30, 36
1935–39	**Marina Script** [29]	Stephenson Blake		14, 18, 24, 36, 42
	Milner Initials [30]	Bespoke		48, 72
	Open Titling	Stephenson Blake		12, 18, 24, 30
1935	**Perpetua Titling** [31]	Monotype		14, 18, 24, 30, 36, 42
1935–39	**Playbill** [32]	Stephenson Blake		24, 36, 48, 72
1930–33	**Prisma** [33]	Klingspor		24, 36, 48
	Ratio Free Initials [34]	Stempel		48, 72
	Ravilious Initials [35]	Bespoke		48
	Record Gothic	Ludlow		6, 8, 10, 12
1938	**Rockwell Light** [36]	Monotype	6, 8, 10, 12	
1938	**Rockwell Medium**	Monotype	6, 8, 10, 12	
1938	**Rockwell Bold**	Monotype	6, 8, 10, 12	
1930–33	**Russian: Baskerville** [37]	Monotype	9, 11	18, 24, 36
	Shaded Black	Klingspor		14, 36, 48
	Square Gothic	Ludlow		6, **8, 10,** 12, 14
1930–33	**Tempo Medium** [38]	Ludlow		8, 10, 12, 18, 24, 30, 36, 48
1930–33	**Tempo Bold** [39]	Ludlow		18, 24, 30, 36, 42, 48, 60, 72
1934	**Thorne Shaded** [40]	Stephenson Blake		18
1938	**Times New Roman** [41]	Monotype	6, 8, 9, 10, 11, 12	
1938	**Times New Roman Bold**	Monotype	6, 8, 9, 10, 11, 12	
	Typewriter	Monotype	12	
1931	**Union Pearl** [42]	Stephenson Blake		22
	Vesta Titling	Berthold		12, 14, 18, 24, 30

Typefaces held by the Kynoch Press in the 1940s

DATE	TYPEFACES	MANUFACTURER	MACHINE SET	HAND SET
	Baskerville[1]	Monotype	6, 8, 9, 10, 11, 12, 14	18, 24, 30, 36
	Baskerville Italic	Monotype	6, 8, 9, 10, 11, 12, 14	18, 24, 30, 36
	Baskerville	Stephenson Blake		18, Paragon on 18, 24, 30, 36, 48, 60, 72
	Bembo	Monotype	6, 8, 10, 11, 12	16, 30, 36
	Bembo Italic	Monotype	10, 12	
	Bembo Bold	Monotype	6, 8, 10, 11, 12	
	Beton Light	Bauersche Giesserei		10, 12, 14, 18, 24, 36
	Beton Medium	Bauersche Giesserei		10, 12, 14, 18, 24, 36
	Beton Bold	Bauersche Giesserei		10, 12, 14, 18, 24, 36
	Black Letter	Bauersche Giesserei		12, 18
1940	**Bodoni** [2]	Monotype	8, 10, 11, 12	
1940	**Bodoni Italic**	Monotype	8, 10, 11, 12	
1940	**Bodoni Bold**	Monotype	8, 10, 11, 12	14
1940	**Bodoni Bold Italic**	Monotype	8, 10, 11, 12	
	Bodoni True Cut	Ludlow		12, 14, 18, 24, 36, 48
	Bodoni Bold	Ludlow		8, 10, 12, 14, 18, 24, 30
	Bold Face	Monotype	6, 8, 10, 11, 12, 14, 18	
	Cartoon Light	Bauersche Giesserei		8, 10, 12, 24, 36
	Cartoon Bold	Bauersche Giesserei		8, 10, 12, 24, 36
	Caslon [3, 4]	Monotype	8, 10, 12	
	Caslon Italic	Monotype	8, 10, 12	
	Caslon Old Face [3]	Stephenson Blake		30, 36, 48, 60, 72
	Caslon Old Face Italic	Stephenson Blake		24, 30, 36, 48
	Caslon [3]	Ludlow		8, 10, 12, 14, 18, 24
	Caslon Italic	Ludlow		8, 10, 12, 14, 18, 24
	Caslon Heavy	Ludlow		12, 14, 18, 24, 30
	Cloister [5]	Monotype	6, 8, 10, 12	
	Cloister Italic	Monotype	6, 8, 10, 12	
	Cloister Bold	Monotype	6, 8, 10, 12	
	Cloister Bold Italic	Monotype	6, 8, 10, 12	
	Cloister [5]	American Type Founders		14, 18, 24, 30, 36, 48, 60
	Cloister Italic	American Type Founders		14, 18, 24, **30**, 36, 48, 60
	Cloister Bold	American Type Founders		14, 18, 24, 30, 36, 48
	Corvinus Medium	Bauersche Giesserei		12, 18, 24, 36, 48
	Corvinus Medium Italic	Bauersche Giesserei		12, 18, 24, 36, 48
	Corvinus Bold	Bauersche Giesserei		12, 18, 24, 36, 48
	Elephant	Stevens Shanks		60
	Elephant Italic	Stevens Shanks		60
	Elongated Roman	Stephenson Blake		12, 16, 24, 30, 36, 48, 60, 72
	Falstaff	Monotype	8, 12	16, 18
	Fat Face 1	Stevens Shanks		30
	Fat Face Italic 1	Stevens Shanks		30
	Fat Face 2	Stephenson Blake		48
	Fat Face Italic 2	Stephenson Blake		48

DATE	TYPEFACES	MANUFACTURER	MACHINE SET	HAND SET
	Garamond [6]	Monotype	8, 10, 12, 14	
	Garamond Italic	Monotype	8, 10, 12, 14	
	Garamond [6]	American Type Founders		18, 24, 30, 36, 48, 60, 72
	Garamond Italic	American Type Founders		18, 24
	Gill Sans Light	Monotype	6, 8, 10, 12, 14	18, 24, 30, 36
	Gill Sans Medium	Monotype	6, 8, 10, 12, 14	18, 24, 30, 36, 42, 48, 60
	Gill Sans Medium Italic	Monotype	10	18
	Gill Sans Bold	Monotype		6, 8, 10, 12, 14, 18, 24
	Gill Sans Bold Condensed	Monotype		**6, 8, 10, 12**, 14
1940	**Gill Sans Extra Bold**	Monotype		10, 12, 14, 18, 24, 30, 36, 60, 72
1940	**Gill Sans Shadow Titling**	Monotype		36
	Granby Condensed	Stephenson Blake		8, 10, 12, 14, 18, 24, 30
	Greek: New Hellenic	Monotype		9, 11
	Greek: Porson	Monotype		8, 12
	Imprint	Monotype	6, 8, 10, 11, 12, 14	18, 24, 30, 36
	Imprint Italic	Monotype	6, 8, 10, 11, 12, 14	
	Imprint Shadow	Monotype		14, 18, 24, 30, 36
	Marina Script	Stephenson Blake		14, 18, 24, 36, 48
	Open Titling	Stephenson Blake		12, 18, 24, 30
	Perpetua Titling	Monotype		14, 18, 24, 30, 36, 42
	Prisma	Klingspor		24, 36, 48
1942	**Plantin Light** [7]	Monotype	6, 8, 10, 12	
1942	**Plantin Light Italic**	Monotype	6, 8, 10, 12	
	Playbill	Stephenson Blake		24, 36, 48, 72
	Record Gothic	Ludlow		6, 8, 10, 12
	Rockwell Light	Monotype	6, 8, 10, 12	
	Rockwell Medium	Monotype	6, 8, 10, 12	
	Rockwell Bold	Monotype	6, 8, 10, 12	
	Russian: Baskerville [8]	Monotype	9, 11	18, 24, 36
pre 1947	**Russian: Plantin Light** [9]	Monotype	6, 8, 10, 12	14, 18, 24, 30
pre 1947	**Russian: Plantin Italic Light**	Monotype	6, 8, 10, 12	14, 18, 24, 30
pre 1947	**Russian: Plantin**	Monotype	6, 8, 10, 12	14, 18, 24, 30, 36
pre 1947	**Russian: Plantin Italic**	Monotype	6, 8, 10, 12	14, 18, 24, 30, 36
	Shaded Black	Klingspor		14, 36, 48
	Square Gothic	Ludlow		6, 8, 10, 12, 14
	Tempo Medium	Ludlow		8, 10, 12, 18, 24, 30, 36, 48
	Tempo Bold	Ludlow		18, 24, 30, 36, 42, 48, 60, 72
	Thorne Shaded	Stephenson Blake		18
	Times New Roman	Monotype	6, 8, 9, 10, 11, 12, **14**	
	Times New Roman Bold	Monotype	6, 8, 9, 10, 11, 12	
by 1947	**Times Titling**	Monotype		
	Typewriter [10]	Monotype	12	
	Union Pearl	Stephenson Blake		22
	Vesta Titling	Berthold		12, 14, 18, 24, 30

Typefaces held by the Kynoch Press in the 1950s

DATE	TYPEFACES	MANUFACTURER	MACHINE SET	HAND SET
post-1953	Albertus [1]	Monotype		14, 18, 24, 36
1953–55	**Annonce Grotesque [2]**	Lettergieterij Amsterdam		8, 10, 12, 14, 18 small & large, 24, 30, 36
	Baskerville	Monotype	6, 8, 9, 10, 11, 12, 14	18, 24, 30, 36
	Baskerville Italic	Monotype	6, 8, 9, 10, 11, 12, 14	18, 24, 30, 36
	Baskerville	Stephenson Blake		18, Paragon on 18, 24, 30, 36, 48, 60, 72
	Bembo [3]	Monotype	6, 8, **9**, 10, 11, 12	**14**, 16, **18, 24,** 30, 36
	Bembo Italic	Monotype	**6, 8, 9**, 10, **11**, 12	**14, 16, 18, 24, 30, 36**
	Bembo Bold	Monotype	6, 8, **9**, 10, 11, 12 [14]	
	Beton Light	Bauersche Giesserei		10, 12, 14, 18, 24, 36
	Beton Medium	Bauersche Giesserei		10, 12, 14, 18, 24, **30**, 36
	Beton Bold	Bauersche Giesserei		10, 12, 14, 18, 24, 36
1952	**Beton Extra Bold**	Bauersche Giesserei		14, 18, 24, 30, 36, 48
	Black Letter	Bauersche Giesserei		12, 18
	Black Letter Shaded [4]	Bauersche Giesserei		14, 36, 48
	Bodoni	Monotype	8, 10, 11, 12	
	Bodoni Italic	Monotype	8, 10, 11, 12	
	Bodoni Bold	Monotype	8, 10, 11, 12	14
	Bodoni Bold Italic	Monotype		14, 18, 24, 30, 36, 48
	Bodoni True Cut	Ludlow		12, 14, 18, 24, 36, 48
	Bodoni Bold	Ludlow		8, 10, 12, 14, 18, 24, 30
	Bold Face	Monotype	6, 8, 10, 11, 12, 14, 18	
	Cartoon Light	Bauersche Giesserei		8, 10, 12, **18**, 24, 36
	Cartoon Bold	Bauersche Giesserei		8, 10, 12, **18**, 24, 36
	Caslon	Monotype	8, 10, 12	
	Caslon Italic	Monotype	8, 10, 12	
	Caslon Old Face	Stephenson Blake		30, 36, **42**, 48, 60, 72
	Caslon Old Face Italic	Stephenson Blake		30, 36, 48
	Caslon	Ludlow		8, 10, 12, 14, 18, 24
	Caslon Italic	Ludlow		8, 10, 12, 14, 18, 24
	Caslon Heavy	Ludlow		12, 14, 18, 24, 30
1952	***Centaur* [5]**	*Monotype*	*9*	
1955	***Clarendon* [6]**	*Monotype*	*6*	
post 1953	**Chisel [7]**	Stephenson Blake		48, 60
	Cloister	Monotype	6, 8, 10, 12	
	Cloister Italic	Monotype	6, 8, 10, 12	
	Cloister Bold	Monotype	6, 8, 10, 12	
	Cloister Bold Italic	Monotype	6, 8, 10, 12	
	Cloister	American Type Founders		14, 18, 24, 30, 36, 48, 60
	Cloister Italic	American Type Founders		14, 18, 24, 30, 36, 48, 60
	Cloister Bold	American Type Founders		14, 18, 24, 30, 36, 48
	Condensed Gothic	Ludlow		6, 8, 10
post 1953	**Cooper Black [8]**	American Type Founders		14, 18, 30, 36
	Corvinus Medium	Bauersche Giesserei		12, 18, 24, 36, 48
	Corvinus Medium Italic	Bauersche Giesserei		12, 18, 24, 36, 48

DATE	TYPEFACES	MANUFACTURER	MACHINE SET	HAND SET
	Corvinus Bold	Bauersche Giesserei		12, 18, 24, 36, 48
	Elephant	Stevens Shanks		60
	Elephant Italic	Stevens Shanks		60
	Elongated Roman	Stephenson Blake		12, 16, 24, 30, 36, 48, 60, 72
1949–51	**Elongated Roman Shaded** [9]	Stephenson Blake		72
	Falstaff [10]	Monotype		**6**, 8, **10**, 12, **14**, 18, **24, 30, 36, 48, 60**
1949–51	**Falstaff Italic**	Monotype		14, 18, 24, 30, 36, 48, 60
	Fat Face 1	Stevens Shanks		30
	Fat Face Italic 1	Stevens Shanks		30
	Fat Face 2	Stephenson Blake		48
	Fat Face Italic 2	Stephenson Blake		48
	Garamond	Monotype	8, 10, 12, 14	
	Garamond Italic	Monotype	8, 10, 12, 14	
	Garamond	American Type Founders		18, 24, 30, 36, 48, 60, 72
	Garamond Italic	American Type Founders		18, 24
	Gill Sans Light	Monotype	6, 8, 10, 12	14, 18, 24, 30, 36, **42, 48**
post 1953	**Gill Sans Light Italic**	Monotype		14
	Gill Sans Medium	Monotype	6, 8, 10, 12	14, 18, 24, 30, 36, 42, 48, 60, **72**
	Gill Sans Medium Italic	Monotype	**6, 8,** 10, **12**	**14,** 18
	Gill Sans Bold	Monotype	6, 8, 10, 12	14, 18, 24, **30, 36, 42, 48**
1949–51	**Gill Sans Bold Italic**	Monotype	6, 8, 10, 12	14, 18, 24, 30, 36, 42
	Gill Sans Extra Bold	Monotype		10, 12, 14, 18, 24, 30, 36, 60, 72
	Gill Sans Bold Condensed	Monotype		6, 8, 10, 12, 14, **18, 24, 30, 36, 42, 48, 60, 72**
	Gill Sans Titling	Monotype		6 *(3 sizes: small, medium and large)*, 36
post 1953	**Gill Ext Bold Con'd Titling**	Monotype		14, 18
	Gill Shadow Titling	Monotype		36
	Granby Condensed	Stephenson Blake		8, 10, 12, 14, 18, 24, 30
	Greek: New Hellenic	Monotype		9, 11
	Greek: Porson	Monotype		8, 12
1959	**Grotesque No 1 [215]** [11]	Monotype	6.5, 8, 9, 10, 11	13, 14, 18, 24, 30
1959	**Grotesque No 1 Italic [215]**	Monotype	6.5, 8, 9, 10, 11	
1959	**Grotesque No 1 Bold [216]**	Monotype	6.5, 8, 9, 10, 11	13, 14, 18, 24, 30
1953	**Grot No1 Bold Extended [150]**	Monotype		6, 8, 10, 12, 14, 18, 24
1949–51	**Grotesque No 9**	Stephenson Blake		8, 10, 12, 14, 18, 24, 30, 36, 42, 48, 60
1949–51	**Grotesque No 9 Italic**	Stephenson Blake		10, 12, 14, 18, 24, 30, 36, 42, 48
1959	**Headline Bold** [12]	Monotype		10, 12
	Imprint	Monotype	6, 8, 10, 11, 12, 14	18, 24, 30, 36
	Imprint Italic	Monotype	6, 8, 10, 11, 12, 14	
	Imprint Shadow	Monotype		14, 18, 24, 30, 36, **42, 48**
	Marina Script	Stephenson Blake		14, 18, 24, 36, 48
1955	***Old Style*** [13]	*Monotype*	*6, 12*	
	Open Titling	Stephenson Blake		12, 18, 24, 30
post 1953	**Perpetua**	Monotype		14, 24
1949–51	**Perpetua Italic**	Monotype		14, 18, 24, 30, 36
	Perpetua Titling	Monotype		14, 18, 24, 30, 36, 42, **48, 60, 72**

DATE	TYPEFACES	MANUFACTURER	MACHINE SET	HAND SET
	Plantin Light	Monotype	6, 8, 10, 12	**14, 18, 24, 30, 36**
	Plantin Light Italic	Monotype	6, 8, 10, 12	**14, 18, 24, 30, 36**
1952	**Plantin Medium** [14]	Monotype	6, 8, 9, 10, 11, 12	14, 18
1952	**Plantin Medium Italic**	Monotype	6, 8, 9, 10, 11, 12	14
post 1953	**Plantin Bold**	Monotype	6, 8, 9, 10, 11, 12	14
	Playbill	Stephenson Blake		24, 36, 48, 72
	Prisma	Klingspor		24, 36, 48
	Record Gothic	Ludlow		6, 8, 10, 12
1953–55	**Reiner Script** [15]	Lettergieterij Amsterdam		36, 48
	Russian: Plantin Light	Monotype	6, 8, 10, 12	14, 18, 24, 30
	Russian: Plantin Light Italic	Monotype	6, 8, 10, 12	14, 18, 24, 30
	Russian: Plantin	Monotype	6, 8, 10, 12	14, 18, 24, 30, 36
	Russian: Plantin Italic	Monotype	6, 8, 10, 12	14, 18, 24, 30, 36
	Rockwell Light	Monotype	6, 8, 10, 12	**14, 18, 24, 30, 36**
	Rockwell Medium	Monotype	6, 8, 10, 12	**14, 18, 24, 30, 36**
	Rockwell Bold	Monotype	6, 8, 10, 12	**14, 18, 24, 30, 36**
	Shaded Black	Klingspor		14, 36, 48
1957	**Spartan Condensed**	Monotype		6
	Square Gothic	Ludlow		6, 8, 10, 12, 14
	Tempo	Ludlow		8, 10, 12, 18, 24, 30, 36, 48
	Tempo Bold	Ludlow		18, 24, 30, 36, 42, 48, 60**,** 72
	Thorne Shaded	Stephenson Blake		18, **24**
	Typewriter	Monotype	12	
	Times New Roman	Monotype	6, 8, 9, 10, 11, 12, 14	**18, 24, 30, 36**
	Times New Roman Italic	Monotype	6, 8, 9, 10, 11, 12, 14	18, 24
	Times Bold	Monotype	6, 8, 9, 10, 11, 12, **14**	**18, 24, 30, 36**
post 1953	**Times Bold Italic**	Monotype	8, 10	
1949–51	**Times Heavy Titling**	Monotype		12, 14, 18, 24, 30, 36, 42, 48
	Union Pearl	Stephenson Blake		22
	Vesta Titling	Berthold		12, 14, 18, 24, 30
post 1953	**Walbaum**	Monotype		14pt, 16d, 20d, 24d

Typefaces held by the Kynoch Press in the 1960s

DATE	TYPEFACES	MANUFACTURER	MACHINE SET	HAND SET
	Albertus	Monotype		14, 18, 24, 36, **48, 60, 72**
	Annonce Grotesque	Lettergieterij Amsterdam		8, 10, 12, 14, 18 small & large, 24, 30, 36
	Baskerville	Monotype	6, 8, 9, 10, 11, 12, 14	18, 24, 30, 36
	Baskerville Italic	Monotype	6, 8, 9, 10, 11, 12, 14	18, 24, 30, 36
	Baskerville	Stephenson Blake		18, paragon on 18, 24, 36, 48, 60, 72
	Bembo	Monotype	6, 8, 9, 10, 11, 12, 14	16, 18, 24, 30, 36
	Bembo Italic	Monotype	6, 8, 9, 10, 11, 12, 14	16, 18, 24, 30, 36
	Bembo Bold	Monotype	6, 8, 9, 10, 11, 12	
	Beton Light	Bauersche Giesserei		10, 12, 14, 18, 24, 36
	Beton Medium	Bauersche Giesserei		10, 12, 14, 18, 24, 30, 36
	Beton Bold	Bauersche Giesserei		10, 12, 14, 18, 24, 36, **48**
	Beton Extra Bold	Bauersche Giesserei		14, 18, 24, 30, 36, 48
	Black Letter	Bauersche Giesserei		12, 18
	Bodoni	Monotype	8, 10, 11, 12	**14, 30**
	Bodoni Italic	Monotype	8, 10, 11, 12	
	Bodoni Bold	Monotype	8, 10, 11, 12	14, **18, 24, 30, 36, 42, 48**
	Bodoni Bold Italic	Monotype		14, 18, 24, 30, 36, 48
	Bodoni True Cut [1]	Ludlow		12, 14, 18, 24, 36, 48
	Bodoni Bold	Ludlow		8, 10, 12, 14, 18, 24, 30
	Bold Face	Monotype	6, 8, 9, 10, 11, 12, 14	18
	Cartoon Light	Bauersche Giesserei		8, 10, 12, 18, 24, 36
	Cartoon Bold	Bauersche Giesserei		8, 10, 12, 18, 24, 36
	Caslon	Monotype	8, 10, 12	**24**
	Caslon Italic	Monotype	8, 10, 12	
	Caslon Old Face [2]	Stephenson Blake		14, 18, 30, 36, 42, 48, 60, 72
	Caslon Old Face Italic	Stephenson Blake		14, 18, 30, 36, 48
	Caslon Wood Letter [3]	Stephenson Blake		6, 8, 10, 12, 14, 16, 18 line
	Caslon	Ludlow		8, 10, 12, 14, 18, 24
	Caslon Italic	Ludlow		8, 10, 12, 14, 18, 24
	Caslon Heavy [4]	Ludlow		12, 14, 18, 24, 30
	Chisel	Stephenson Blake		48, 60
	Cloister	Monotype	6, 8, 10, 12	
	Cloister Italic	Monotype	6, 8, 10, 12	
	Cloister Bold	Monotype	6, 8, 10, 12	
	Cloister Bold Italic	Monotype	6, 8, 10, 12	
	Cloister	American Type Founders		14, 18, 24, 30, 36, 48, 60
	Cloister Italic	American Type Founders		14, 18, 24, 30, 36, 48, 60
	Cloister Bold	American Type Founders		14, 18, 24, 30, 36, 48
pre 1962	**Condensed Sans No 1**	Stephenson Blake		18, 24, 30, 36, 48
	Condensed Gothic [5a]	Ludlow		6, 8, 10
	Cooper Black	American Type Founders		14, 18, 30, 36
	Corvinus Medium	Bauersche Giesserei		12, 18, 24, 36, 48
	Corvinus Medium Italic	Bauersche Giesserei		12, 18, 24, 36, 48
	Corvinus Bold	Bauersche Giesserei		12, 18, 24, 36, 48
	Elephant	Stevens Shanks		60

DATE	TYPEFACES	MANUFACTURER	MACHINE SET	HAND SET
	Elephant Italic	Stevens Shanks		60
	Elongated Roman	Stephenson Blake		12, 16, 24, 30, 36, 48, 60, 72
	Elongated Roman Shaded	Stephenson Blake		72
pre 1961	**Erbar** [6]	Ludwig and Mayer		8, 12
pre 1961	**Erbar Italic**	Ludwig and Mayer		8, 10
pre 1961	**Erbar Bold**	Ludwig and Mayer		8, 30
	Falstaff	Monotype		6, 8, 10, 12, 14, 18, 24, 30, 36, 48, 60
	Falstaff Italic	Monotype		**10, 12**, 14, 18, 24, 30, 36, 48, 60
	Fat Face 1	Stevens Shanks		30
	Fat Face Italic 1	Stevens Shanks		30
	French Canon	Stephenson Blake		48
	French Canon Italic	Stephenson Blake		48
pre 1961	**Ganton Titling**	Stephenson Blake		36
	Garamond	Monotype	8, 10, 12, 14	**24, 72**
	Garamond Italic	Monotype	8, 10, 12,	14, **24**
pre 1961	**Garamond Bold** [7]	Monotype		12, 42
1961	**Garamond Bold Italic**	Monotype		18, 42, 60
	Garamond	American Type Founders		18, 24, 30, 36, 48, 60, 72
	Garamond Italic	American Type Founders		18, 24
	Gill Sans Light	Monotype	6, 8, 10, 12	14, 18, 24, 30, 36, 42, 48
	Gill Sans Light Italic	Monotype	**8**	14
	Gill Sans Medium	Monotype	6, 8, 10, 12, 14	**5,** 18, 30, 36, 42, 48, 60, 72
	Gill Sans Medium Italic	Monotype	6, 8, 10, 12, 14,	**5,** 18
	Gill Sans Bold	Monotype	6, 8, 10, 12	14, 18, 24, 30, 36, 42, 48
	Gill Sans Bold Italic	Monotype	6, 8, 10, 12	14, 18, 24, 30, 36, 42
	Gill Sans Extra Bold	Monotype		10, 12, 14, 18, 24, 30, 36, 60, 72
	Gill Sans Bold Condensed	Monotype		6, 8, 10, 12, 14, 18, 24, 30, 36, 42, 48, 60, 72
	Gill Sans Titling	Monotype		6 *(3 sizes: small, medium and large)*, 36
pre 1961	**Gill Condensed Titling**	Monotype		14, 18
	Gill Shadow Titling	Monotype		36
	Gill Woodletter [8]	Stephenson Blake		6, 8, 10, 12, 14, 16, 18 line
pre 1961	**Gill Bold Condensed**	Stephenson Blake		20 line
pre 1961	**Gill Extra Bold**	Stephenson Blake		12 lines
	Granby Condensed	Stephenson Blake		8, 10, 12, 14, 18, 24, 30
	Greek: New Hellenic	Monotype		9, 11
	Greek: Porson	Monotype		**6,** 8, **10,** 12
	Grotesque No 1 [215]	Monotype	6.5, 8, 9, 10, 11	13, 14, 18, 24, 30, **36, 48**
	Grotesque No 1 Italic [215]	Monotype	6.5, 8, 9, 10, 11, **13**	
	Grotesque No 1 Bold [216]	Monotype	6.5, 8, 9, 10, 11	13, 14, 18, 24, 30
	Grot No1 Bold Extended[150]	Monotype		6, 8, 10, 12, 14, 18, 24, **36**
	Headline Bold	Monotype		**8,** 10, 12, **14, 18, 24, 30, 36, 42, 48, 60, 72**
pre 1961	**Headline Bold Italic**	Monotype		8, 10, 12, 14, 18, 24, 30, 36, 42, 48, 60, 72
1968	***Hebrew: Levinim*** [9]	*Monotype*		*18*
1968	**Helvetica**	Monotype		
	Imprint	Monotype	6, 8, **9,** 10, 11, 12, 14	18, 24, 30, 36

DATE	TYPEFACES	MANUFACTURER	MACHINE SET	HAND SET
	Imprint Italic	Monotype	6, 8, **9,** 10, 11, 12, 14	
	Imprint Shadow	Monotype		14, 18, 24, 30, 36, 42, 48
pre 1962	**Klang** [10]	Stephenson Blake		14, 18
	Marina Script	Stephenson Blake		14, 18, 24, **30**, 36, 48
1963	***Modern Condensed*** [11]	*Monotype*	*6*	
	Open Titling	Stephenson Blake		12, 18, 24, 30
	Perpetua [12]	Monotype		**10, 12**, 14, 24
	Perpetua Italic	Monotype		**12**, 14, 18, 24, 30, 36
pre 1961	**Perpetua Bold** [13]	Monotype		30, 42, 48, 60, 72
	Perpetua Titling	Monotype		14, 18, 24, 30, 36, 42, 48, 60, 72
pre 1961	**Phosphor** [14]	Ludwig and Mayer		18
	Plantin Light	Monotype	6, 8, 10, 12	14, 18, 24, 30, 36
	Plantin Light Italic	Monotype	6, 8, 10, 12	14, 18, 24, 30, 36
	Plantin Medium	Monotype	6, 8, 9, 10, 11, 12	14, 18
	Plantin Medium Italic	Monotype	6, 8, 9, 10, 11, 12	14, **18**
	Plantin Bold	Monotype	6, 8, 9, 10, 11, 12	14, **18**
pre 1962	Playbill	Stephenson Blake		24, 36, 48, 72
pre 1961	**Playbill Titling** [15]	Stephenson Blake		72
pre 1961	**Playbill Woodletter**	Stephenson Blake		20, 30 line
	Prisma	Klingspor		24, 36, 48
	Reiner Script	Lettergieterij Amsterdam		36, 48
	Record Gothic [5b]	Ludlow		6, 8, 10, 12
	Russian: Baskerville	Monotype	9, 11	18, 24, 36
	Russian: Plantin [16]	Monotype	6, 8, 10, 12	14, 18, 24, 30, 36
	Russian: Plantin Italic	Monotype	6, 8, 10, 12	14, 18, 24, 30, 36
1960	**Russian: Gill Sans**	Monotype	6, 8, 10, 12, 14	
1960	**Russian: Gill Sans Italic**	Monotype	6, 8, 10, 12	
pre 1966	**Russian: Gill Sans Bold**	Monotype	6, 8, 10, 12	14, 18, 24
pre 1966	**Russian: Gill Bold Cond**	Monotype		18, 24
	Rockwell Light	Monotype	6, 8, 10, 12	14, 18, 24, 30, 36
	Rockwell Medium	Monotype	6, 8, 10, 12	14, 18, 24, 30, 36
	Rockwell Bold	Monotype	6, 8, 10, 12	14, 18, 24, 30, 36
	Shaded Black [17]	Klingspor		15, 38, 51
	Spartan Condensed	Monotype		5/6
	Square Gothic [5c]	Ludlow		6, 8, 10, 12, 14
	Tempo [18]	Ludlow		8, 10, 12, 18, 24, 30, 36, 48
	Tempo Bold	Ludlow		18, 24, 30, 36, 42, 48, 60, 72
	Thorne Shaded	Stephenson Blake		18, 24, **30**
	Typewriter	Monotype		12
	Times New Roman	Monotype	6, 8, 9, 10, 11, 12, 14	18, 24, 30, 36
	Times New Roman Italic	Monotype	6, 8, 9, 10, 11, 12, 14	18, 24
	Times Bold	Monotype	6, 8, 9, 10, 11, 12, 14	18, 24, 30, 36
	Times Bold Italic	Monotype	8, 10	
	Times Heavy Titling	Monotype		12, 14, 18, 24, 30, 36, 42, 48
	Union Pearl	Stephenson Blake		22

DATE	TYPEFACES	MANUFACTURER	MACHINE SET	HAND SET
1964	**Univers Light**	Monotype	6d, 8d, 9d, 10d, 12d	14d, 18d, 22d, 28d, 36d
1964	**Univers Light Italic**	Monotype	6d, 8d, 9d, 10d, 12d	14d
1964	***Univers Light Cond.*** [20]	*Monotype*	*6d, 8d, 9d, 10d, 12d*	
1964	**Univers Medium** [19]	Monotype	6d, 8d, 9d, 10d, 12d	14d, 18d, 22d
1964	**Univers Medium Italic**	Monotype	6d, 8d, 9d, 10d, 12d	
1964	***Univers Medium Cond.*** [21]	*Monotype*	*8*	
1964	**Univers Bold**	Monotype	6d, 8d, 9d, 10d, 12d	14d, 18d, 22d
1964	**Univers Bold Italic** [22]	Monotype	6d, 8d, 9d, 10d, 12d	14d, 18d, 22d, 28d, 36d
1964	***Univers Bold Cond***	*Monotype*	*8d*	
1964	**Univers Extra Bold**	Monotype	6d, 8d, 9d, 10d, 12d	14d, 22d, 28d
pre 1966	**Univers** [23]	Deberny and Peignot		24
	Vesta Titling	Berthold		12, 14, 18, 24, 30
	Walbaum	Monotype		14d, 16d, 20d, 24d

Typefaces held by the Kynoch Press in the 1970s

DATE	TYPEFACES	MANUFACTURER	MACHINE SET	HAND SET
	Albertus	Monotype		14, 18, 24, 36, 48, 60, 72
	Annonce Grotesque	Lettergieterij Amsterdam		8, 10, 12, 14, 18 small and large, 24, 30, 36
1973	**Arnold Brocklin**	Letraset		
1974	**Avant Garde Gothic Light**	Letraset		
1974	**Avant Garde Gothic Bold**	Letraset		
	Baskerville	Monotype	6, 8, 9, 10, 11, 12, 14	18, 24, 30, 36
	Baskerville Italic	Monotype	6, 8, 9, 10, 11, 12, 14	18, 24, 30, 36
	Baskerville	Stephenson Blake		18, Paragon on 18, 24, 36, 48, 60, 72
1976	**Baskerville**	Linotype		
	Bembo	Monotype	6, 8, 9, 10, 11, 12,14	16, 18, 24, 30, 36
	Bembo Italic	Monotype	6, 8, 9, 10, 11, 12, 14	16, 18, 24, 30, 36
	Bembo Bold	Monotype	6, 8, 9, 10, 11, 12	
1976	**Bembo**	Linotype		
	Beton Light	Bauersche Giesserei		10, 12, 14, 18, 24, 36
	Beton Medium	Bauersche Giesserei		10, 12, 14, 18, 24, 30, 36
	Beton Bold	Bauersche Giesserei		10, 12, 14, 18, 24, 36, 48
	Beton Extra Bold	Bauersche Giesserei		14, 18, 24, 30, 36, 48
	Black Letter	Bauersche Giesserei		12, 18
	Bodoni	Monotype	8, 10, 11, 12	14, 30
	Bodoni Italic	Monotype	8, 10, 11, 12	
	Bodoni Bold	Monotype	8, 10, 11, 12	14, 18, 24, 30, 36, 42, 48
	Bodoni Bold Italic	Monotype		14, 18, 24, 30, 36, 48
1976	**Bodoni**	Linotype		
	Bold Face	Monotype	6, 8, 10, 11, 12, 14	18
1971	**Bookman Bold Italic**	Letraset		
1973	**Busorama Bold**	Letraset		
1970	**Cable Heavy**	Letraset		
	Cartoon Light	Bauersche Giesserei		8, 10, 12, 18, 24, 36
	Cartoon Bold	Bauersche Giesserei		8, 10, 12, 18, 24, 36
	Caslon	Monotype	8, 10, 12	24
	Caslon Italic	Monotype	8, 10, 12	
	Caslon	Stephenson Blake		14, 18, 30, 36, 42, 48, 60, 72
	Caslon Italic	Stephenson Blake		14, 18, 30, 36, 48
	Caslon Wood Letter	Stephenson Blake		6, 8, 10, 12, 14, 16, 18 line
1973	**Caslon Black**	Letraset		
1970	**Century Schoolbook Bold**	Letraset		
	Chisel	Stephenson Blake		48, 60
	Cloister	Monotype	6, 8, 10, 12	
	Cloister Italic	Monotype	6, 8, 10, 12	
	Cloister Bold	Monotype	6, 8, 10, 12	
	Cloister Bold Italic	Monotype	6, 8, 10, 12	
	Cloister	American Type Founders		14, 18, 24, 30, 36, 48, 60
	Cloister Italic	American Type Founders		14, 18, 24, 30, 36, 48, 60
	Cloister Bold	American Type Founders		14, 18, 24, 30, 36, 48
	Condensed Sans No. 1	Stephenson Blake		18, 24, 30, 36, 48

DATE	TYPEFACES	MANUFACTURER	MACHINE SET	HAND SET
	Cooper Black	American Type Founders		14, 18, 30, 36
1970	**Cooper Black**	Letraset		
1970	**Cooper Black**	Letraset		
	Corvinus Medium	Bauersche Giesserei		12, 18, 24, 36, 48
	Corvinus Medium Italic	Bauersche Giesserei		12, 18, 24, 36, 48
	Corvinus Bold	Bauersche Giesserei		12, 18, 24, 36, 48
1974	**Dempsey Medium**	Letraset		
	Elephant	Stevens Shanks		60
	Elephant Italic	Stevens Shanks		60
	Elongated Roman	Stephenson Blake		12, 16, 24, 30, 36, 48, 60, 72
	Elongated Roman Shaded	Stephenson Blake		72
	Erbar	Ludwig and Mayer		8, 12
	Erbar Italic	Ludwig and Mayer		8, 10
	Erbar Bold	Ludwig and Mayer		8, 30
	Falstaff	Monotype		6, 8, 10, 12, 14, 18, 24, 30, 36, 48, 60
	Falstaff Italic	Monotype		10, 12, 14, 28, 24, 30, 36, 48, 60
	Fat Face 1	Stevens Shanks		30
	Fat Face Italic 1	Stevens Shanks		30
1973	**Flash**	Letraset		
1973	**Frankfurter**	Letraset		
	French Canon	Stephenson Blake		48
	French Canon	Stephenson Blake		48
1970	**Futura Display**	Letraset		
1973	**Futura Light**	Letraset		
	Ganton Titling	Stephenson Blake		36
	Garamond	Monotype	8, 10, 12, 14	24, 72
	Garamond Italic	Monotype	8, 10, 12,	14, 24
	Garamond Bold	Monotype		12, 42
	Garamond Bold Italic	Monotype		18, 42, 60
	Garamond	American Type Founders		18, 24, 30, 36, 48, 60, 72
	Garamond Italic	American Type Founders		18, 24
	Gill Sans Light	Monotype	6, 8, 10, 12	14, 18, 24, 30, 36, 42, 48
	Gill Sans Light Italic	Monotype	8	14
	Gill Sans Medium	Monotype	6, 8, 10, 12, 14	5, 18, 30, 36, 42, 48, 60, 72
	Gill Sans Medium Italic	Monotype	6, 8, 10, 12, 14,	5, 18
	Gill Sans Bold	Monotype	6, 8, 10, 12	14, 18, 24, 30, 36, 42, 48
	Gill Sans Bold Italic	Monotype	6, 8, 10, 12	14, 18, 24, 30, 36, 42
	Gill Sans Extra Bold	Monotype		10, 12, 14, 18, 24, 30, 36, 60, 72
	Gill Sans Bold Condensed	Monotype		6, 8, 10, 12, 14, 18, 24, 30, 36, 42, 48, 60, 71
	Gill Sans Titling	Monotype		6, 36
	Gill Condensed Titling	Monotype		14, 18
	Gill Shadow Titling	Monotype		36
	Gill Woodletter	Stephenson Blake		6, 8, 10, 12, 14, 16, 18 line
	Gill Bold Condensed	Stephenson Blake		20 line
	Gill Extra Bold	Stephenson Blake		12 lines

DATE	TYPEFACES	MANUFACTURER	MACHINE SET	HAND SET
	Gill Sans	Linotype		
1973	**Glaser Stencil Bold**	Letraset		
	Granby Condensed	Stephenson Blake		8, 10, 12, 14, 18, 24, 30
	Greek: New Hellenic	Monotype		9, 11
	Greek: Porson	Monotype		8, 12
	Grotesque No 1 [215]	Monotype	6.5, 8, 9, 10, 11	13, 14, 18, 24, 30, 36, 48
	Grotesque No 1 Italic [215]	Monotype	6.5, 8, 9, 10, 11	
	Grotesque No 1 Bold [216]	Monotype	6.5, 8, 9, 10, 11	13, 14, 18, 24, 30
	Grot No1 Bold Extended [150]	Monotype		6, 8, 10, 12, 14, 18, 24, 36
	Headline Bold	Monotype		8, 10, 12, 14, 18, 24, 30, 36, 42, 48, 60, 72
	Headline Bold Italic	Monotype		8, 10, 12, 14, 18, 24, 30, 36, 42, 48, 60, 72
	Helvetica	Monotype		
1976	**Helvetica**	Linotype		
	Imprint	Monotype	6, 8, 9, 10, 11, 12, 14	18, 24, 30, 36
	Imprint Italic	Monotype	6, 8, 10, 11, 12, 14	
	Imprint Shadow	Monotype		14, 18, 24, 30, 36, 42, 48
	Klang	Stephenson Blake		14, 18
1974	**Lazybones**	Letraset		
	Marina Script	Stephenson Blake		14, 18, 24, 36, 48
	Open Titling	Stephenson Blake		12, 18, 24, 30
1970	**Palace Script**	Letraset		
	Perpetua	Monotype		10, 12, 14, 24
	Perpetua Italic	Monotype		12, 14, 18, 24, 30, 36
	Perpetua Bold	Monotype		30
	Perpetua Titling	Monotype		14, 18, 24, 30, 36, 42, 48, 60, 72
	Phosphor	Ludwig and Mayer		18
1974	**Piccadilly**	Letraset		
	Plantin Light	Monotype	6, 8, 10, 12	14, 18, 24, 30, 36
	Plantin Light Italic	Monotype	6, 8, 10, 12	14, 18, 24, 30, 36
	Plantin	Monotype	6, 8, 9, 10, 11, 12	14, 18,
	Plantin Italic	Monotype	6, 8, 9, 10, 11, 12	14, 18
	Plantin Bold	Monotype	6, 8, 9, 10, 11, 12	14, 18
1973	**Plantin Bold Condensed**	Letraset		
1976	**Plantin**	Linotype		
	Playbill	Stephenson Blake		24, 36, 48, 72
	Playbill Titling	Stephenson Blake		72
	Playbill Woodletter	Stephenson Blake		20, 30 line
	Prisma	Klingspor		24, 36, 48
1973	**Pump**	Letraset		
1973	**Pretorian**	Letraset		
	Reiner Script	Lettergieterij Amsterdam		36, 48
1970	**Romantiques No 5**	Letraset		
	Rockwell Light	Monotype	6, 8, 10, 12	14, 18, 24, 30, 36
	Rockwell Medium	Monotype	6, 8, 10, 12	14, 18, 24, 30, 36
	Rockwell Bold	Monotype	6, 8, 10, 12	14, 18, 24, 30, 36

DATE	TYPEFACES	MANUFACTURER	MACHINE SET	HAND SET
	Russian: Baskerville	Monotype	9, 11	18, 24, 36
	Russian: Plantin	Monotype	6, 8, 10, 12	14, 18, 24, 30, 36
	Russian: Plantin Italic	Monotype	6, 8, 10, 12	14, 18, 24, 30, 36
	Russian: Gill Sans	Monotype	6, 8, 10, 12, 14	
	Russian: Gill Sans Italic	Monotype	6, 8, 10, 12	
	Russian: Gill Sans Bold	Monotype	6, 8, 10, 12	14, 18, 24
	Russian: Gill Bold Cond	Monotype		18 24
1973	**Sans Serif Shaded**	Letraset		
	Shaded Black	Klingspor		15, 38, 51
1974	**Souvenir Light**	Letraset		
1974	**Souvenir Bold**	Letraset		
	Spartan Condensed	Monotype		5/6
1970	**Stencil Bold**	Letraset		
1974	**Tangui**	Letraset		
	Thorne Shaded	Stephenson Blake		18, 24
	Typewriter	Monotype		12
	Times New Roman	Monotype	6, 8, 9, 10, 11, 12, 14	18, 24, 30, 36
	Times New Roman Italic	Monotype	6, 8, 9, 10, 11, 12, 14	18, 24
	Times Bold	Monotype	6, 8, 9, 10, 11, 12, 14	18, 24, 30, 36
	Times Bold Italic	Monotype	8, 10	
	Times Heavy Titling	Monotype		12, 14, 18, 24, 30, 36, 42, 48
1976	**Times**	Linotype		
1973	**Tintoretto**	Letraset		
	Union Pearl	Stephenson Blake		22
	Univers Light	Monotype	6d, 8d, 9d, 10d, 12d	14d, 18d, 22d, 28d, 36d
	Univers Light Italic	Monotype	6d, 8d, 9d, 10d, 12d	14d
	Univers Medium	Monotype	6d, 8d, 9d, 10d, 12d	14d, 18d, 22d
	Univers Medium Italic	Monotype	6d, 8d, 9d, 10d, 12d	
	Univers Bold	Monotype	6d, 8d, 9d, 10d, 12d	14d, 18d, 22d
	Univers Bold Italic	Monotype	6d, 8d, 9d, 10d, 12d	14d, 18d, 22d, 28d, 36d
	Univers Extra Bold	Monotype	6d, 8d, 9d, 10d, 12d	14d, 22d, 28d
	Univers Cond Bold	Monotype		14d, 18d, 22d
	Univers	Founders		24
1976	**Univers**	Linotype		
	Vesta Titling	Berthold		12, 14, 18, 24, 30
	Walbaum	Monotype		14d, 16d, 20d, 24d
1970	**Windsor Bold**	Letraset		

The Kynoch Press

Typefaces through the decades

KEY

● = a full range of sizes was available

◗ = the typeface was abandoned part way through the decade

○ = the typeface was still available but with a reduced number of sizes

TYPEFACE	1920	1930	1940	1950	1960	1970
Albertus (Monotype)				●	●	●
Annonce Grotesque (Lettergieterij Amsterdam)				●	●	●
Baskerville (Monotype)	●	●	●	●	●	●
Baskerville Italic (Monotype)	●	●	●	●	●	●
Baskerville (Stephenson Blake)	●	●	●	●	●	●
Bembo (Monotype)		●	●	●	●	●
Bembo Italic (Monotype)		●	●	●	●	●
Bembo Bold (Monotype)		●	●	●	●	●
Beton Light (Bauersche Giesserei)		●	●	●	●	●
Beton Medium (Bauersche Giesserei)		●	●	●	●	●
Beton Bold (Bauersche Giesserei)			●	●	●	●
Beton Extra Bold (Bauersche Giesserei)				●	●	●
Black Letter [Ancient Black, Gothic] (Bauersche Giesserei)	●	●	●	●	●	●
Bold Face [Old Style Bold] (Monotype)	●	●	●	●	●	●
Bodoni True Cut (Ludlow)	●	●	●	●	◗	
Bodoni Bold (Ludlow)		●	●	●	◗	
Bodoni (Monotype)			●	●	●	●
Bodoni Italic (Monotype)			●	●	●	●
Bodoni Bold (Monotype)			●	●	●	●
Bodoni Bold Italic (Monotype)			●	●	●	●
Cartoon Light (Bauersche Giesserei)		●	●	●	●	●
Cartoon Bold (Bauersche Giesserei)		●	●	●	●	●
Caslon (Monotype)	●	●	●	●	●	●
Caslon Italic (Monotype)	●	●	●	●	●	●
Caslon Old Face (Stephenson Blake)	●		○	○	○	○
Caslon Old Face Italic (Stephenson Blake)	●	◗	○	○	○	○
Caslon Poster Type [Wood Letter] (Stephenson Blake)	●				●	●
Caslon (Ludlow)		●	●	●	◗	
Caslon Italic (Ludlow)		●	●	●	◗	
Caslon Heavy (Ludlow)	●	●	●	●	◗	
Centaur (Monotype)				●		
Clarendon (Monotype)				●		
Chisel (Stephenson Blake)				●	●	●
Cloister (Monotype)	●	●	●	●	●	●
Cloister Italic (Monotype)	●	●	●	●	●	●
Cloister Bold (Monotype)	●	●	●	●	●	●
Cloister Bold Italic (Monotype)	●	●	●	●	●	●
Cloister (American Type Founders)	●	○	○	○	○	○
Cloister Italic (American Type Founders)	●	○	○	○	○	○
Cloister Bold (American Type Founders)	●	○	○	○	○	○
Cloister Bold Italic (American Type Founders)	●					
Condensed Gothic (Ludlow)		●		●	◗	
Condensed Sans (Stephenson Blake)					●	●
Cooper Black (American Type Founders)					●	●
Corvinus Medium (Bauersche Giesserei)			●	●	●	●
Corvinus Medium Italic (Bauersche Giesserei)			●	●	●	●
Corvinus Bold (Bauersche Giesserei)			●	●	●	●
Delphian Titling (Ludlow)	●					
Elephant (Stevens Shanks)			●	●	●	●
Elephant Italic (Stevens Shanks)			●	●	●	●
Elongated Roman (Stephenson Blake)				●	●	●
Elongated Roman Shaded (Stephenson Blake)				●	●	●
Erbar (Ludwig and Mayer)					●	●
Erbar Italic (Ludwig and Mayer)					●	●
Erbar Bold (Ludwig and Mayer)					●	●
Falstaff (Monotype)		●	●	●	●	●

The Kynoch Press

Typefaces through
the decades

TYPEFACE	1920	1930	1940	1950	1960	1970
Falstaff Italic (Monotype)				●	●	●
Fat Face 1 (Stevens Shanks)		●	●	●	●	●
Fat Face Italic 1 (Stevens Shanks)		●	●	●	●	●
Fat Face 2 *[French Canon]* (Stephenson Blake)	●	●	●	●	●	●
Fat Face Italic 2 *[French Canon]* (Stephenson Blake)	●	●	●	●	●	●
Ganton Titling (Stephenson Blake)					●	●
Garamond (Monotype)	●	●	●	●	●	●
Garamond Italic (Monotype)	●	●	●	●	●	●
Garamond Bold (Monotype)					●	●
Garamond Bold Italic (Monotype)					●	●
Garamond (American Type Founders)	●	●	●	●	●	●
Garamond Italic (American Type Founders)	●	●	●	●	●	●
Gill Sans Light (Monotype)		●	●	●	●	●
Gill Sans Light Italic (Monotype)				●	●	●
Gill Sans Medium (Monotype)	●	●	●	●	●	●
Gill Sans Medium Italic (Monotype)		●	●	●	●	●
Gill Sans Bold (Monotype)		●	●	●	●	●
Gill Sans Bold Italic (Monotype)				●	●	●
Gill Sans Bold Condensed (Monotype)		●	●	●	●	●
Gill Sans Extra Bold (Monotype)			●	●	●	●
Gill Sans Extra Bold Condensed (Monotype)				●		
Gill Sans Titling (Monotype)	●	●		●	●	●
Gill Condensed Titling (Monotype)					●	●
Gill Sans Shadow Titling (Monotype)			●	●	●	●
Gill Sans Poster Type *[Woodletter]* (Stephenson Blake)		●			●	●
Gill Bold Condensed (Stephenson Blake)					●	●
Gill Extra Bold (Stephenson Blake)					●	●
Granby Condensed (Stephenson Blake)		●	●	●	●	●
Greek: New Hellenic (Monotype)		●	●	●	●	●
Greek: Porson (Monotype)		●	●	●	●	●
Grotesque No 1 [215] (Monotype)				●	●	●
Grotesque No 1 Italic [215] (Monotype)				●	●	●
Grotesque No 1 Bold [2126] (Monotype)				●	●	●
Grotesque No 1 Bold Extended [150] (Monotype)				●	●	●
Grotesque No 9 (Stephenson Blake)				●		
Grotesque No 9 Italic (Stephenson Blake)				●		
Headline Bold (Monotype)				●	●	●
Headline Bold Italic (Monotype)					●	●
Hebrew Levinim *(Monotype)*					●	
Imprint (Monotype)	●	●	●	●	●	●
Imprint Italic (Monotype)	●	●	●	●	●	●
Imprint Open *[Imprint Shadow]* (Monotype)	●	●	●	●	●	●
Klang (Stephenson Blake)					●	●
Marina Script (Stephenson Blake)		●	●	●	●	●
Milner Initials (Bespoke)	●	●				
Modern Condensed *(Monotype)*					●	
Old Style *(Monotype)*				●		
Open Titling (Stephenson Blake)	●	●	●	●	●	●
Perpetua (Monotype)				●	●	●
Perpetua Italic (Monotype)				●	●	●
Perpetua Bold (Monotype)				●	●	○
Perpetua Titling (Monotype)			●	●	●	●
Phosphor (Ludwig and Mayer)					●	●
Plantin Light (Monotype)			●	●	●	●
Plantin Light Italic (Monotype)			●	●	●	●
Plantin Medium (Monotype)				●	●	●

The Kynoch Press

Typefaces through
the decades

TYPEFACE	1920	1930	1940	1950	1960	1970
Plantin Medium Italic (Monotype)				•	•	•
Plantin Bold (Monotype)				•	•	•
Playbill (Stephenson Blake)		•	•	•	•	•
Playbill Titling (Stephenson Blake)					•	•
Playbill Woodletter (Stephenson Blake)					•	•
Prisma (Klingspor)		•	•	•	•	•
Ratio Free Initials (Stempel)	•	•				
Ravilious Initials (Bespoke)	•	•				
Record Gothic [Gothic Sans Serif] (Ludlow)	•	•	•	•	◗	
Reiner Script (Lettergieterij Amsterdam)					•	•
Rockwell Light (Monotype)		•	•	•	•	•
Rockwell Medium (Monotype)		•	•	•	•	•
Rockwell Bold (Monotype)		•	•	•	•	•
Russian: Baskerville (Monotype)		•	•		•	•
Russian: Plantin Light (Monotype)				•	•	
Russian: Plantin Light Italic (Monotype)				•	•	
Russian: Plantin Medium (Monotype)				•	•	•
Russian: Plantin Medium Italic (Monotype)				•	•	
Russian: Gill Sans Medium (Monotype)					•	•
Russian: Gill Sans Medium Italic (Monotype)					•	•
Russian: Gill Sans Bold (Monotype)					•	•
Russian: Gill Bold Condensed (Monotype)					•	•
Shaded Black (Klingspor)	•	•	•	•	•	•
[Black Letter Shaded, Shaded Gothic, Ornamented Fraktur]						
Spartan Condensed (Monotype)				•	•	•
Square Gothic (Ludlow)	•	•	•	•	◗	
Tempo Medium (Ludlow)		•	•	•	◗	
Tempo Bold (Ludlow)		•	•	•	◗	
Thorne Shaded (Stephenson Blake)		•	•	•	•	•
Times New Roman (Monotype)		•	•	•	•	•
Times New Roman Italic (Monotype)				•	•	•
Times New Roman Bold (Monotype)			•	•	•	•
Times Bold Italic (Monotype)				•	•	•
Times Heavy Titling (Monotype)				•	•	•
Times Titling (Monotype)			•			
Typewriter (Monotype)			•	•	•	•
Typefounder's Initials (Various)	•					
Union Pearl (Stephenson Blake)	•	•	•	•	•	
Univers Light (Monotype)					•	•
Univers Light Italic (Monotype)					•	•
Univers Light Condensed (Monotype)					•	•
Univers Medium (Monotype)					•	•
Univers Medium Italic (Monotype)					•	•
Univers Medium Condensed (Monotype)					•	•
Univers Bold (Monotype)					•	•
Univers Bold Italic (Monotype)					•	•
Univers Bold Condensed (Monotype)					•	•
Univers Extra Bold (Monotype)					•	•
Univers (Deberny & Peignot)					•	•
Vesta Titling (Berthold)	•	•	•	•	•	•
Walbaum (Monotype)					•	•

The Curwen Press

Typefaces through the decades

TYPEFACE	1920	1930	1940	1950	1960	1970
Albertus (Monotype)					•	
Albertus Titling (Monotype)				•	•	
Baskerville (Monotype)	•	•	•	•	•	
Baskerville Italic (Monotype)	•	•	•	•	•	
Baskerville Bold (Monotype)					•	
Baskerville Semi Bold (Monotype)						
Baskerville (Stephenson Blake)		•			•	
Baskerville Italic (Stephenson Blake)		•				
Baskerville Titling (Stephenson Blake)				•		
Bell (Monotype)					•	
Bembo (Monotype)		•	•	•	•	
Bembo Italic (Monotype)		•	•	•	•	
Bernhard Roman (Founders)		•	•			
Bodoni Bold (Monotype)				•	•	
Bodoni Bold Condensed (Monotype)				•	•	
Bodoni Ultra (Monotype)				•	•	
Bodoni Bold (Founders)		•	•			
Bodoni Ultra (Founders)		•	•			
Bodoni Ultra Extra Condensed (Founders)		•	•	•	•	
Cable Light (Klingspor)		•	•	•		
Cable Bold (Klingspor)		•	•	•		
Cable Heavy (Klingspor)		•	•	•		
Caslon (Monotype)	•	•	•		•	
Caslon Italic (Monotype)	•	•	•		•	
Caslon Old Face (Stephenson Blake)	•	•		•	•	
Caslon Old Face Italic (Stephenson Blake)	•	•				
Chisel (Stephenson Blake)			•	•	•	
Clarendon (Monotype)		•				
Cloister Bold (American Type Founders)	•	•	•	•	•	
Cloister Black (American Type Founders)	•	•	•	•		
Columna (Bauersche Giesserei)				•	•	
Consort (Stephenson Blake)					•	
Consort Condensed (Stephenson Blake)					•	
Consort Light (Stephenson Blake)					•	
Consort Bold (Stephenson Blake)					•	
Consort Bold Condensed (Stephenson Blake)					•	
Curwen Poster Type (Bespoke)	•	•	•	•		
Curwen Sans Titling (Bespoke)		•	•	•		
Curwen Sans Serif (Bespoke)		•				
Dante (Monotype)				•	•	
Egyptian Expanded (Stephenson Blake)					•	
Ehrhardt (Monotype)			•	•	•	
Ehrhardt Semi Bold (Monotype)				•	•	
Elongated Roman (Stephenson Blake)			•	•		
Elongated Roman Shaded (Stephenson Blake)				•		
Fat Face (Stephenson Blake)		•	•	•	•	
Fat Face Italic (Stephenson Blake)		•	•	•	•	
Figgins' Shaded (Stevens Shanks)		•	•			
Flamme (Schelter & Giesecke)		•	•			
Fry's Ornamented (Stephenson Blake)		•	•	•	•	
Garamond (Monotype)	•	•	•	•	•	
Garamond Italic (Monotype)	•	•	•	•	•	
Garamond Bold Italic (Monotype)					•	
Garamond (American Type Founders)	•	•	•	•	•	
Garamond Italic (American Type Founders)	•	•	•	•	•	
Gill Sans Light (Monotype)		•	•	•	•	

The Curwen Press

Typefaces through
the decades

TYPEFACE	1920	1930	1940	1950	1960	1970
Gill Sans Medium (Monotype)		●	●	●	●	
Gill Sans Bold (Monotype)		●	●	●	●	
Gill Sans Bold Condensed (Monotype)			●	●	●	
Gill Sans Extra Bold (Monotype)			●	●	●	
Gill Sans Bold Extra Condensed (Monotype)			●	●		
Gill Sans Extra Bold Condensed (Monotype)			●			
Gill Sans Heavy Titling Condensed (Monotype)					●	●
Gill Sans Titling (Monotype)					◐	
Gothic 150 (Monotype)					●	
Grotesque Condensed [33] (Monotype)					●	
Grotesque [215] (Monotype)					●	
Grotesque [216] (Monotype)					●	
Grotesque No 9 (Stephenson Blake)					●	
Grotesque Italic No 9 (Stephenson Blake)					●	
Hyperion (Bauersche Giesserei)					●	
Imprint (Monotype)	●	●	●	●	●	
Imprint Italic (Monotype)	●	●	●	●	●	
Initial Letters (Bespoke)	●	●	●			
Ionic (Monotype)					●	
Kennerley Italic (Stephenson Blake)	●	●	●	●		
Koch Kursive (Klingspor)	●	●	●	●		
Latin Antique (Monotype)		◐				
Lutetia Roman (Lettergieterij Enschedé)	●	●	●	●	●	
Lutetia Italic (Lettergieterij Enschedé)		●	●	●	●	
Lutetia (Monotype)	●	●	●	●	●	
Lutetia Italic (Monotype)	●	●	●	●	●	
Maximilian (Klingspor)	●	●	●	●		
Modern No 20 (Stephenson Blake)					●	
Micro–Gramma (Nebiolo)					●	
New Clarendon (Monotype)					●	
New Clarendon Bold (Monotype)					●	
Old English (Monotype)					●	
Old Face Open Titling (Stephenson Blake)	●	●	●	●	●	
Old Style (Monotype)		◐				
Ornata (Klingspor)		●		●	●	
Orplid (Klingspor)		●	●	●		
Perpetua (Monotype)				●	●	●
Perpetua Bold (Monotype)					●	●
Perpetua Titling (Monotype)					●	●
Perpetua Light Titling (Monotype)						●
Placard (Monotype)						●
Placard Medium Condensed (Monotype)						●
Placard Bold Condensed (Monotype)						●
Plantin Medium (Monotype)		●	●	●		●
Plantin Bold (Monotype)					●	●
Plantin (Founders)			●			
Rockwell Light (Monotype)		●	●	●		
Rockwell Medium (Monotype)		●	●	●		
Rosart (Lettergieterij Enschedé)					●	
Sans 15 (Monotype)					●	
Sans Condensed No 7 (Founders)					●	
Thorne Shaded (Stephenson Blake)			●	●	●	
Times New Roman (Monotype)		●	●	●	●	
Times New Roman Bold (Monotype)		●	●	●	●	
Times Book (Monotype)					◐	
Times Heavy Titling (Monotype)		●	●	●		

The Curwen Press

TYPEFACE	1920	1930	1940	1950	1960	1970
Times Titling (Monotype)		●	●	●	●	
Times Extended Titling (Monotype)		●	●	●	●	
Times Wide (Monotype)				●		
Typefounder's Initials (Various)	●	●	●	●		
Univers Light (Monotype)					●	
Univers Medium (Monotype)					●	
Univers Bold (Monotype)					●	
Univers Extra Bold (Monotype)					●	
Van Krimpen Open (Lettergieterij Enschedé)					●	●
Vesta Titling (Berthold)	●	●	●	●		
Walbaum (Monotype)		●	●	●	●	
Walbaum Medium (Monotype)		●	●	●	●	
Walbaum (Founders)	●	●	●	●		
Walbaum Italic (Founders)	●	●	●	●		

Typefaces through
the decades

Percy, Lund Humphries

Typefaces through the decades

TYPEFACE	1920	1930	1940	1950	1960	1970
Albion (Monotype)	•					
Albertus (Monotype)				•	•	•
Antique (Monotype)	•	•				
Antique (Founders)	•	•				
Antique No 6 (Stevens Shanks)				•	•	•
Ashley Script (Monotype)				•	•	
Baskerville (Monotype)	•	•	•	•	•	•
Baskerville Semi Bold (Monotype)					•	•
Baskerville Italic (Monotype)			•	•	•	•
Bembo (Monotype)					•	•
Bembo Italic (Monotype)					•	•
Bembo Bold (Monotype)					•	•
Beton Light (Bauersche Giesserei)		•	•	•	•	•
Beton Medium (Bauersche Giesserei)		•	•	•	•	•
Beton Bold (Bauersche Giesserei)		•	•			
Beton Extra Bold (Bauersche Giesserei)		•	•	•	•	•
Beton Open (Bauersche Giesserei)		•				
Bifur (Deberny & Peignot)		•	•	•	•	
Bodoni (Monotype)	•	•	•	•	•	•
Bodoni Italic (Monotype)		•	•	•	•	•
Bodoni Bold (Monotype)		•	•	•	•	•
Bodoni Bold Italic (Monotype)				•	•	•
Bodoni Bold Condensed (Monotype)				•	•	•
Bodoni Heavy (Monotype)		•	•			
Bodoni Heavy Italic (Monotype)		•	•			
Bodoni Ultra (Monotype)						
Bold Face Outline (Monotype)	•	•	•			
Bold Latin (Monotype)	•	•	•			
Broadway (American Typefounder's)		•	•			
Cable Bold (Klingspor)		•	•			
Cable Heavy (Klingspor)		•	•			
Cable Shaded (Klingspor)		•	•			
Caslon (Monotype)	•	•	•	•	•	•
Caslon Italic (Monotype)	•	•	•	•	•	•
Caslon Bold (Monotype)	•	•	•			
Caslon Bold *[Caslon Heavy]* (Stephenson Blake)	•	•	•	•	•	
Caslon Poster Type *[Wood Letter]* (Stephenson Blake)	•	•	•			
Caslon Titling (Stephenson Blake)	•	•				
Centaur (Monotype)		•	•			
Centaur Italic (Monotype)		•	•			
Chatsworth (Stephenson Blake)	•	•				
Cheltenham [Gloucester] (Monotype)	•	•	•			•
Cheltenham Italic [Gloucester Italic](Monotype)	•	•	•			•
Cheltenham Bold [Gloucester Bold](Monotype)	•	•	•			•
Cheltenham (Stephenson Blake)	•	•				
Cheltenham Bold (Stephenson Blake)		•				
Cheltenham Bold Italic (Stephenson Blake)	•	•				
Cheltenham Bold Expanded (Stephenson Blake)	•	•	•			
Cheltenham Bold Condensed (Stephenson Blake)	•	•				
Chiswell Old Face (Monotype)	•					
City (Berthold)		•	•	•	•	
Clear Face Bold (Monotype)	•	•				
Cochin (Monotype)	•	•	•			
Cochin Italic (Monotype)		•	•			
Cochin Open (Founders)	•	•	•			
Cochin (Founders)		•	•			

Percy, Lund Humphries

Typefaces through
the decades

TYPEFACE	1920	1930	1940	1950	1960	1970
Colonna (Monotype)	●	●				
Columna (Bauersche Giesserei)				●	●	
Condensed Sans (Stephenson Blake)	●					
Condensed Sans No 7 (Stephenson Blake)				●	●	●
Consort (Stephenson Blake)					●	
Corvinus Light Italic (Bauersche Giesserei)		●	●	●	●	
Corvinus Medium (Bauersche Giesserei)		●	●	●	●	
Corvinus Medium Italic (Bauersche Giesserei)		●	●	●	●	
Corvinus Heavy (Bauersche Giesserei)				●	●	
Cushing (Monotype)	●	●				
De Vinne (Stephenson Blake)	●	●				
De Vinne Italic (Stephenson Blake)	●	●				
De Vinne Condensed (Stephenson Blake)	●	●				
Doric Light (Stephenson Blake)	●	●				
Doric Heavy (Stephenson Blake)	●	●				
Egyptian (Monotype)				●		
Elongated Roman (Stephenson Blake)				●	●	
Erbar Light (Ludwig & Mayer)		●	●	●	●	
Erbar Light Italic (Ludwig and Mayer)		●	●			
Erbar Medium (Ludwig and Mayer)		●	●	●	●	
Erbar Medium Italic (Ludwig and Mayer)		●	●			
Erbar Medium Condensed (Ludwig and Mayer)				●	●	
Erbar Bold (Ludwig and Mayer)		●	●	●	●	
Erbar Bold Condensed (Ludwig & Mayer)		●	●	●	●	
Falstaff (Monotype)		●	●	●	●	●
Falstaff Italic (Monotype)		●	●	●	●	●
Falstaff (Founders)		●	●			
Flamingo (Founders)		●	●			
French Old Style (Founders)	●					
Garamond (Monotype)	●	●	●	●	●	●
Garamond Italic (Monotype)	●	●	●	●	●	●
Garamond Bold (Monotype)	●	●	●	●	●	●
Garamond (Founders)	●	●				
Garamond Italic (Founders)	●	●				
Garamond Bold (Founders)	●	●				
Gill Sans Light (Monotype)				●	●	●
Gill Sans Light Italic (Monotype)				●	●	●
Gill Sans Extra Light (Monotype)		●	●			
Gill Sans Extra Light Italic (Monotype)		●	●			
Gill Sans Medium (Monotype)	●	●	●	●	●	●
Gill Sans Medium Italic (Monotype)		●	●	●	●	●
Gill Sans Bold (Monotype)		●	●	●	●	●
Gill Sans Bold Italic (Monotype)		●	●	●	●	●
Gill Sans Bold Condensed (Monotype)		●	●	●	●	●
Gill Sans Extra Bold (Monotype)		●	●	●	●	●
Gill Sans Extra Heavy (Monotype)		●				
Gill Sans Titling (Monotype)		●	●			
Gill Sans Shadow (Monotype)		●	●			
Gillies Gothic (Bauersche Giesserei)		●	●			
Gillies Gothic Bold (Bauersche Giesserei)		●	●			
Goudy Bold (Monotype)	●	●	●			

Percy, Lund Humphries

Typefaces through
the decades

TYPEFACE	1920	1930	1940	1950	1960	1970
Goudy Bold Italic (Monotype)		●	●			
Goudy Catalogue (Monotype)		●				
Goudy Heavy (Monotype)		●	●			
Goudy Modern (Monotype)		●	●			
Goudy Modern Italic (Monotype)		●	●			
Goudy Hand-tooled (American Type Founders)		●	●	●	●	
Granby Shaded (Stephenson Blake)			●	●	●	
Granjon (Monotype)	●	●				
Grotesque No 1 [215] (Monotype)				●	●	●
Grotesque No 1 Italic [215] (Monotype)				●	●	●
Grotesque No 1 Bold [216] (Monotype)				●	●	●
Grotesque No 2 Bold Condensed [15] (Monotype)				●	●	●
Grotesque Condensed [33] (Monotype)		●	●	●	●	●
Grotesque Light [126] (Monotype)					●	●
Grotesque Light Italic [126] (Monotype)					●	●
Grotesque Condensed [383] (Monotype)					●	●
Grotesque No 8 (Stephenson Blake)				●	●	●
Grotesque No 9 (Stephenson Blake)	●	●		●	●	●
Grotesque Italic No 9 (Stephenson Blake)				●	●	●
Grotesque Bold (Stephenson Blake)	●	●				
Hawden (Founders)	●					
Heyer (Founders)	●					
Holla (Klingspor)		●	●			
Imprint (Monotype)	●	●	●	●	●	●
Imprint Italic (Monotype)		●	●	●	●	●
Imprint Bold (Monotype)			●	●	●	●
Imprint Bold Italic (Monotype)				●	●	●
Imprint Shadow *[Imprint Open]* (Monotype)	●	●	●			
Imprint Shadow Italic (Monotype)	●	●				
Klang (Monotype)					●	●
Latin Condensed (Founders)	●					
Lining Gothic (American Type Founders)	●	●	●			
Lining Grotesque (Stephenson Blake)	●	●				
Lining Grotesque Bold Condensed (Stephenson Blake)		●				
Locarno Light Face (Klingspor)		●	●			
Locarno Bold Face (Klingspor)		●	●			
Locarno Bold Face Italic (Klingspor)		●	●			
Luxor (Founders)		●	●			
Luxor Bold Condensed (Founders)		●	●	●	●	
Mistral (Lettergieterij Amsterdam)				●	●	
Modern No 1 (Monotype)				●	●	●
Modern No 1 Italic (Monotype)				●	●	●
Modern No 1 Extended (Monotype)				●	●	●
Modern No 1 Italic Extended (Monotype)				●	●	●
Modern Bold (Monotype)						●
Morland (Stephenson Blake)	●	●				
Narciss (Klingspor)	●	●				
New Clarendon (Monotype)					●	●
New Clarendon Bold (Monotype)					●	●
Neo Didot *(Monotype)*	●					
Old English (Founders)	●					

Percy, Lund Humphries

Typefaces through
the decades

TYPEFACE	1920	1930	1940	1950	1960	1970
Old Face No 45 (Monotype)	•	•	•			
Old Face No 45 Italic (Monotype)		•	•			
Old Style (Monotype)	•	•	•	•	•	•
Old Style Italic (Monotype)		•	•	•	•	•
Old Style Bold 1 [Bold Face] (Monotype)	•	•	•	•	•	•
Old Style Bold 2 (Monotype)				•	•	•
(Old Face) Open Titling (Stephenson Blake)				•	•	
Othello (Monotype)	•	•				
Othello Shadow (Monotype)	•	•				
Perpetua (Monotype)		•	•	•	•	•
Perpetua Italic (Monotype)		•	•	•	•	•
Perpetua Bold (Monotype)				•	•	•
Perpetua Titling (Monotype)		•	•	•	•	•
Phosphor Bold (Ludwig & Mayer)		•	•	•	•	
Plantin Light *(Monotype)*			•			
Plantin Medium (Monotype)	•	•	•	•	•	•
Plantin Medium Italic (Monotype)		•	•	•	•	•
Plantin Bold (Monotype)		•	•	•	•	•
Plantin Bold Italic (Monotype)				•	•	•
Plantin Old Face (Monotype)	•					
Poliphilus Titling (Monotype)		•				
Reiner Script (Lettergieterij Amsterdam)				•	•	
Rockwell Light (Monotype)		•	•	•	•	•
Rockwell Medium (Monotype)		•	•	•	•	•
Rockwell Bold (Monotype)		•	•	•	•	•
Rockwell Condensed (Monotype)		•	•	•	•	•
Rockwell Shadow [Shaded] (Monotype)		•	•	•	•	•
Roman (Founders)	•					
Roman Italic (Founders)	•	•				
Ronaldson (Monotype)	•					
Sabon (Monotype)						•
Sabon Italic (Monotype)						•
Sabon Semi Bold (Monotype)						•
Sans Serif (Monotype)	•	•	•			
Sans Serif Condensed (Stephenson Blake)		•				
Script (Founders)	•					
Slimback (Deberny & Peignot)			•	•	•	
Studio (Lettergieterij Amsterdam)				•	•	
Thorne Shaded (Stephenson Blake)		•	•	•	•	
Tieman (Klingspor)		•	•	•	•	
Times New Roman (Monotype)		•	•	•	•	•
Times New Roman Italic (Monotype)		•	•	•	•	•
Times New Roman Bold (Monotype)		•	•		•	•
Times Bold Italic (Monotype)						•
Times Titling (Monotype)		•				
Times Bold Titling (Monotype)				•	•	•
Times Extended Titling (Monotype)				•	•	•
Times Bold Extended (Monotype)			•			
Titling Victoria Condensed (Monotype)				•	•	•
Trafton Script (Bauersche Giesserei)			•	•	•	
Typewriter (Monotype)					•	

Percy, Lund Humphries

Typefaces through the decades

TYPEFACE	1920	1930	1940	1950	1960	1970
Ultra Bodoni (American Type Founders)		●	●			
Univers Light (Monotype)					●	●
Univers Light Italic (Monotype)					●	●
Univers Medium (Monotype)					●	●
Univers Medium Italic (Monotype)					●	●
Univers Bold (Monotype)					●	●
Univers Bold Italic (Monotype)					●	●
Univers Extra Light Condensed (Monotype)					●	
Univers Extra Bold (Monotype)					●	●
Univers Extra Bold Italic (Monotype)					●	●
Venetian (Stephenson Blake)	●					
Walbaum (Monotype)			●	●	●	●
Walbaum Italic (Monotype)			●	●	●	●
Walbaum Medium (Monotype)			●	●	●	●
Walbaum Medium Italic (Monotype)			●	●	●	●
Westminster (Stephenson Blake)	●	●				
Wide Gothic (Monotype)		●				
Windsor (Stephenson Blake)	●	●				
Windsor Condensed (Stephenson Blake)	●	●				

Notes to the typeface tables

Kynoch Press 1920s

[1] Ancient Black is re-named Black Letter or Gothic in later Kynoch Press specimen books. Seldom seen in the type specimen books of other printers it was the first of two German Gothic faces purchased by the Press.

[2] Kynoch Press installed its first Monotype caster in 1920. Although Baskerville was not manufactured by the Corporation until 1924, Baskerville 8, 10, 11, 12, and 14 point are recorded as the first, albeit undated, purchases by the Press from Monotype. It is unlikely that the Press would have waited four years before ordering its first matrice cases. It must be assumed, therefore, that the undated entries in the Monotype ledgers are not necessarily in purchase date order.

Despite 8, 10, 11, 12, and 14 point being Kynoch's first recorded order by the Monotype Corporation, the Press only gradually advertised their availability. 10 and 12 point appear in the 1924 Broadsheet; 10, 12 and 14 point are displayed in the 1927 Specimen; 8, 10, 11, 12, and 14 point are advertised in the 1930 Supplement.

Kynoch Press' choice of faces for its initial Monotype installation was influenced by the already proven popularity of a number of foundry faces. Baskerville, having already demonstrated its worth and value as a founder fount, was a natural first choice when it came to machine setting. Monotype Baskerville went on to justify its purchase by remaining the most popular of all faces at the Press until it ceased trading in 1979. The Press itself later remarked of Baskerville that 'no type is more used than this at the present time for all kinds of printing. Its clean-cut and architectural forms are a welcome relief from the archaism of many machine set types.' (*Kynoch Press Specimen of Types*, 1934.)

[3] Although Kynoch Press was encouraging its customers towards Monotype composition, it still maintained the founders versions of all founts and so Baskerville was also available from Stephenson Blake. This version was available only in roman, with no italic, and only in those sizes which were too large for Monotype composition. The Press informed its customers that this fount was an eighteenth-century type cut in emulation of Baskerville, and it considered the larger sizes to be 'particularly well engraved'.

[4] Bold Face is the Kynoch Press name for Monotype Old Style Bold (53) which was released in 1911. Bold Face 11 point does not appear in a Kynoch Press specimen book until 1934 but is listed in the Monotype *Purchase Ledger* as one of the five sizes (6, 8, 10, 11, 12 point) which represent the ninth, undated, Kynoch Press purchase. The Press educated its clients into the origins of Bold Face stating that it was 'introduced as a successor to Fat Face when Modern types were displaced by Old Face for text. It is very clear and readable, but only the capitals are well shaped.' (*Kynoch Press Specimen of Types*, 1934). It advised it be used for headings and emphasising paragraphs.

[5] Ludlow Bodoni True Cut was only available in display sizes of upper and lower case roman. There was no italic. Bodoni True Cut was the only type of the Modern category available at Kynoch Press in the 1920s.

Kynoch Press 1920s

⁶ Issued between 1915–17, Monotype Caslon was the second, albeit undated, purchase of the Kynoch Press from the Corporation. Strangely, the availability of the face was not advertised by the Press until the 1930 *Supplement*. It was purchased following on from the success of Stephenson Blake's Caslon.

⁷ Stephenson Blake's Caslon Old Face was purchased for the Kynoch Press by Donald Hope on his arrival in 1901 on the advice of Emery Walker as a replacement to the dated nineteenth-century faces then in use at the Press. Available in text sizes which overlapped with its Monotype equivalent, it was additionally available in display sizes and included alternative swash characters. The type displayed in the 1924 Broadsheet and the 1927 *Specimen Book* was over twenty years old and was showing distinct signs of wear and tear.

A display version of Caslon was also available on the Ludlow which the Press suggested provided a particularly 'careful cutting of Caslon's letters' but it also warned that customers might find an unfamiliar look to the larger sizes which were unusually far spaced.

⁸ There is no mention in the Monotype Purchase ledger of Kynoch Press ever having bought a fount of Cloister—either roman, italic or bold. Cloister is first advertised in the 1930 Kynoch Press *Supplement*. It must be assumed that Monotype Cloister was purchased from sources other than the Corporation itself—possibly from a printer who had ceased trading or from a county fair. It was purchased following the success of founder's Cloister.

Cloister was viewed by Kynoch Press as being one of the best of the revived old types and it was particularly admiring of the smaller sizes, but admitted it was 'hardly a book type according to present day tastes' but that it was excellent for jobs in which 'an element of the picturesque is not objectionable'. The bold was recommended for use in headings and emphatic passages.

Also available with swash characters.

⁹ The American Type Founders version of Cloister, Cloister Italic and Cloister Bold may have been purchased by Mr Forbes (Press Manager 1903–13). There is great similarity between the ATF and Monotype cutting of this fount, but the alphabet length shown in the 1927 *Specimen Book* is longer than that of the Monotype sample in the 1930 *Supplement*. I assume the 1927 sample is not, therefore, Monotype. ATF Cloister was available in overlapping text sizes with the Monotype version, but additionally was available in the larger display sizes. Cloister Bold Italic had disappeared by the 1930s.

¹⁰ Ludlow Delphian Titling was designed by Robert Hunter Middleton and manufactured by the Ludlow Typograph Corporation of Chicago in 1928. Although it was acquired by the Press immediately on its release, it proved to be a face of short-lived popularity as it was withdrawn from the specimen books by 1934. Although the type was withdrawn from the specimen books, it was not dispensed with entirely, for occasional use of this face can be found on work produced by the Kynoch Press over the ensuing decades. With the absence of Ludlow from both Lund Humphries and Curwen Press, Delphian was a face unusual to the Press.

¹¹ Fat Face 2 is one of the most rare and interesting of all the Kynoch Press type faces which, according to the Press, dates from around 1820. It first appears in the 1930 *Supplement* to the 1927 specimen book, where it was merely referred to by its

Kynoch Press 1920s   category name, Fat Face, but was later listed in the 1960s specimen book as French Canon. BERRY, JOHNSON AND JASPERT in their *Encyclopedia of Typefaces* refer to it as Fry's Canon. This type, originally from Fry and Steel's foundry was re-cast from the original matrices by Stephenson Blake for both the Kynoch Press and Curwen Press who privately held the fount [although Curwen did not acquire the face until the late 1930s]. 'It is one of the earliest of the Fat Faces dating from 1808. The design is that of a modern face, with an exaggeration of the contrast between thick and thin strokes. The exaggeration is however less than in the contemporary type Thorowgood'. BERRY, JOHNSON AND JASPERT. The Press passed no comment on this face in its 1930 *Supplement*, no mention of its antecedents and no intimation as to its exclusivity—which seems rather a missed advertising opportunity!

The Press regarded this as a 'particularly handsome' face and it was to remain in its specimen books until the Press closed in 1979.

[12] Garamond was issued by Monotype between 1922–24, but there is no Monotype record of the date when the Kynoch Press first purchased Garamond. Garamond 8, 10 and 12 point are, however, listed as its fifth undated Monotype purchase. Sizes 10, 12, and 14 point are first advertised in the 1924 Broadsheet, but 8 point is curiously not displayed until the 1927 *Specimen Book*.

In 1927 Garamond was erroneously displayed in the 'machine-set' section of the *Specimen Book* in sizes 8–72 point. The larger sizes could not have been machine-set, nor were they, from 18 point upwards, even Monotype.

Garamond remained a popular text face throughout the best part of the century.

[13]   The 1927 *Specimen Book* makes no distinction between the founder's and Monotype versions of Garamond and lists them both together as 'machine-set'. There are, however marked differences between the two versions, especially noticeable is the variations in the lower case roman 'g' and the italic capital 'Q'.

From sizes 18–72 point, ATF Garamond has misleadingly been reproduced in the machine-set section of the *Specimen Book*.

[14]   Monotype have no record of the date on which Kynoch Press purchased Gill Sans Medium. It is, however, listed as the Press' fourth purchase with the acquisition of 6, 8, 10 and 12 point. It first appears in the *Supplement* of 1930. As Gill Sans was first manufactured in 1929–30 it shows an immediate commitment to the face. The Press noted in its type specimen of 1934 that Gill Sans was to the present age what Cheltenham was to 1910, and that it was a face which 'no jobbing printer could possibly do without.' Gill was the first of the Press' new sans faces and it would transpire to be the most enduring of sans faces, frequently added to.

[15]   Gill Sans Titling 6 point, was the Kynoch Press' sixth undated Monotype purchase and first appears in the *Supplement* of 1930.

[16]   Imprint was manufactured by Monotype between 1913–15 and Imprint 6, 8, 10, 11, 12, and 14 point are the seventh and eighth, undated, Kynoch Press purchases from Monotype. Imprint does not appear in the specimen books until the *Supplement* of 1930. Imprint was displayed in sizes 6–36 point in the machine-set section of the *Specimen Book*, but on the Monotype system only sizes up to and including 14 point could be cast by machine. The larger sizes, although Monotype, would have had to be set by hand. The description of 'machine-set' is imprecise; 'machine cast' might have been a more accurate term.

Kynoch Press 1920s

[17] Imprint Open is the Kynoch Press name for Monotype Imprint Shadow.

[18] Milner Initials is a bespoke face which was unique to the Kynoch Press; it remained both unacknowledged and unidentified by the Press. I believe the designer to have been Donald Ewart Milner, Headmaster of The Aston School of Art and Crafts in Birmingham. Milner had a reputation as a painter, stained glass artist and book decorator. He was the artist responsible for the illustrations in the first Kynoch Press Notebook and Diary in 1929.

[19] Open Titling first appeared in Fry's specimen book of 1788 having been issued as a companion to Fry's Baskerville. It was a face common to both the Kynoch and Curwen Press'. In the Kynoch Press Broadsheet of 1924 and the 1927 *Specimen* it exhibits many battered characters. The 24 point size of Stephenson Blake's Open Titling was abandoned by 1930, but re-appears in 1934.

[20] Ratio Free Initials were designed by Professor F. W. Klenkens for Stempel, who advertised the face as 'Freie Versalien zur Ratio'. It was also advertised by H. W. Caslon and Company, who acted as agents for Stempel, and who sold the face under the name of 'Hiawatha'.

[21] Ravilious Initials were decorated woodletters designed for the Kynoch Press by Eric Ravilious. Tirzah Garwood, wife to Ravilious, also cut six continuous strips for the Press at about the same date.

[20] The Kynoch Press also referred to Shaded Black as Black Letter Shaded; Ornamented Fraktur and Shaded Gothic also known as Deutsche Zierschrift. Like Ancient Black it is seldom, if ever, found in the specimen books of other UK printers. It was the second of the Press' German display faces and it remained in its specimen books until the Press closed in 1979.

[22] Ludlow Record Gothic was designed by R. H. Middleton and issued in 1927; it was based on the nineteenth century model of sans serif types.

[24] Ludlow Square Gothic was designed by R. H. Middleton, a square lineal based on the nineteenth century model.

[25] Typewriter was displayed in the Kynoch Press broadsheet of 1924, but was then withdrawn from all its specimen books until the 1940s.

[26] Vesta Titling was the third of the German faces purchased by the Kynoch Press; it was designed by Albert Augspurg for Berthold AG in 1926 and was quickly obtained by the Press for inclusion in its 1927 *Type Specimen Book*.

[27] On the 1924 Broadsheet, the Kynoch Press had displayed a variety of unspecified typefounder's initials. These initials had been abandoned by the 1927 *Book of Type Specimens*.

Kynoch Press 1930s

[1] With its quickly proven popularity Monotype Baskerville was expanded and augmented with six additional sizes. Baskerville 6 point was not purchased from Monotype until 28 June 1938, too late to be included in any Kynoch Press type specimen book of the 1930s.

[2] Monotype Bembo had been issued by the Corporation between 1930–35. Monotype have no record of the date on which Kynoch Press first purchased Bembo, but 10 and 12 point Bembo were entered as the third purchases made by the Press from Monotype, although 10 and 12 point do not appear in any specimen books until 1934. Bembo 6, 8 and 11 point do not appear in the 1930s specimens books as they were not purchased from Monotype until 28 June 1938, too late to appear in any specimen of the 1930s.

Bembo 30 and 36 point were available only as capitals.

The Press recommended that as 'a regular book type of handsome appearance it is best set solid in a rather narrow measure.'

[3] Monotype Bembo Bold was purchased by Michael Clapham on his arrival at the Kynoch Press in 1938 in an attempt to resurrect the Monotype list which had been neglected by H. V. Davis during his term of management in the mid-1930s.

[4] The Beton family was one of several continental faces purchased by the Kynoch Press in the 1930s. It was manufactured between 1931–36 and was quickly purchased by the Press in 1934. The Press commented that it was a 'modern version of the old-established Egyptian style of types, which, as Johnson said in his *Typographica* (1824) are "all the rage just now".' It was a particularly popular face with ICI who used it on much of its internal publicity.

[5] Black Letter, previously listed as Ancient Black.

[6] Ludlow Bodoni Bold, an accompaniment to Bodoni True Cut, was available only as upper and lower case roman. There was no italic.

[7] Monotype Bold Face 18 point varies through the decades as to whether it is specified for hand- or machine-setting.

[8] Cartoon, another newly purchased Continental face, was designed by H. A. Trafton for Bauersche Giesserei in 1936 and quickly bought by the Kynoch Press between 1936–38.

[9] By 1934, the Kynoch Press was promoting the use of Monotype Caslon text sizes in preference to founders Caslon text sizes.

[10] Ludlow's version of Caslon was a new addition, providing those intervening sizes which were not covered by either the Monotype or Stephenson Blake.

[11] Stephenson Blake's Caslon Old Face, roman and italic, appears to have been abandoned by the 1934 *Specimen*. The roman re-appears in the 1950s when it is available in the range of 30–72 point. The italic makes a re-appearance in the 1935 *Supplement* with newly re-purchased versions of 24, 30, 36 and 48 point—presumably to replace the old, and very obviously, worn founts that had been in use for over thirty years.

NOTE

Caslon defied the trend to rationalise hand- and machine-set sizes which was prevalent in the 1930s and is one of the most erratic of all faces to pursue

Kynoch Press 1930s

through the decades as its variants rise and fall in favour. The position of Monotype Caslon never altered—it was initially purchased in roman and italic 8, 10 and 12 point and the range was never extended or changed—with the exception of the addition of a single purchase of 24 point in the 1960s. Not only was the range of sizes never increased, further orders were never placed for those sizes already held. A face once regarded as *de rigor* for printers of quality had ceased to be the customers favourite as the century progressed. It had become a printer's standard face, retained through custom rather than popular appeal.

Although Monotype Caslon may have had a stable placing in the Kynoch specimen books the foundry versions of this fount had a changeable and confusing existence.

Stephenson Blake's Caslon Old Face roman was available at the Kynoch Press from 1900, but had been completely withdrawn by the early 1930s only to make a re-appearance in the late 1940s in a reduced range of sizes (30–72 point). In the 1960s 14 and 18 point re-appear in the specimen books.

A similar story lies with Stephenson Blake's Calson Old Face italic. Abandoned for the early part of the 1930s, it made a return in 1935 being advertised as a 'new' face in the *Supplement* of that year. Only half the original sizes were available—8–18 point had been jettisoned and 24–48 point had been retained. They were purchased to replace the obviously worn types which had been displayed in the 1927 *Specimen Book*, which were, by that stage, 30 years old.

Ludlow's version of Caslon, in both its italic and roman form, is rather more stable with sizes 8 to 24 point being available from the 1930s through to 1966, when the Ludlow Typograph was abandoned.

[12] Although the ATF Cloister 8, 10 and 12 point were still being advertised in 1930, by the 1934 *Specimen Book*, these sizes have been abandoned from the list, presumably to encourage the use of machine-setting in the smaller text sizes which were available on the Monotype.

[13] Ludlow Condensed Gothic was a sans serif face of the European model.

[14] The Corvinus family of display faces was issued by Bauersche Giesserei, the favoured foundry of the Kynoch Press, in 1929–34 after a design by Imre Reiner, and was purchased by Michael Clapham on his arrival at the Press in 1938.

[15] This Elephant face by Stevens Shanks is a genuine nineteenth-century face, an outrageous development of the Fat Faces. It was a face favoured by the Press in distinct preference to Bodoni Extra Bold which, in its view, did not possess such 'pleasant curves'.

[16] Stephenson Blake's Elongated Roman was a revival of the Victorian condensed and elongated fat faces and was purchased by the Kynoch Press between 1935–39.

[17] Although the Kynoch Press were already displaying Falstaff in its 1934 *Specimen Book*, there are no Monotype records showing its purchase until 1939 when records show 8d and 12d were bought. The Press later purchased many sizes of Falstaff which were never noted in the Monotype purchase ledger which suggests a source of supply other than Monotype. Having been acquired immediately at the date of manufacture, it is peculiar that the Press does not appear to have purchased the fount direct from Monotype.

[11] Fat Face 1, which is unrelated to Fat Face 2, dates from around the same period—

Kynoch Press 1930s

1820. Fat Face 1 was made available through Stevens Shanks. It was experimentally re-cast from the original matrices. The experiment was abandoned when the matrices were found to be defective. In his Preface to a *Specimen of Printing Types* (Sheffield 1819) Austin questioned 'how can it be expected that types cut nearly as thin as the edge of a razor can retain their form for any reasonable length of time'. His point was admirably proved by the Kynoch Press, because the quality of the printing of this face is poor, the italic having completely lost its rounded finials on the lower case 'f' and 'j'. It is odd that the Press, who prided itself on the quality of its work, should allow a *Specimen Book* to be issued with such a badly reproduced specimen of type.

[19] With the issuing of the 1934 *Specimen Book*, the Kynoch Press was making the distinction between the Monotype and founders versions of Garamond. Garamond was only available as a Monotype fount in the smaller sizes (8–14 point) whilst the larger sizes were provided by ATF (18–72 point) and this division of sizes was noted through to the 1970s.

[20] Monotype record Gill Sans Light [12 point], as being an early, but undated, purchase of the Kynoch Press, but it is not advertised until the *Supplement* of 1934. Further purchases of Gill Sans Light [6, 8, and 10 point] were made on 28 June 1938, too late to be included in any of the Specimen Books of the 1930s.

[21] Gill Sans Bold 8 point, was only available as capitals.

[22] The purchases of Gill Sans Bold Condensed, would not be apparent from the Monotype *Purchase Ledger* which do not recorded the acquisition of display sizes.

[23] Gill Sans Poster Type in sizes 14, 16 and 18 point was available as capitals only.

[24] Stephenson Blake's Granby Condensed was manufactured in the 1930s and was quickly available at the Kynoch Press for inclusion in its 1934 *Specimen*. It was a sans serif face of the Continental model.

[25] Greek New Hellenic 11 and 9 point were the eleventh and fifteenth undated purchases from the Monotype Corporation, but their availability is not advertised until the *Specimen Book* of 1934.

[26] Greek Porson was available in small founts for quotations. The Monotype *Purchase Ledger*s record the first Kynoch Press purchase of this fount to have been 12 point in 1950. As both 8 and 12 point are advertised in the 1934 Kynoch *Specimen Book*, they may have been purchased from sources other than Monotype.

[27] Imprint 11 point appears as the seventh undated purchase from Monotype. It s availability was first advertised in the 1930 *Supplement*.

[28] Imprint Shadow 14 point was added in 1934. The 1930 *Supplement* retains the old name of Imprint Open, but by the 1934 *Type Specimen Book* the name Imprint Shadow is adopted.

[29] Marina Script was produced by Stephenson Blake in 1936 and bought by the Kynoch Press by Michael Clapham, on his arrival in 1938. It is the first of the Press script typefaces.

[30] Milner Initials appear to have been abandoned by the close of the 1930s for they cease to appear in any type list after 1934.

Kynoch Press 1930s

[31]   The purchase of Perpetua Titling would not have been apparent from the Monotype Ledgers which do not record the purchase of display sizes.

[32]   Stephenson Blake's Playbill was designed after sketches by Robert Harling. It was a revival of a Victorian type of which the style was at first called French Antique or sometime Italian. It was manufactured by Stephenson Blake in 1938 and was swiftly purchased by the Kynoch Press as a contemporary companion to their its of nineteenth century revivals.

[33]   Prisma, one of Kynoch Press' few continental faces, was manufactured in 1931 and bought for inclusion in the 1934 *Specimen Book*. Supplied only as capitals with ranging figures, the Press recommended it as 'a decorative letter useful in display for matching the grays of halftone blocks. It looks particularly brilliant on art paper.'

[34]   Ratio Free Initials appear to have been abandoned by the close of the 1930s, for they cease to appear in any type list after 1934.

[35]   Ravilious Initials appear to have been abandoned by the close of the 1930s for they cease to appear in any type list after 1934.

[36]   The Rockwell family of faces, three weights of which were purchased on 28 June 1938, were too late an acquisition to appear in any of the Kynoch Press *Type Specimen Books* of the 1930s.

[37]   This Russian type had been made in five sizes, and was specifically designed to work with Baskerville Roman. It had been designed by Harry Carter during his employment at the Kynoch Press. The specimen sheet, issued by the Corporation in January 1932 to advertise the face, had been printed by the Press and carried an introduction which echoed Kynoch's own pragmatic voice:

> The demand for British machinery and tools from Russian is giving rise to an increased interest in Russian printing in this country. Catalogues and similar commercial jobs set in Russian are needed for the trade between the two countries. In the case of bilingual settings it is very desirable to have a type of uniform design of letters of the Roman and Russian alphabets so that the pages in which the two languages occur side by side may appear as even in colour and texture as the differences between the two alphabets permit.

Monotype never recorded any purchase of Russian Baskerville by the Kynoch Press. It may be assumed that as the creators of the face, it was, at least, entitled to complimentary matrices.

[38]   Ludlow Tempo was designed by R. H. Middleton and manufactured between 1930–42. It was an early acquisition by the Kynoch Press and was included in its 1934 *Specimen*.

[39]   Tempo Bold 36, 42, 48 and 72 point were only available in capitals.

[40]   Thorne Shaded was first used by the Kynoch Press in a Nonesuch Press book published in December 1933, and displayed in its type *Supplement* of 1934. It was a small fount cast from matrices dating from about 1803 and, as is evident from the specimen books, they were 'showing some honourable scars'.

[41]   Times New Roman was too late a purchase to appear in the specimen books of the 1930s. Times New Roman and Times Bold 6, 8, 9, 10, 11 and 12 point were purchased on 28 June 1938, with additional purchases of 10 and 12 point on 21 October 1938.

[42] Union Pearl does not appear in any type specimen book, or list, issued by the Kynoch Press at any time. The face was, though, used by the Press on the Nonesuch edition of *Astrophel and Stella* published in 1931. It was also used on a number of subsequent publications. Michael Clapham writes:

> In my copy of *Kynoch Press Specimen of Types*, acquired on my arrival there, were *Supplements* 1, 2 and 3, the last for types acquired since 1935. It also had tucked in, I think by me, the enclosed print of a small fount of Union Pearl, and the case was then in the composing room rack. Davis . . . saw no use for type specimens, which would explain its non-appearance in a Supplement. That it wasn't included in the two volume specimen book was due, I would guess, to the fact that the fount is too small for anything much more than titling: you could print a sonnet with it but hardly two.'

Although Kynoch was using this fount by 1931, it does not appear in any Stephenson Blake specimen book of the 1920s or 1930s. It is not advertised by the foundry until 1950.

Kynoch Press 1940s

[1] The 1948 type list does not distinguish between Monotype and Stephenson Blake Baskerville. Because the two versions were still running concurrently both in the 1930s and 1950s, I have assumed they were both still available in the 1940s.

[2] Bodoni was one of only three new type acquisitions in the 1940s. It was purchased before the full impact of the war was felt. Monotype records show 10 and 12 point Bodoni and Bodoni Bold to have been purchased in April 1940, whilst 8 and 11 point Bodoni and Bodoni Bold were purchased twelve months later in May 1941. Both Bodoni Italic and Bodoni Bold Italic were available during the 1940s, but the 1948 type list merely documents founts and their various weights, it does not differentiate between roman and italic.

[3] The 1948 type list does not distinguish between either Monotype, Ludlow or Stephenson Blake Caslon, but merely lists them generically as 'Caslon'. As all three versions of Caslon were available both in the 1930s and 1950s, I am assuming that all versions were retained throughout the 1940s.

[4] The 1948 type list makes mention of Calson Light and Caslon Bold, but these founts do not occur in any other decade.

[5] The 1948 type list makes no distinction between Monotype or American Type Founders Cloister. As both versions were available in both the 1930s and 1950s I have assumed both were available through the 1940s.

[6] The 1948 list makes no distinction between Monotype or American Type Founders Garamond. As both versions were available in both the 1930s and 1950s I have assumed both were available through the 1940s.

[7] Plantin was the last significant Monotype purchase of the 1940s having been bought as a companion to Russian Plantin.

[8] The 1948 type list merely catalogues 'Russian' and does not distinguish between the various founts of Russian. There was a large volume of Cyrillic typesetting

required during the war for propaganda purposes, because of the volume of work it is likely that Russian Baskerville would have been retained.

[9] Russian Plantin does not appear in the type specimen books until the 1950s, and there is no Monotype entry for its purchase. It was, though, available in the 1940s and used in the setting of *Endeavour* and other war-time propaganda literature. It is possible that the Kynoch Press did not purchase this version of Russian itself. Much of the materials and the production costs of publishing *Endeavour* were funded by the Government, and therefore Russian Plantin may have been a Government purchase on behalf of the Press.

[10]   Although Typewriter appears as an early Monotype purchase, and its availability was advertised on the 1924 Broadsheet, it was then withdrawn from the specimen books and does not re-appear until the 1948 type list.

Kynoch Press 1950s

[1] Albertus had been designed by Berthold Wolpe and issued by Monotype between 1932–40, but it was not purchased by the Kynoch Press until after 1953. These sizes of Albertus are too large to have been recorded in the purchase ledgers of Monotype.

[2] Annonce Grotesque, issued by Lettergieterij Amsterdam, was one of the most widely distributed faces appearing under various names in many European Foundries.

[3] Bembo and Bembo Bold proved popular faces and their range of sizes were expanded during the 1950s.

[4] Black Letter Shaded was previously listed as Shaded Gothic.

[5] Monotype record the Kynoch Press as having bought Centaur in 1952, but this face never appears in any Kynoch specimen books.

[6] Monotype record the Kynoch Press as having bought Clarendon in 1955, but this face does not appear in any Kynoch specimen books.

[7] Stephenson Blake's Chisel was issued between 1939–56 and purchased by the Press in 1953, it was designed on the suggestion of Robert Harling.

[8] Cooper Black was designed by Oswald B. Cooper for Barnhardt Brothers and Spindler in 1921 and was purchased by Kynoch Press soon after 1953.

[9] Elongated Roman Shaded was a display face which owed its origins to the condensed and elongated fat faces of the nineteenth century. It was bought by the Kynoch Press in the early 1950s as a complimentary face to Elongated Roman.

[10] The popularity of Falstaff is evidenced by the particularly large number of new sizes purchased in the 1950s and the addition of Falstaff italic as a companion to the roman.

[11] Grotesque No 1 is how Kynoch termed the more generally known Grotesque 215 and 126. Grotesque was a popular face amongst British printers being a sans face of the nineteenth-century model.

[12]   Headline Bold was a Monotype fount which bore great resemblance to Grotesque No 9.

[13] Monotype record the Kynoch Press as having bought Old Style in 1955, but this face does not appear in any Kynoch specimen book.

[14] Plantin and Plantin Bold proved to be particularly popular faces. Throughout the first six months of 1952 the Kynoch Press made 16 separate purchases of this face.

[15] Reiner Script, an informal cursive type designed by Imre Reiner, which was Kynoch Press' only contemporary script.

Kynoch Press 1960s

[1] Ludlow Bodoni True Cut and Bodoni Bold, although available in 1963 had been withdrawn by 1966, along with all other Ludlow founts.

[2] Stephenson Blake's 14 and 18 point Caslon Old Face roman and Caslon Old Face italic are a re-appearance from the 1930s.

[3] Stephenson Blake's Caslon Wood Letter makes a re-appearance from the 1930s.

[4] Ludlow Caslon was available in 1963 but had been abandoned by 1966, along with all other Ludlow founts.

[5 a b c] Ludlow Condensed, Record and Square Gothic are all available in 1963 but have been withdrawn by 1966, along with all other Ludlow founts.

[6] Erbar, a modern sans, had been designed by J. Erbar and release by Ludwig and Mayer between 1922–30 and found great popularity before the war. The Kynoch Press failed to take up the face before the war, but when it was re-launched in 1960 added it to its type list.

[7] There are no Monotype records to show the purchase of Garamond Bold or Garamond Bold Italic.

[8] Gill Wood Letter, previously named Gill Poster Type, is a re-appearance from the 1930s.

[9] There are no Kynoch Press records showing Hebrew Levinim, but it is shown as a Monotype purchase of 1968.

[10] Klang was purchased from by the Kynoch Press from Stephenson Blake rather than the Monotype Corporation.

[11] There are no Kynoch Press records showing that it possessed Modern Condensed, but it is shown as a Monotype purchase of 1963.

[12] There are no Monotype records showing a Kynoch purchase of 10 and 12 point Perpetua, but it appears in the 1962 type list.

[13] Perpetua Bold in sizes 42, 48, 60 and 72 point were available in 1963 but were abandoned by 1966.

[14] Phosphor, a sans display face, acted as a companion face to Erbar.

[15] The popularity of Playbill is evidenced by its expansion during this decade.

[16] Russian: Plantin Light and Plantin Italic had been withdrawn by 1962.

[17] By the 1960s Shaded Black is specified in terms of Didots rather than points.

[18] Ludlow Tempo and Tempo Bold were available in 1963 but were abandoned by 1966, along with all other Ludlow founts.

[19] Univers, designed by Adrian Frutiger, had originally been released by Deberny and Peignot of Paris in 1957, and was further released by the Monotype Corporation in 1961. Because of the commitment of the Kynoch Press to Monotype and the great investment it had made in the system, the Press, like most other British printers, did not purchase Univers until it was manufactured by Monotype.

[20] There are no Kynoch Press records showing Univers Light Condensed, which was purchased from Monotype on 16 April 1964.

[21] There are no Kynoch Press records showing Univers Medium Condensed, which was purchased from Monotype on 19 November 1969, too late for inclusion in the last known Kynoch type list of 1966.

[22] There are no Kynoch Press records showing Univers Bold Condensed, which was purchased from Monotype on 19 November 1969, too late for inclusion in the last known Kynoch type list of 1966.

[23] There are no Monotype records showing Univers Extra Bold but its availability was advertised in the 1966 type list.

Kynoch Press membership of the Birmingham Typographic Association

Year	Total	Press-room total	Composing total	Compositors	Monotype operators	Caster operators	Overseers	Readers	Apprentices
1921	25	9	16	16	1				
1922	26								
1924	24								
1925	27								
1926	30								
1927	37								
1928	47								
1929	56	23	32	24	2	2	1	2	1 comp, 1 press
1930	60	24	36	25	3	2	2	2	2 comp, 2 press
1931	61	20	41	24	4	2	1	5	5 comp, 1 press
1932	59	20	39	23	3	1	2	4	3 comp, 3 mono
1933	58	22	36	21	3	2	1	4	3 comp, 2 mono
1934	59	22	37	21	3	3	2	4	3 comp, 1 mono
1935	56	23	33	19	3	2	2	4	2 comp, 1 mono
1936	55	23	32	21	3	2	1	3	2 comp
1937	55	24	31	20	3	3	1	3	1 comp, 1 press
1938	55	24	31	21	3	3	1	3	2 press
1939	54	24	30				1		1 press
1940	53	24	29	21	2	1	1	3	2 comp, 2 press
1941	50	19	31	23	2	1	1	2	2 comp, 1 press
1942	47	20	27	14	3	2	2	3	3 comp
1943	46	19	27	17	3	2	2	3	
1944	48	18	30	22	4	1	1	2	
1945	53	21	32	22	3	2	1	3	1 comp
1946	66	27	39	27	3	3	1	4	1 comp

Year	Total	Press-room total	Composing total	Compositors	Monotype operators	Caster operators	Overseers	Readers	Apprentices
1947	68	30	38	25	4	3	1	4	1 comp
1948	69	32	37	22	3	3	1	5	3 comp
1949	77	35	42	23	5	3	1	6	4 comp
1950	70	31	39	27	3	2		6	1 comp
1951	76	34	42	29	3	3		6	1 comp
1952	75	29	46	28	4	3		7	4 comp
1953	79	32	47	30	4	4		7	2 comp
1954	72	28	44	27	5	4		7	1 comp
1955	66	25	41	26	4	3		7	1 comp
1956	70	28	42	26	4	4		7	1 comp
1957	75	30	45						2 comp
1958	71	26	45	26	5	4		7	3 comp
1959	71	25	46	28	5	2		6	5 comp
1960	78	28	50	35	4	2		7	2 comp
1961	80	28	52	32	5	2		6	7 comp
1962	77	30	62	41	3	2		6	7 comp
1963	73	28	45	29	5	2		4	5 comp
1964	75	30	45	27	5	2		5	6 comp
1965	78	28	50	32	5	2		5	6 comp
1966	83	29	54	35	6	3		5	5 comp
1967	81	26	55	38	6	2		4	5 comp
1968	77	28	49	34	4	1		4	6 comp
1969	70	23	47		5	1		5	6 comp
1970	83	39	44	25	5	2		6	6 comp
1971	78	38	40	25	4	2		6	3 comp
1972	71	32	39	26	4	1		6	2 comp
1973	66	28	38	24	6			6	2 comp
1974	61	28	33	20	4	2		7	
1975	65	31	34	20	4	2		6	2 comp
1976	66	29	37	19	5	1		6	6 comp
1977	67	28	39	17	9	2		7	4 comp
1978	65	27	38	18	9	2		7	2 comp
1979	58	24	34	16	8			7	3 comp

Catalogue of works

Examples of work produced by the Kynoch Press can be found in the libraries of many institutions including: Birmingham Central Reference Library; Birmingham Museum of Science; Birmingham and Midland Institute; Birmingham Proof House; BBC Written Archives, Reading; Bodleian Library, John Johnson Collection, Oxford; The British Library, St Pancras, London; ICI Library, Millbank, London; Imperial War Museum, London; John Jarrold Printing Museum, Norwich; Manchester Metropolitan University Library; Ministry of Defence Pattern Room, Nottingham; Private collections; Royal Armouries, London and Leeds; St Bride Printing Library, London; Victoria and Albert Museum, London

The largest single collection of work printed by the Kynoch Press is housed in the Birmingham Central Reference Library. The archive department of this library hold records which comprise the extensive business annals of the former Metals Division of Imperial Chemical Industries Limited, ICI Metals Limited. These records pre-date 1962 when the Metals Division became a new operating company—Imperial Metals Division [Kynoch] Limited. Some of the earliest records of the collection relate to the firm of Kynoch and Co. which opened its factory for the manufacture of ammunition at Witton in 1862. This company was twice reformed and expanded dramatically—G. Kynoch & Co. Ltd, and Kynoch Ltd—before becoming a component part of ICI Metals in 1928/29. ICI Metals itself absorbed many other metal manufacturing companies in the 1930s and 1940s and the business records of these and other firms are included in this considerable archive. Although predominantly a business archive, it contains a not insignificant quantity of printed ephemera which has been produced by the Kynoch Press. In addition to these business records, the library also holds a vast and diverse collection of

Kynoch Press and ICI material in the local history, science technology and management, and arts and literature departments. Additionally, examples of Kynoch fine printing can be found in the Rare Books collection of the Birmingham library. Some of the material has been catalogued by the library under the reference 'Local printing, Kynoch Press', but most of the material remains uncharted, its discovery has been a matter of serendipity and perseverance.

The John Johnson Collection at the Bodleian Library, Oxford, supports three boxes of Kynoch Press material: one contains assorted ephemera most of which pre-dates 1945; the remainder contain samples of the Notebook and Diary. The John Jarrold Printing Museum, Norwich, also holds a collection of Kynoch Notebooks, but the only complete set, of which I am aware, belongs to a private individual. Indeed, individual collections have provided a valuable source for the compilation of this catalogue.

The vast majority of material that can be found within library collections was produced for ICI, or Kynoch's other parent companies, between 1920 and 1945. There is little material that either pre- or post-dates this period. For work produced either at the beginning or end of Kynoch's trading history, I have been dependent upon the collections of individuals.

BOOKS-TRADE

Architectural Press
London

HOLMES John M., *Colour in Interior Decoration* (with a foreword by L. H. Bucknell); The Architectural Press; 1931; 310 x 220 mm; 106 pp; Monotype Gill Sans, Monotype Imprint, Ratio Free Initials; Tipped-in, full-colour architectural drawings; Stock: toned laid; Binding: hard-cased, thread-sewn.

Bernard Sleigh
London

SLEIGH Bernard, *A Faery Pageant* ['With illustrations drawn by Bernard Sleigh and engraved on wood by Ivy A. Ellis and the author, and bound by Frank Garrett. 'This edition is printed at the Kynoch Press and is limited to 475 copies and is sold by Bernard Sleigh, 3 Newhall Street, Birmingham and Frank Garrett, Cornwall Chambers.' December 1924; 122 x 156 mm; 28 pp; Monotype Garamond and hand-decorated initials; Monochrome wood engravings; Stock: toned wove; Binding: hard-cased, thread-sewn.

The Bulletin Press
Hertford

RUSSELL W. G. A., *The City of Birmingham Choir, 1921–46*; The Bulletin Press, Hereford; 1946; 227 x 178 mm; 54 pp; Monotype Times New Roman, Monotype Perpetua; Monochrome half-tones; Stock: toned book wove and art paper; Binding: hard-cased, thread-sewn.

Butterworth's
Scientific Publications
London

CHALMERS Bruce (ed), *Progress in Metal Physics*; Butterworth's Scientific Publications; 1949; 245 x 152 mm; 410 pp; Monotype Baskerville; Monochrome half-tones and line illustrations; Stock: toned laid; Binding: hard-cased, thread-sewn.

Cornish Brothers
Publishers to
The University of
Birmingham

DOWNING Ida M., *The Twilight Book*; Cornish Brothers Limited, Birmingham; 1926; 183 x 120 mm; 78 pp; Monotype Imprint, Stephenson Blake Caslon; Monochrome and full-colour illustrations by Stavert Cash; Stock: toned, wove; Binding: hard-cased, thread-sewn.

HILL Joseph, and MIDGLEY William, *The History of the Royal Birmingham Society of Artists*—a century of Birmingham art with a chapter of personal reminiscence by E. S. Harper; The Society and Cornish Brothers Limited, Birmingham; 1928; 264 x 204 mm; 65 pp, plus 302 pp plates; Monotype Baskerville; 151 monochrome half tones; Stock: toned book wove and toned art; Binding: hard-cased, thread-sewn.

RODWAY Phyllis, RODWAY-SLINGSBY Lois, *Philip Rodway—and a tale of two theatres*; Cornish Brothers Limited, Birmingham; 1934; 234 x 150 mm; 644 pp; Fry's Baskerville, Monotype Baskerville; full-colour and monochrome half tones; Stock: toned book wove and art; Binding: hard-cased, thread-sewn.

STAFFORDIA i.e. WHITEHOUSE E., *Guide to the History of Haywood and its old church near Stafford in the Valley of Trent*; Cornish Brothers Limited, Birmingham; 1924; 174 x 118 mm; 148 pp; Monotype Imprint; Monochrome line illustrations by the author; Stock: toned book wove; Binding: hard-cased, thread-sewn.

Cassell and
Company Limited
London

NEWMAN Ernest, *The Life of Richard Wagner*, Volume I, 1813–1848; Cassell and Company Limited; 1933; 232 x 155 mm; 496 pp; Monotype Imprint, Bauersche Giesserei Shaded Black; Monochrome half tones; Stock: toned wove and art; Binding: hard-cased, thread-sewn.

NEWMAN Ernest, *The Life of Richard Wagner*, Volume II, 1848–1860; Cassell and Company Limited; 1937; 232 x 155 mm; 588 pp; Monotype Imprint, Bauersche Giesserei Shaded Black; Monochrome half tones; Stock: toned wove and art; Binding: hard-cased, thread-sewn. [the final two volumes of this work were printed by Jarrold and Sons Limited, Norwich, using Shaded Black, and it is possible that Kynoch Press produced the typesetting whilst Jarrold printed.]

Dryad Press
Leicester

COTTINS A. F., *Book Crafts for Schools—an approach to Bookbinding*; Dryad Press, Leicester, 1932; 208 x 135 mm; 228 pp; Monotype Baskerville, Gill Sans; illustrated with many photographs of technical processes and specimens of work, together with numerous line drawings by the author; Stock: toned book wove; Binding: hard-cased, thread-sewn.

FAIRBANK Alfred J., *A Handwriting Manual* (with bibliography); Dryad Press, Leicester; 1932; 217 x 138 mm; 46 pp; Monotype Bembo, Stephenson Blake Union Pearl; Monochrome half tone and line illustrations; Stock: toned book wove; Binding: hard-cased, thread-sewn.

GREGORY A., *The Art of Woodworking and Furniture Making* (with a foreword by B. Fletcher and a bibliography); The Dryad Press, Leicester; 1929; 254 x 189 mm;

86 pp; Monotype Gill Sans, Monotype Baskerville, Fry's Baskerville; Monochrome half tones and line illustrations; Stock: toned art; Binding: hard-cased, thread-sewn.

GREGORY A., *Constructive Woodworking for Schools* (with a foreword by T. Reed and a bibliography); The Dryad Press, Leicester; 1933; 246 x 182 mm; 100 pp; Monotype Gill Sans, Monotype Baskerville, Milner Initials; Monochrome half tones and line illustrations; Stock: toned book wove and art; Binding: hard-cased, thread-sewn.

JUDSON Muriel, *Lettering for Schools*; Dryad Press, Leicester; 1928; 238 x 154 mm; 40 pp; Monotype Baskerville, Berthold Vesta Titling; Stock: toned wove; Binding: hard-cased, thread-sewn.

LUNN Dora, *Pottery in the Making—a handbook for teachers and individual workers* (with a foreword by P. B. Ballard, glossary, recipes and a bibliography); The Dryad Press; 1931; 210 x 133 mm; 124 pp; Monotype Imprint; Monochrome half tones and line illustrations; Stock: toned book wove; Binding: hard-cased, thread-sewn.

SIMON Herbert, CARTER Harry, *Printing Explained—an elementary practical handbook for schools and amateurs* (with a foreword by F. M. W. Meynell and bibliography); Dryad Press, Leicester; 1931; 209 x 134 mm; 68 pp; Monotype Baskerville; Monochrome lino-block illustrations by G. M. Freebairn; Stock: George Parsons and Co.'s toned antique book wove; Binding: A. W. Bain and Co. Ltd, hard-cased binding, thread-sewn.

Effingham Wilson
London

MENNELL Robert O., *Tea—an historical sketch* (including annals of the tea firm of William Tuke and Son and references to the East India Company); Effingham Wilson, London; 1926; 240 x 180 mm; 64 pp; Stephenson Blake Caslon, Monotype Baskerville; Monochrome half tones and full-colour illustrations; Stock: toned, laid; Binding: hard-cased, thread-sewn.

Elkin Mathews
London

CLAWSON H Phelps, *Transmutation and other poems;* Elkin Mathews Limited; 1923; 189 x 126 mm; 48 pp; Stephenson Blake Open Titling, Monotype Imprint; Stock: toned Abbey Mills, Greenfield; Binding: hard-cased, thread-sewn.

KAYE-SMITH Sheila, *Saints in Sussex* (of this book only 250 copies have been printed and the type distributed); Elkin Mathews Limited; 1923; 245 x 167 mm; 32 pp; Monotype Garamond; Monochrome line illustrations; Stock: toned laid; Binding: hard-cased, thread-sewn.

ROSTREVOR George, *Pieces of Eight*; Elkin Mathews; 1923; 186 x 124 mm; 38 pp; Monotype Imprint; Stock: toned book wove; Binding: hard-cased, thread-sewn.

Office of the Fleuron
London

MORISON Stanley, JACKSON Holbrook, *A Brief Survey of Printing History and Practice*; At the Office of the Fleuron; 1923; 216 x 137 mm; 88 pp; Monotype Garamond; Monochrome line illustrations; Stock: toned wove; Binding: hard-cased, thread-sewn.

George Allen and Unwin
London

PEACH Harry, CARRINGTON Noel, *The Face of the Land—the yearbook of the Design and Industries Association 1929–30* (with an introduction by Clough William-Ellis and a bibliography); George Allen and Unwin Limited; 1930; 219 x 140 mm; 172 pp; Fry's Baskerville, Monotype Baskerville; Monochrome half tones; Stock: toned art; Binding: hard-cased, thread-sewn.

James Moran
London

HUTCHINGS R. S. (ed), *Alphabet—International Annual of Letterforms*; James Moran Limited, London; 1964; 280 x 214 mm; 166 pp; Amsterdam Annonce Grotesque, Monotype Albertus Titling, Nebiolo Augustea, Inter-type photosetter Baskerville, Monotype Baskerville, Monotype Bembo, Bauersche Giesserei Beton, Ludlow Bodoni, Monotype Bodoni, Monotype Cloister, Bauersche Giesserei Cartoon, Intertype Cornell, Monotype Caslon, Monotype Grotesque, Monotype Gill Sans, Monotype Imprint, Stephenson Blake Mole Foliate, Monotype Old English Text, Klingspor Prisma, Stephenson Blake Playbill, Monotype Plantin, Bauersche Giesserei Shaded Black, Monotype Times Titling; Monochrome half-tones and line illustrations, full-colour half-tones, adverts; Stock: various; Binding: hard-cased, thread-sewn, dust jacket.

John Lane at the Bodley Head
London

CLOUD Yvonne (ed), *Beside the Seaside* (2nd edition); John Lane, The Bodley Head; 1938; 220 x 140 mm; 274 pp; Monotype Baskerville; Monochrome half tones; Stock: toned book wove; Binding: hard-cased, thread-sewn.

The Nonesuch Press
London

BUNYAN John, *The Pilgrim's Progress and the Life and Death of Mr Badman* (Edited with an introduction by G. G. Harrison); The Nonesuch Press; 1928; 195 x 120 mm; 490 pp; Stephenson Blake Caslon, Monotype Caslon, Bauersche Giesserei Ancient Black and Shaded Black; Illustrated by K. Mitchell and woodblocks coloured stencilled by the Curwen Press; Edition limited to 1,600 copies—1,000 UK, 600 USA; Stock: toned Arches paper; Binding: hard-cased, thread-sewn.

COLERIDGE S. T., *Selected Poetry and Prose* (edited with an introduction and notes by Stephen Potter); The Nonesuch Press; 1933; 189 x 116 mm; 852 pp; Stephenson Blake Thorne Shaded, Monotype Baskerville; Stock: toned Bible paper; Binding: hard-cased, buckram, thread-sewn.

DONNE John, *X Sermons* (preached by the late and learned and reverend divine John Donne, doctor in divinity, and Dean of the Cathedral Church of St Paul. Chosen from the whole body of Donne's sermons by Geoffrey L. Keynes); Nonesuch Press; 1923; 292 x 190 mm; 168 pp; American Type Founders Garamond, Monotype Garamond, Bauersche Giesserei Ancient Black; Edition limited to 725 copies; Stock: toned Dutch mould made paper; Binding: hard-cased, thread-sewn.

GRANT Bartle [ed], *The Receipt Book of Elizabeth Raper—and a portion of her cipher journal*, (written 1756–1770 and never before printed); Nonesuch Press; 1924; 230 x 145 mm; 104 pp; Stephenson Blake Open Titling, Monotype Baskerville; Monochrome line illustrations by Duncan Grant; Edition limited to 850 copies; Stock: Dutch mould made paper; Binding: hard-cased, buckram, thread-sewn.

HOOPINGTON Ambrose, *A Letter to a Young Lady on the Occasion of her Approaching Marriage and Possible Divorce*; The Nonesuch Press; 1934; 224 x 142 mm; 42 pp; Monotype Gill Sans, Monotype Baskerville, Bauersche Giesserei

Shaded Black, Stevens Shanks Fat Face; Stock: toned laid; Binding: hard-cased boards printed with a design by Leonard Beaumont, thread-sewn.

The Letters of George Meredith to Alice Meynell, 1896–1907 (with annotations thereto); Nonesuch Press; 1923; 235 x 155 mm; 108 pp; Monotype Garamond and Caslon; Edition limited to 850 copies; Stock: toned Ingres rag paper; Binding: quarter inch canvas, thread-sewn, dust jacket.

MARVELL Andrew, *Poems*; The Nonesuch Press; 1923; 274 x178 mm; 132 pp; Monotype Garamond; Edition limited to 850 copies; Stock: Pernsia hand-made paper; Binding: velum, thread-sewn.

McKENNA Michael, *Poems*; Privately printed under the supervision of The Nonesuch Press; 1932; 178 x 124 mm; 69 pp; Monotype Imprint; Stock: Abbey Mills cream laid machine made paper.

McKENNA Michael, *Michael 31 January 1910–6 October 1931*; Privately printed under the supervision of The Nonesuch Press; 1932; 192 x 124 mm; 488 pp and 22pp of inserts; Monotype Imprint, Monotype Caslon; Half tones tipped-in and printed by collotype; Stock: Abbey Mills cream laid machine made paper.

SECUNDUS Johannes, *Kisses* (rendered into English verse by Thomas Stanley, 1647); Nonesuch Press; 1923; 256 x 165 mm; 28 pp; Bauersche Giesserei Ancient Black, Stephenson Blake Open Titling; Monotype Garamond; Edition limited to 725 copies; Stock: toned Vidalon; Binding: hard-cased, thread-sewn.

SIDNEY Sir Philip, *Astrophel and Stella (*edited with an introduction by Mona Wilson); The Nonesuch Press; 1931; 228 x 142 mm; 234 pp; Monotype Bembo, Stephenson Blake Union Pearl; Edition limited to 1,210 copies—725 UK, 485 USA; Stock: toned Van Gelder paper; Binding: hard-cased, thread-sewn.

THOMSON James, *The Seasons* (with an introduction by J. Beresford); Nonesuch Press; 1927; 265 x 180 mm; 122 pp; Fry's Baskerville, Stephenson Blake Open Titling, Monotype Baskerville, Fournier ornaments; 5 colour illustrations by Jacquier; pictures by A. Alexander and Sons; Copper plates engraved by C. Sigrist; water colour through stencil by the Curwen Press; Edition limited to 1,500 copies; Stock: Dutch mould made paper; Binding: hard-cased, thread-sewn.

VAUGHAN Henry, *Poems* (from Poems, Olor Iscanus, Silex Scintillanus, Thalia Rediviva; an essay from The Mount of Olives; two letters from MSS in the Bodleian Library); Nonesuch Press; 1924; 260 x 170 mm; 170 pp; Monotype Baskerville; Stephenson Blake Open Titling and Caslon; Edition limited to 850 copies; Stock: toned Wolvercote rag; Binding: hard-cased, thread-sewn.

Norman Gale
Rugby, Northamptonshire

GALE Norman, *Verse in Bloom*; Norman Gale, Rugby; 1924; 189 x 128 mm; 166 pp; Fry's Baskerville, Monotype Baskerville; Stock: toned Basingwerk Parchment; Binding: hard-cased, thread-sewn.

GALE Norman, *A Flight of Fancies;* Norman Gale, Rugby; 1926; 189 x 128 mm; 172 pp; Monotype Baskerville; Stock: toned book wove; Binding: hard-cased, thread-sewn.

GALE Norman, *Messrs Bat and Ball*; Norman Gale, Rugby; 1930; 175 x 120 mm; 62 pp; Monotype Imprint; Stock: toned book wove, Dutch; Binding: hard-cased, thread-sewn.

Oliver and Boyd
Edinburgh

MEINERTZHAGEN Colonel R., *Birds of Arabia;* Oliver and Boyd, Edinburgh; 1954; 266 x 186 mm; 638 pp; Monotype Baskerville; full-colour half-tones and monochrome half-tones; Stock: toned coated; Binding: hard-cased, thread-sewn.

OAKES Clifford, *The Birds of Lancashire;* Oliver and Boyd, Edinburgh; 1953; 224 x 145 mm; 396 pp; Monotype Baskerville; Monochrome half-tones; Stock: toned book wove; Binding: hard-cased, thread-sewn.

Oxford University Press
Oxford

READER W. J., *Imperial Chemical Industries—a history, Volume I, The Forerunners 1870–1926;* Oxford University Press; 1970; 235 x 150 mm; 580 pp; Fry's Baskerville, Monotype Baskerville; Monochrome half-tones and line illustrations; Stock: toned book wove; Binding: hard-cased, thread-sewn, dust jacket.

READER W. J., *Imperial Chemical Industries—a history, Volume II, The First Quarter-century, 1926–1952;* Oxford University Press; 1975; 235 x 150 mm; 586 pp; Fry's Baskerville, Monotype Baskerville; Monochrome half-tones and line illustrations; Stock: toned book wove; Binding: hard-cased, thread-sewn, dust jacket.

The Porpoise Press
Edinburgh

FERGUSON Robert, *Scots Poems* (fully re-printed from *The Weekly Magazine* and the editions of 1773 and 1779, edited by Bruce Dickins); The Porpoise Press, Edinburgh; 1925; 220 x 140 mm; 108 pp; Monotype Garamond; Edition limited to 550 copies; Stock: toned laid, mould-made, deckle edged; Binding: hard-cased, thread-sewn.

HENRYSON Robert, *The Testament of Cresseid—a poem* (Edited anew by Bruce Dickins with a bibliographical note); The Porpoise Press, Edinburgh; 1925; 220 x 140 mm; 52 pp; Monotype Garamond; Edition limited to 500 copies; Stock: toned, laid, mould made, deckle edged; Binding: hard-cased, thread-sewn.

Selwyn and Blount
London

DE LA MARE Walter, *The Riddle and Other Stories;* Selwyn and Blount; 1923; 184 x 122 mm; 312 pp; Monotype Garamond; an edition limited to 310 copies; Stock: toned laid; Binding: hard-cased, thread-sewn.

MOORE, Clement Clarke; *The Night Before Christmas;* Selwyn and Blount; 1923; Originally published as *A Visit from St Nicholas* in *The New York Book of Poetry,* New York, 1830.

PERRAULT Mr, *Tales of Past Times;* Selwyn and Blount; 1922; 214 x 168 mm; 64 pp; Monotype Caslon; Colour and monochrome illustrations; Stock: toned wove; Binding: hard-cased, thread-sewn.

TAYLOR Frederic Irving, *Azal and Edras* (an epic poem with a foreword by T. W. Crossland, Part 1 only printed at Kynoch Press); Selwyn and Blount; 1923; 207 x 140 mm; 92 pp; Monotype Imprint; Stock: toned laid; Binding: hard-cased, thread-sewn.

The Society of SS Peter and Paul
London

KAYE-SMITH Sheila, *The Mirror of the Months;* The Society of SS Peter and Paul Limited, London; 1934; 218 x 142 mm; 78 pp; Monotype Garamond, Bauersche Giesserei Black Letter; Stock: toned Ellerslie laid paper; Binding: hard-cased, thread-sewn.

MACKAY H. F. B., *The Message of Francis of Assisi* [H. F. B. Mackay, Prebendary of

St Paul's and Vicar of All Saints Margaret Street London W]; Society of SS Pater and Paul Limited, London; 1924; 217 x 140 mm; 84 pp; Monotype Baskerville, Monotype Caslon; Stock: toned wove; Binding: hard-cased, thread-sewn.

Stanley Nott
London

FENOLLOSA Ernest, *The Chinese Written Character as a Medium for Poetry—an ars poetica* (foreword and notes by Ezra Pound); Ideogramatic series; Stanley Nott; 1936; 210 x 166 mm; 52 pp; Monotype Bembo, Stephenson Blake Union Pearl; Monochrome line illustrations; Stock: toned book wove; Binding: hard-cased, thread-sewn.

POUND Ezra (ed) *Ta Hio—the great learning*; edited into the American language by Ezra Pound; Stanley Nott, London; 1936; 203 x 136 mm; 32 pp; American Type Founders Garamond, Monotype Garamond, Stempel Ratio Free Initials; Stock: toned book wove; Binding: hard-cased, thread-sewn.

BOOKS AND BOOKLETS

Local and national industry

Architectural Lighting; Best and Lloyd Limited, Handsworth, Birmingham; 1950; 247 x 180 mm; 64 pp; Monotype Baskerville, Stephenson Blake Baskerville, Ludlow Delphian, Stempel Ratio Free Initials; Monochrome half-tones; Stock: toned, art; Binding: hard-cased, thread-sewn. Book

The Birmingham Chamber of Commerce; The Birmingham Chamber of Commerce; 1960; 277 x 175 mm; 16 pp; Monotype Grotesque No 1; Monochrome and full-colour half-tones; Stock: toned, wove; Binding: hard-cased, thread-sewn. Booklet

The Birmingham Guild Limited—architectural and decorative workers; The Birmingham Guild Limited, Grosvenor Works, Grosvenor Street West, Birmingham; 1930; 279 x 214 mm; 128 pp; Monotype Baskerville, Stempel Ratio Free Initials; Monochrome half-tones; Stock: toned, art; Binding: hard-cased, thread-sewn. Book

Bulletin of the International Seismological Centre, 1968, January; International Seismological Centre; 1968–1971; 210 x 135 mm; 369 pp; Monotype Times, Monotype Univers; Tables, equations; Stock: toned Bible paper; Binding: hard case, thread-sewn. Book

British Technology Index; Edited by E. J. Coates; The Library Association; 1969; 292 x 200 mm; Monotype Times; Monochrome diagrams; Stock: toned wove; Binding: hard case, thread-sewn. Book

Bickford Smith and Company Limited 1931–1931; Tuckingmill, Cornwall; 1931; 238 x 180 mm; 28 pp; Monotype Baskerville; Monochrome half-tones; Stock: toned wove and art; Binding: hard-cased, thread-sewn. Book

The Development of Birmingham—an essay; With designs and drawings by William Haywood. An introduction by Neville Chamberlain. This edition is limited to 250 copies; 243 x 183 mm; 102 pp; Stephenson Blake Caslon, Cheltenham; Monochrome half-tones and line illustrations, colour illustrations; Stock: toned wove; Binding: hard-cased, thread-sewn. Book

EDE John F., *The History of Wednesbury*; Wednesbury Corporation; Monotype Baskerville; Monochrome half-tones; Stock: Toned, book wove; Binding: hard-cased, thread-sewn. Book

Exhibition of English Medieval Art; Victoria and Albert Museum and The Board of Education; 1930; 208 x 160 mm; 202 mm; Monotype Cloister, Monotype Baskerville, Fry's Baskerville; Stock: Toned, book wove; Binding: hard-cased, thread-sewn. Book

Forth Road Bridge Superstructure; Forth Road Bridge Joint Board; 1964; 297 x 237 mm; 92 pp; Stephenson Blake Grotesque No 9 Condensed, Monotype Grotesque No 1; Monochrome half-tones, full-colour half tone, two colour wood engravings; Stock: toned, art; Binding: hard-cased, thread-sewn. Book

Handbook of the Barber Institute of Fine Arts; The University of Birmingham, published for the trustees; 1949; 202 x 135 mm; 62 pp; Monotype Bembo; Monochrome half-tones; Stock: Toned, book wove and art; Binding: hard-cased, thread-sewn. Book

HILTON Roger N., *Maladies of Heva in Malaya*; Rubber Research Institute, Kuala Lumpur, Malaya; 1959; 273 x 206 mm; 104 pp; Fry's Baskerville, Monotype Baskerville; Full-colour illustrations reproduced from watercolours by Hoh Choo Chuan; Stock: toned book wove; Binding: hard-cased with dust jacket, thread-sewn. Book

HULL, M. F., *Magadi—the story of the Magadi soda company*; Kynoch Press for the Magadi Soda Company; 1964; 254 x 186 mm; 200 pp; Monotype Baskerville, Stephenson Blake Baskerville; Monochrome and colour half-tones, colour fold-out map; Stock: toned wove; Binding: cased, thread-sewn. Book

The Institute of Metals—Silver Jubilee Programme, Autumn Meeting, September 18–21, 1933; Institute of Metals; 1933; 215 x 140; 34 pp; Fry's Baskerville, Monotype Baskerville; Stock: toned, wove; Binding: hard-cased, thread-sewn; Booklet

International Tables for X-ray Crystallography; Edited by Norman F. M. Henry and Kathleen Lonsdale; Published for the International Union of Crystallography by the Kynoch Press; 1952–67; 275 x 200 mm; 570 pp; Monotype Times; Tables, equations, diagrams; Stock: toned wove; Binding; hard case, thread-sewn. Book

LOWE Frank, *Our Centenary Year—an historical note on the company of Edwin Lowe Limited* (thimble and ferule makers); Edwin Lowe; 1952; 214 x 138 mm; 10 pp; Berthold Vesta Titling, Monotype Baskerville; Monochrome half-tones; Stock: toned, book wove; Binding: hard-cased, thread-sewn; Booklet

MACKENZIE Compton, *Brockhouse—a study in Industrial Evolution*; J. Brockhouse and Co., Limited, Victoria Works, Hill Tops, West Bromwich; 1945; 54 pp; Monotype Times New Roman; full-colour illustration; Designed by Adprint, London; Stock: Toned, book wove; Binding: hard-cased, thread-sewn. Book

MACKENZIE Compton, *The Vital Flame;* A British Gas Council Publication; 1947; 245 x 182 mm; 88 pp; Monotype Times New Roman; 42 pictures in colour photography and 7 pages of isotype charts; Colour plates by Thomas Foreman and Sons Limited, and isotype charts by Brown, Knight and Truscott; Designed and produced by Adprint, London for A. N. Holden and Company Limited London and Birmingham; Stock: Mellotex book paper by Tullis Russell and Co. Limited; Binding: hard-cased, thread-sewn. Book

PATTERSON H. J., *Handbook for Electrical Welders;* Murex Welding Processes

Limited, Waltham Cross, London; 1936 and 1945; 210 x 137 mm; 188 pp; Monotype Gill Sans, Monotype Imprint, Monotype Bold Face; Monochrome half-tones and line illustrations; stock: toned art; Binding: hardcased, thread-sewn. Book

Sheet Copper-work for Building; Copper Development Association; 1934; 246 x 173 mm; 70 pp; Monotype Gill Sans; Monochrome line illustrations; toned wove stock; hard-cased, laced binding. Book

Henry Hope and Sons
Birmingham

Hope's—British Empire Exhibition; Henry Hope and Sons Limited; 1924; 203 x 130 mm; 22 pp; American Type Founders Garamond; Monotype Garamond; full-colour illustrations by Mrs G. Barraclough; Stock: Arnold hand made paper; Binding: hard-cased, thread-sewn; A special edition consisting of 200 copies. Booklet

Hope's Bronze Windows 1918–1932; Hope's Windows Inc, Jamestown, New York; October 1932; 267 x 177 mm; 36 pp; Monotype Baskerville, Monotype Caslon; Monochrome half-tones and diagrams, duo-tones; Stock: toned art; Binding: cased, thread-sewn. Booklet

Hope's Hardware 1818–1930 (catalogue); Henry Hope and Sons; 1930; 262 x 178 mm; 106 pp; Stephenson Blake Caslon, Monotype Imprint; Monochrome half-tones; Stock: toned, art; Binding: hard-cased, thread-sewn; Book

Hope's Heating and Lighting; Henry Hope and Sons; 308 x 220 mm; 56 pp; Monotype Caslon; Duo-tones, map, diagrams; Stock: toned art; Binding: separate cover, thread-sewn. Book

Hope's Leadwork; BCM/Hope; 1927; 267 x 175 mm; 88 pp; Monotype Garamond; Monochrome half-tones; Stock: toned art; Binding: separate cover, thread-sewn. Book

Hope's Metal Windows and Casements; Henry Hope and Sons Limited; 1926; 371 x 245 mm; 152 pp; American Type Founders Garamond, American Type Founders Cloister, Stephenson Blake Caslon; Monochrome half-tones and line illustrations, full-colour illustrations by Mrs G. Baraclough; Stock: toned, coated; Binding: hard-cased, thread-sewn; Book

Hope's Standard Windows; Henry Hope and Sons Limited; 1927; 201 x 128 mm; 48 pp; Monotype Garamond; Monochrome and full-colour line illustrations by Mrs G. Baraclough; Stock: toned, book wove; Binding: hard-cased, thread-sewn; Booklet

Hope's Windows for Hospitals and Schools 1818–1932 [catalogue 99]; Henry Hope and Sons Limited; November 1932; 266 x 178 mm; 28 pp; Stephenson Blake Caslon, Monotype Baskerville, Monotype Bodoni; Monochrome half-tones and line illustrations, duo-tones; Stock: toned art; Binding: separate cover, thread-sewn. Booklet

Imperial Chemical Industries

Alfred Nobel—a century appreciation of his life's work: ICI; Published on the occasion of a dinner presided over by Sir Harry McGowan KBE, on 5th January 1933, in commemoration of the Alfred Nobel Centenary, 1933; 260x 184 mm; 24 pp; Monotype Baskerville; Monochrome half-tone on frontispiece; Stock: toned laid, deckle edge; Binding: hard-cased, thread-sewn; Booklet

Ancestors of an Industry; ICI; 1950; 215 x 140 mm; 164 pp; Monotype Garamond; Monochrome line illustrations; Stock: toned book wove; Binding: hard-cased, thread-sewn. Book

Billingham; ICI; 250 x 300 mm; 60 pp; Monotype Baskerville, Grotesque; Monochrome and full-colour half-tones; Stock: toned art; Binding: Rexine leather cloth, thread-sewn. Book

'Cassel' Heat-treatment and Casehardening Handbook [2nd edition]; ICI; 1938; 137 x 100 mm; 128 pp; Monotype Imprint, Monotype Bold Face; Monochrome half-tones; Stock: toned wove and art; Binding: cloth cover, thread-sewn. Booklet

'Cassel' Heat-treatment and Casehardening Handbook' [4th edition]; ICI; 1943; 137 x 100 mm; 128 pp; Monotype Imprint, Monotype Bold Face; Monochrome half-tones; Stock: toned wove and art; Binding: cloth cover, thread-sewn. Booklet

'Cassel' Heat-treatment and Casehardening Handbook [6th edition]; ICI; 1953; 216 x 138 mm; 216 pp; Monotype Times; Monochrome half-tones, 2-colour graphs; Stock: toned art; Binding: cased, thread-sewn. Book

Colour from Britain; ICI; 1949; 260 x 200 mm; 44 pp; Monotype Times, Monotype Perpetua; Colour illustrations from paintings by Gordon Nicoll RI, FRSA; Stock: toned wove; Binding: hard-cased, thread-sewn. Book

The Control of Water Softening and Boiler Water Conditioning; ICI; 1935; 210 x 136 mm; 40 pp; Monotype Gill Sans, Monotype Garamond, ATF Garamond, Stempel Ratio Free Initials; Monochrome half-tones, 2-colour graphs; Stock: toned art; Binding: cased, thread-sewn. Booklet

The Control of Water Softening and Boiler Water Conditioning [4th edition]; ICI; 1937; 210 x 140 mm; 44 pp; Monotype Gill Sans, Monotype Garamond, ATF Garamond, Stempel Ratio Free Initials; Monochrome half-tones, 2-colour graphs; Stock: toned art; Binding: cased, thread-sewn. Booklet

CULPEPER Nicholas, *The Complete Herbal* (this book is re-printed from an original edition of 1653 preserving all the typographical inconsistencies); ICI; 1953; 246 x 154 mm; 616 pp; Monotype Caslon, Stephenson Blake Caslon; full-colour illustrations (these have been reproduced by auto-lithography in order to retain their original character); Stock: toned book wove; Binding: hard-cased, with slip case. Book

The Dyeing of 'Terylene' Polyester Fibre; ICI, Dyestuffs Division; 1951; 240 x 152 mm; 26 pp; Monotype Times; Monochrome and colour half-tones, monochrome tables and graphs; Stock: toned art; Binding: cased, thread-sewn. Booklet

Ethylene Glycol; ICI; 1948; 215 x 138 mm; 28 pp; Monotype Gill Sans, Monotype Times; Monochrome graphs; Stock: toned art; Binding: cased, thread-sewn. Booklet

Ethelene Glycol; ICI; 1938; 215 x 138 mm; 28 pp; Monotype Bodoni; 2-colour graphs; Stock: toned art; Binding: cased, thread-sewn. Booklet

Equipment of an Industry; ICI; 276 x 214 mm; 72 pp; (a selection of examples taken from a series of press announcements published by ICI in 1946–7 under the title 'Equipment of an Industry' Monotype Times; Monochrome half-tones; Stock: toned art; Binding: hard-cased, thread-sewn. Book

Fifty Years of Progress 1895–1945—the story of the Castner-Kellner Alkali Company (told to celebrate the fiftieth anniversary of its formation); ICI; 1945; 245 x 182 mm; 66 pp; Monotype Bembo, Monotype Garamond; Monochrome half-tones; Stock: toned laid and toned art; Binding: cased, thread-sewn. Book

Fundamentals of Rubber Technology—eight lectures delivered at Newton Heath Technical School; ICI, Dyestuffs Division; 1955; 246 x 182 mm; 176 pp; Monotype Times; Monochrome half-tones, tables, illustrations, diagrams; Stock: toned art; Binding: cased, thread-sewn. Book

Galvene and A.C.P. Rodines 40, 106, 110—restrainers for the acid, pickling of iron, steel and stainless ferrous alloys; ICI; 1938; 215 x 138 mm; 20 pp; Monotype Gill Sans, Monotype Bodoni, Monotype Baskerville; Monochrome half-tones, 2-colour tables; Stock: toned art; Binding: cased, thread-sewn. Booklet

Imperial Chemical Industries Limited—a short account of the activities of the company; ICI; February 1929; 255 x 190 mm; 48 pp; Monotype Caslon, Imprint; Monochrome half-tones, one full-colour half-tone; Stock: toned wove; Binding: Rexine leather cloth, an ICI product, thread-sewn. Book

ICI in Focus; ICI; 1965; 210 x 147 mm; 68 pp; Monotype Baskerville; Full-colour half-tones, diagrams; Stock: toned wove, with toned and textured dividing papers; Binding: hard-cased, square backed, thread-sewn. Book

IRVINE A. S., *A History of the Alkali Division (formerly Brunner, Mond & Co)—a booklet for newly joined managerial staff;* ICI; 1950; 204 x 138 mm; 56 pp; Monotype Bembo; Monochrome half-tones; Stock: toned wove and art; Binding: hard-cased, dust-jacket, thread-sewn. Book

Landmarks of the Plastics Industry—1862–1962; ICI; 242 x 162 mm; 128 pp; Monotype Baskerville; Full-colour and monochrome half-tones; Stock: toned art; Binding: hard-cased, thread-sewn. Book

The Metals Division of Imperial Chemicals Industries Limited; ICI; 1949; 247 x 180 mm; 34 pp; Monotype Bodoni, Monotype Baskerville; Full-colour illustrations by Henry Rushbury, monochrome illustrations by Ruth Hurley; Stock: toned wove; Binding: hard-cased, thread-sewn. Book

MILES F. A., *A History of Research in the Nobel Division of ICI*; ICI; 1955; 214 x 138 mm; 210 pp; Monotype Imprint; Monochrome half-tones and line illustrations; Stock: toned wove and art; Binding: hard-cased, thread-sewn. Book

Nobel Industries Limited—a record of Nobel Exhibits at the British Empire Exhibition 1924; Nobel Industries; 1924; 305 x 207 mm; 52 pp; Monochrome half-tones and line illustrations; Caslon; Stock: toned art; Binding: hard-cased, thread-sewn. Book

The Neutralisation of Chrome Leather; ICI; 1935; 184 x 118 mm; 24 pp; Bauersche Giesserei Beton, Monotype Bodoni; Monochrome Tables, tipped-in leather sample; Stock: toned wove; Binding: cased, thread-sewn. Booklet

Notes on First Aid in Industrial Injuries—section 1; ICI, Medical Services; 1934; 170 x 114 mm; 52 pp; Monotype Gill Sans, Monotype Imprint, Monotype Bold Face; Monochrome half-tones; Stock: toned art and wove; Binding: cased, thread-sewn. Booklet

An Outline of the Chemistry and Technology of the Dyestuffs Industry; ICI; 1968; 215 x 139 mm; 88 pp; Linotype Baskerville and Linotype Helvetica; Stock: white wove; Binding: separate cover, thread-sewn. Paperback book

PEACOCK F. C. (ed), *Jealott's Hill—fifty years of agricultural research, 1928–1978*; ICI; 1978; 230 x 150 mm; 160 pp; Phototypeset in Baskerville; Monochrome and full-colour half-tones, and monochrome line illustrations; Stock: Paladin 115 g/m^2; Binding: hard-cased, thread-sewn. Book

Pharmaceutical Research in ICI—1936–57; Introduction by Sir Alexander Fleck (Chairman od ICI); ICI; 1957; 252 x 202 mm; 78 pp; Monotype Bembo; Full-colour and monochrome half-tones and line illustrations; Stock: toned wove; Binding: hard case, thread-sewn. Book

In Search of Colour; ICI, Dyestuffs Division; 1949; 276 x 210 mm; 42 pp; Stephenson Blake Marina Script, Monotype Bembo; full-colour illustrations, map, diagrams; Designed and illustrated by Vernon Shearer and Arthur Smith; Stock: toned book wove; Binding: hard-cased, thread-sewn. Book

SCOTT C. A., *Background of Discovery—pictures of an industrial research unit;* ICI Alkali Division Information Service; December 1959; 305 x 240 mm; 56 pp; Monotype Bembo; Monochrome half--tones; Stock: white art; Binding: case bound, thread-sewn. Book

Under Five Flags—the Story of the Kynoch Works 1862–1962; ICI The Kynoch Press; 1962; 272 x 220 mm; 100 pp; Monotype Grotesque No. 1, Monotype Baskerville; Monochrome half-tones and line illustrations; Stock: Toned, book wove; Binding: hard-cased, thread-sewn. Book

Sulphuric acid—manufacture and uses; ICI; 1955; 210 x 140 mm; 40 pp; Monotype Times; Monochrome half-tones and line illustrations; Stock: toned wove and art; Binding: case bound, thread-sewn. Book

This is Your Concern; ICI; 1947; 183 x 120 mm; 70 pp; Monotype Garamond; Stock: toned wove; Binding: cover with flaps, square backed, thread-sewn. Book

This is Our Concern; ICI; 1955; 210 x 135 mm; 92 pp; Monotype Bembo, Monotype Times; Stock: toned book wove; BInding: separate cover, thread-sewn. Paperback book

This is Our Concern; ICI; 1961; 246 x 182 mm; 80 pp; Monotype Baskerville, Lettergieterij Amsterdam Annonce Grotesque; Full-colour illustrations; Stock: toned wove; Binding: cover with flaps, square backed, thread-sewn; Book

This is Our Concern; ICI; 1962; 246 x 182 mm; 80 pp; Monotype Baskerville, Lettergieterij Amsterdam Annonce Grotesque; Full-colour illustrations; Stock: toned wove; Binding: cover with flaps, square backed, thread-sewn; Book

Titanium Abstract Bulletin [abstracts 5918–6063] Volume 6, No. 1; ICI Metals Limited; July–August 1960; 240 x 148 mm; 318 pp; Monotype Gill Sans, Monotype Times; Tables; Stock: toned wove; Binding: cased, thread-sewn. Book

Water Sterilisation; ICI: 1937; 210 x 135 mm; 52 pp; Monotype Gill Sans; Monotype Garamond, Stempel Ratio Free Initials; Monochrome half-tones, 2-colour tables; Stock: toned wove; Binding: cased, thread-sewn. Booklet

Zip Fasteners—an instructional handbook for teachers; Lightning Fasteners (a subsidiary of IMI); 1966; 204 x 330 mm; 44 pp; Monotype Univers; Two colour line illustrations; Stock: toned, wove; Binding: lever-arch. Book

Kynoch Limited   *The Colliery Fireman and his Duties;* Nobel Industries Limited; 1925; 208 x 127 mm; 86 pp; Monotype Imprint; Monochrome half-tones and line illustrations, full-colour half-tones; Stock: toned, art; Binding: hard-cased, thread-sewn. Book

Kynoch Limited Birmingham—notes on Kynoch's war work; Lion Works Witton; 23 March 1918; 216 x 135 mm; 18 pp; Stephenson Blake Caslon; Stock: toned, hand-made, deckle-edged; Binding: cased, thread-sewn. Booklet

Kynoch Ammunition and Gunpowder—price list; Kynoch Limited; 1900–1901; 214 x 138 mm; 70 pp; De Vinne, Grotesque, Caledonian italic, hand-lettering; Monochrome line illustrations; Stock: toned art; Binding: cased, thread-sewn. Booklet

Shooting Notes and Comments—a book containing matters of interest to sportsmen; Kynoch Limited; First edition, July 1910 [limited to 200 copies], re-printed September 1910; 215 x 136 mm [limited edition] 182 x 120 mm[ordinary edition]; 94 pp; Stephenson Blake Caslon, Cheltenham Old Style; Monochrome half-tones and line illustrations; Stock: toned, laid; Binding: hard-cased, thread-sewn. Book

Sporting Ammunition: Nobel Industries Limited; 1925; 240 x 182 mm; 120 pp; Stephenson Blake Caslon; Monochrome half-tones, illustrations, tabular matter; Stock: toned art; Binding: separate cover, thread-sewn. Book

The Witton Book of Non-ferrous Metals and Alloys; Kynoch Limited and Kings Norton Metal Company Limited, Birmingham, constituent companies of Nobel Industries Limited; 1924; 171 x 116 mm; 48 pp; Stephenson Blake Caslon; Monotype Imprint; Monochrome half-tones, tables, 2-colour graphs; Stock: toned, art; Binding: hard-cased, thread-sewn; Booklet

Kynoch Press   *An Example of Printing from the Kynoch Press—notes on Kynoch war work*; Kynoch Press, Lion Works, Witton; February 1919; 221 x 142 mm; 20 pp; Stephenson Blake Caslon, floral initials; Monochrome half-tones, single-coloured tail-piece; Paper: toned laid; Binding: cased, thread-sewn. Booklet

IMI Kynoch Press—printers for one hundred years; Kynoch Press; 1979; 207 x 207 mm; 152 pp; Linotype Univers; Monochrome line illustrations; Stock: white laid; Binding: hard case, dust jacket, thread-sewn. Book

Magnesium Elektron Limited   BULIAN Walter, FAHRENHORST Eberhard, *Metallography of Magnesium and its Alloys* (a translation from the German by the technical staffs of F. A. Hughes and Company Limited and Magnesium Elektron Limited of *Metallographie des Magnesiums und seiner technischen Legierungen*); F. A. Hughes and Company Limited, London; 1945; 230 x 148 mm; 128 pp; Monotype Times; Monochrome half-tones, tables; Stock: toned art; Binding: hard-cased, thread-sewn. Book

Magnesium Alloys (compiled for the use of engineers and designers by the producers, suppliers and manufacturers of Elecktron Magnesium Alloys); Magnesium Elektron Limited; 1947; 243 x 160 mm; 224 pp; Bauersche Giesserei Beton,

Monotype Imprint; Monochrome half-tones and line illustrations; Stock: toned art; Binding: hard-cased, thread-sewn. Book

PAMPHLETS AND LEAFLETS

British Broadcasting Corporation

BEVAN Edwyn R., *Our Debt to the Past* (Broadcast Talks Pamphlet No 608, with a bibliography); British Broadcasting Corporation; 1932; 215 x 136 mm; 56 pp; Monotype Baskerville; Cover illustrated by McKnight Kauffer; Monochrome half-tones; Stock: toned, art; Binding: separate cover, thread-sewn. Pamphlet

BURT Cyril, *How the Mind Works* (Broadcast Talks Pamphlet, with a bibliography); British Broadcasting Corporation; 1932; 215 x 136 mm; 60 pp; Monotype Baskerville; Cover illustrated by McKnight Kauffer; Monochrome half-tones and diagrams, one cull colour diagram; Stock: toned, art; Binding: separate cover, thread-sewn. Pamphlet

CARRINGTON Noel (intro), *Design in Modern Life* (Broadcast Talks Pamphlet; synopsis of broadcast talks with an introduction) British Broadcasting Corporation; 1933; 215 x 136 mm; 48 pp; Monochrome half-tones; Stock: toned, art and book wove; Binding: separate cover, thread-sewn. Pamphlet

CAVE Dr Sydney, *Living Religions of the East* (Broadcast Talks Pamphlet No. 70, with bibliography); British Broadcasting Corporation; 1931; 215 x 136 mm; 44 pp; American Type Founders Cloister, Monotype Cloister, Monotype Imprint; Monochrome half-tones; Stock: toned, art; Binding: separate cover, thread-sewn. Pamphlet

COUPLAND R., T*he British Empire* (Broadcast Talks Pamphlet, with bibliography); British Broadcasting Corporation; 1933; 215 x 136 mm; 56 pp; Monotype Gill Sans Shadow,, Monotype Gill Sans, Monotype Baskerville; Monochrome half-tones and maps; Stock: toned, art; Binding: separate cover, thread-sewn. Pamphlet

DE LAGUNA Maria, *Spanish—a second year course 1933–43* (Broadcast Talks Pamphlet, with a bibliography); British Broadcasting Corporation; 1933; 215 x 136 mm; 32 pp; Monotype Baskerville; Stock: toned, wove; Binding: separate cover, thread-sewn. Pamphlet

GLEADOWE R. M. Y., *British Art* (Broadcast Talks Pamphlet, with an introductory essay by G. W. Constable); British Broadcasting Corporation; 1934; 248 x 183 mm; 44 pp; Ravilious Initials, Monotype Gill Sans, Monotype Baskerville; Monochrome half-tones; Cover illustration by Eric Ravilious; Stock: toned, wove; Binding: separate cover, thread-sewn. Pamphlet

HILTON John, *Industrial Britain* (Broadcast Talks Pamphlet; an essay introduction to 12 talks); British Broadcasting Corporation; 1934; 215 x 136 mm; 48 pp; Hand lettering, Monotype Baskerville, Monotype Gill Sans; Monochrome half-tones, graphs; Stock: toned, art; Binding: separate cover, thread-sewn. Pamphlet

JENKS Edward, *The Law of the Land* (Broadcast Talks Pamphlet No 609, with a bibliography); British Broadcasting Corporation; 1932; 215 x 136 mm; 42 pp;

Monotype Baskerville; Cover illustrated by McKnight Kauffer; Monochrome half-tones; Stock: toned, art; Binding: separate cover, thread-sewn. Pamphlet

KROEMER Max, *German—a first year course 1933–34* (Broadcast Talks Pamphlet with a bibliography); British Broadcasting Corporation; 1933; 215 x 136 mm; 32 pp; Monotype Baskerville; Stock: toned, book wove; Binding: separate cover, thread-sewn. Pamphlet

LEVY, Professor H., *The Changing World [3] Science in Perspective* (Broadcast Symposium); British Broadcasting Corporation; 1931/32; 215 x 136 mm; 48 pp; Monotype Baskerville, Berthold Vesta; Monochrome line illustrations; Stock: toned art; Binding: self-cover, wire stitched. Pamphlet

MCDOUGALL Prof William, *Love and Hate—the story of the energies of men and nations* (Broadcast Talks Pamphlet No 68); British Broadcasting Corporations; 1931; 215 x 136 mm; 28 pp; Stempel Ratio Free Initials, Stephenson Blake Fat Face, Monotype Imprint; Monochrome line illustrations; Stock: toned, art; Binding: separate cover, thread-sewn. Pamphlet

MACMURRAY John, *The Modern Spirit* (Broadcast Talks Pamphlet; an introductory essay to 12 talks on some members of the modern spirit); British Broadcasting Corporation; 1933; 215 x 136 mm; 48 pp; Monotype Baskerville; Cover illustration by McKnight Kauffer; Monochrome half-tones; Stock: toned, art; Binding: separate cover, thread-sewn

NEVINSON Henry W., *Ourselves—an essay on the national character* (Broadcast Talks Pamphlet, with a bibliography); British Broadcasting Corporation; 1933; 215 x 136 mm; 48 pp; Monotype Baskerville; Monochrome half-tones; Stock: toned, art; Binding: separate cover, thread-sewn. Pamphlet

NEWTON Eric, *An Approach to Art* (a pictorial guide to 12 broadcast talks and discussion on the artist and his public); British Broadcasting Corporation; 1935; 146 x 180 mm; 40 pp; Hand-drawn lettering by Blair Hughes-Stanton, Stempel Ratio Free Initials, Monotype Baskerville; Monochrome half-tones; Stock: toned, book wove and art; Binding: separate cover, thread-sewn. Pamphlet

RUSHBROOK-WILLIAMS Prof. L. F., *India* (Broadcast Talks Pamphlet No. 67, with a bibliography); British Broadcasting Corporation; 1931; 215 x 136 mm; 44 pp; Stephenson Blake Open Titling, Stempel Ratio Free Initials, Monotype Baskerville; Monochrome half-tones and graphs; Stock: toned, art; Binding: separate cover, thread-sewn. Pamphlet

TOYNBEE Arnold and HAMMOND J. L. Le B., *Britain and the Modern World Order* (Broadcast Talks Pamphlet No. 571); British Broadcasting Corporation; 1932; 215 x 136 mm; 48 pp; Fry's Baskerville, Monotype Baskerville; Monochrome half-tones and line illustrations; Stock: toned, art; Binding: separate cover, thread-sewn. Pamphlet

VIVIAN Mrs S. P., GREENWOOD Prof. M., GRANVILLE-EDGE Major P., *The Story of the Census and its Meaning* (Broadcast Talks Pamphlet No 65; copy of the census form is included [the form is not printed at Kynoch Press]); British Broadcasting Corporation; 1931; 215 x 136 mm; 28 pp; Bauersche Giesserei Black Letter, Ludlow Delphian Titling, Milner Initials, Monotype Gill Sans, Monotype Imprint; Monochrome half-tones; Stock: toned, art; Binding: separate cover, thread-sewn. Pamphlet

WATSON Seton, DANUBAIN R. W., *Clues to European Peace* (Broadcast Talks Pamphlets; synopsis of 10 talks with a bibliography); British Broadcasting Corporation; 1935; 215 x 136 mm; 48 pp; Bauersche Giesserei Corvinus, Monotype Baskerville, Monotype Gill Sans; Monochrome half-tones and maps; Stock: toned, art; Binding: separate cover, thread-sewn. Pamphlet

The World and Ourselves (Broadcast Talks Pamphlet No 69; on themes of 6 talks on 6 European countries) British Broadcasting Corporation; 1931; 215 x 136 mm; 40 pp; Hand drawn initials, Stempel Ratio Free Initials, Monotype Imprint; Monochrome half-tones; Stock: toned, art; Binding: separate cover, thread-sewn. Pamphlet

Local and national industry

The Birmingham Advisory Art Committee, Annual Reports; 1925–28; 240 x 180 mm; 8 pp; Stephenson Blake Caslon, Monotype Caslon; Stock: toned, art; Binding: self cover, thread-sewn. Leaflet

The Birmingham Law Society's Library (an appendix to the Society's Report for the year ending 31 December 1934); Birmingham Law Society; 1935; 210 x 140 mm; 24 pp; Monotype Bembo; Monochrome half-tones; Stock: toned, art; Binding: separate cover, thread-sewn. Pamphlet

Brierley Crystal; Stevens and Williams Limited, Brierley Hill, Staffordshire; 207 x 153 mm; Monotype Gill Sans; Monochrome half-tones; Stock: toned art; Binding: wallet with 12 loose leaf inserts

The Chemist in the Midlands (exhibition catalogue); Royal Institute of Chemistry of Great Britain and Ireland; 1948; 213 x 138 mm; 18 pp; Monotype Baskerville; Stock: toned, wove; Binding: separate cover, thread-sewn. Leaflet

COATES R. H. *In Memoriam—Robert Hall Best* (an address delivered by R. H. Coates at the funeral service, Hampstead Road Baptist Church on Thursday June 4th 1925); 1925; 220 x 130 mm; 8 pp; Monotype Garamond, and display initials; Monochrome half-tone; Stock: toned, laid, deckle-edged; Binding: self cover, thread-sewn. Leaflet

COSSONS W. E., *The Bournville Dramatic Society 1912–1933* (a chronical compiled by W. E. Cossons and issued by the Society in commemoration of the 21st anniversary of its foundation, 8 November 1933); The Bournville Dramatic Society; 1933; 250 x 182 mm; 24 pp; Fry's Baskerville, Monotype Baskerville; Monochrome half-tones and line illustrations; Stock: toned, art; Binding: separate cover, thread-sewn. Pamphlet

FERGUSON R. W., ABBOTT A., *Day Continuation Schools* (Pamphlet No. 22; with an address by Lord Eustace Percy; a foreword by G. Cadbury; a bibliography; issued in connection with the 21st anniversary of the Day Continuation School carried on at Bournville by the Education Authority of the City of Birmingham); Works Publications Department Bournville and Sir Isaac Pitman and Sons Limited; 1935; 210 x 130 mm; 92pp; Stephenson Blake Caslon, Monotype Imprint; Monochrome half-tones and diagrams; Stock: toned, art; Binding: separate cover, thread-sewn. Pamphlet

The Lygon Arms, Broadway, Worcestershire; Russell and Sons; 189 x 125 mm; 4 pp; Monotype Bembo; Ravilious illustration; Stock: toned wove; Binding: Separate cover, wire stitched. Pamphlet

MANDER G. B., *A Visit to Bobbington and Enville* (by the Wolverhampton Archeological Society; some notes circulated among members by their president); Wolverhampton Archeological Society; 1924 and 1926; 228 x 149; 12 pp; Milner Initials, Monotype Baskerville; Stock: toned, laid; Binding: self cover, thread-sewn. Leaflets

Motor Control and Power Distribution Centres—indoor and outdoor; G.E.C. (Engineering) Limited, Birmingham; 1964; 297 x 210 mm; 22 pp; Monotype Grotesque No 1; Stock: toned art; Binding: separate cover, wire stitched. Pamphlet

HANDFORTH, J. R., TOWNS ROBINSON, J., *The Manufacture and Production of Aluminium Alloy Forgings and Stampings;* Issued by the Technical Committee Wrought Alloys Association, Birmingham; 1945; 245 x 187 mm; 48 pp; Monotype Caslon, Monotype Imprint, Monotype Bold Face; Stock: toned wove; Binding: separate cover, wire stitched. Pamphlet

In Memory of Arthur Chamberlain (born Highbury, London April 11th, 1842; died Cadhay House, Ottery St Mary, October 19th, 1913); 1913; 214 x 170 mm; 16 pp; Stephenson Blake Caslon, hand drawn initials; Stock: toned, laid; Binding: hard-cased, vellum, thread-sewn; Booklet for memorial service

Salient-pole Synchronous Motors; G.E.C. (Engineering) Birmingham; 297 x 210 mm; 14 pp; Monotype Univers; Monochrome half-tones, diagrams; Stock: toned art; Binding: separate cover, wire stitched. Pamphlet

University Service and Dedication of War Memorial; The University of Birmingham; 8 October 1922; 225 x 146 mm; 20 pp; Monotype Garamond; Stock: De Haesbeek toned laid, deckle edged; Binding: self cover. Leaflet.

The Aluminium Development Association—aims and objectives; The Aluminium Development Association; August 1946; 220 x 142 mm; 16 pp; Monotype Baskerville; Stock: toned wove; Binding: separate cover, thread-sewn. Pamphlets

Die Britischen Inseln—Shakespeare Land und Westliches Mittelengland; 1930; 229 x 101 mm [folded], 229 x 404 [flat]; 8 pp; Monotype Gill Sans Monotype Imprint, Blackletter Shaded, Bauersche Giesserei Beton; Duo-tones; Stock: toned art; Binding: 3 folds. Leaflet

Die Britischen Inseln: Oxford die Cotswolds—die taler der severn und Wye; 1930; 229 x 101 mm [folded], 229 x 404 [flat]; 8 pp; Hand-drawn lettering, Bauersche Giesserei Beton, Monotype Gill Sans; Monochrome half-tones, map; Stock: toned art; Binding: 3 folds. Leaflet

Elektron' Magnesium Review and Abstracts (Volume III No 1–Volume VIII No 1–4); Magnesium Elektron Limited and F. A. Hughes and Company Limited, London; September 1943–December 1952; 206 x 135 mm;   28 pp each number; Monotype Perpetua Titling, Monotype Times; Monochrome half-tones, graphs, line illustration, table; Stock: toned, art; Binding: Self-cover, thread-sewn. Leaflets

Kronos Titanium Pigments (pamphlet describing the factory, organisation and products); British Titanium Products Company Limited, Billingham; 1934; 266 x 180 mm; 16 pp; Ludlow Tempo, Monotype Garamond, Monotype Gill Sans; Monochrome half-tones, tipped-in; Stock: toned, laid; Binding: separate cover, thread-sewn. Pamphlet

Research Laboratories (for investigations in electrical insulation and transition); Callender's Cable and Construction Company Limited; 1934; 245 x 180 mm; 44 pp; Hand drawn lettering, Monotype Gill Sans, Monotype Baskerville, Klingspor Prisma; Monochrome half-tones, duo-tones, monochrome line illustrations; Designed and printed by Kynoch Press. The photographs have been taken by Maurice Beck; The plates in photogravure have been engraved and printed by the Sun Engraving Company; The cover design is by Gerard Baker and Charles Wormald; Stock: toned, art; Binding: separate cover, thread-sewn. Pamphlet

Roads around the World—a career with Limmer and Trinidad Company Limited; Limmer and Trinidad Company Limited, Trinidad Lake House, London; *circa* 1960s; 199 x 210 mm; 12 pp; American Type Founders Cooper Black, Monotype Univers; Monochrome half-tones; Stock: toned, art; Binding: separate cover, wire stitched. Pamphlet

Some Facts about Copper Tubing for those interested in Houses; Copper Development Association; 1934; 126 x 226 mm; 22 pp; Hand drawn letters, Monotype Gill Sans; Monochrome half-tones; Stock: toned, art; Binding: spiral binding. Pamphlet

Thermit repair Process for Worn Tracks; Thermit Limited [a constituent company of Nobel Industries]; 1921; 217 x 135 mm; 8 pp; Stephenson Blake Caslon; Monochrome half-tones; Stock: toned, art; Binding: separate cover, thread-sewn. Pamphlet

Coronation Planting Committee   ADAMS, Thomas, *Playparks—with suggestions for their design, equipment and planting;* The Coronation Planting Committee; 226 x 150 mm; 56 pp; Ludlow Bodoni, Monotype Bembo; Monochrome half-tones; Stock: toned art; Binding: Separate cover, wire stitched. Pamphlet

For King and Countryside—towards a more beautiful Britain; The Coronation Planting Committee; 228 x 152 mm; 20 pp; Stephenson Blake Fat Face, Stevens Shanks Fat Face, Ludlow Bodoni, Monotype Bembo; Monochrome half-tones; Stock: toned art; Binding: separate cover, wire stitched. Pamphlet

The Village—how to make and keep it beautiful; The Coronation Planting Committee; 277 x 152 mm; 24 mm; Ludlow Bodoni, Monotype Bembo; Monochrome half-tones; Stock: toned art; Binding: self cover, wire stitched. Leaflet

Coventry Cathedral Festival   *Coventry Cathedral Festival—Iolanthe;* (Programme); Coventry Cathedral and the Arts Council of Great Britain; 1962; 230 x 166 mm (folded) 130 x 498 mm (open); 6 pp; Monotype Grotesque No 1, Monotype Bembo; Monochrome half-tones; Stock: gray, wove; Binding: folded x 2. Leaflet

Coventry Cathedral Festival—La Traviata; (Programme); Coventry Cathedral and the Arts Council of Great Britain; 1962; 230 x 166 mm (folded) 130 x 498 mm (open); 6 pp; Monotype Grotesque No 1, Monotype Bembo; Monochrome half-tones; Stock: gray, wove; Binding: folded x 2. Leaflet

Coventry Cathedral Festival—The Raising of Lazarus; (Programme); Coventry Cathedral and the Arts Council of Great Britain; 1962; 230 x 166 mm (folded) 130 x 498 mm (open); 6 pp; Monotype Grotesque No 1, Monotype Bembo; Monochrome half-tones; Stock: gray, wove; Binding: folded x 2. Leaflet

Coventry Cathedral Festival—International Festival of Folk Dance; (Programme); Coventry Cathedral and the Arts Council of Great Britain; 1962; 230 x 166 mm (folded) 130 x 498 mm (open); 6 pp; Monotype Grotesque No 1, Monotype Bembo; Monochrome half-tones; Stock: gray, wove; Binding: folded x 2. Leaflet

Coventry Cathedral Festival—War Requiem; Coventry Cathedral Festival and the Arts Council of Great Britain; 1962; 356 x 204 mm; 2pp; Monotype Grotesque No 1, Monotype Bembo; Stock: gray, wove; Binding: single sheet

Coventry Cathedral Festival—a service for the servants of the church; Coventry Cathedral Festival and the Arts Council of Great Britain; 1962; Monotype Grotesque No 1, Monotype Bembo. Leaflet

FORTUNE Dr Nigel (assistant editor) *Coventry Cathedral Festival* (Programme) Coventry Cathedral Festival and the Arts Council of Great Britain; 1962; 240 x 185 mm; 96 pp; Monotype Grotesque No 1, Monotype Bembo; Monochrome half-tones and line illustrations; Stock: toned, laid; Binding: separate cover, square backed, glued. Pamphlet

Design and Industry Association

WILLIAMS-ELLIS Clough, *The DIA Cautionary Guide to St Albans;* Design and Industry Association; 1929; 240 x 150 mm; 32 pp; Milner Initials, American Type Founders Cloister, Monotype Cloister; Monochrome half-tones; Stock: toned, book wove; Binding: separate cover, thread-sewn. Pamphlet

WILLIAMS-ELLIS Clough, *The DIA Cautionary Guide to Carlisle;* Design and Industry Association; 1930; 214 x 135 mm; 24 pp; Fry's Baskerville, Monotype Baskerville, Ratio Free Initials; Monochrome half-tones, map; Stock: toned, art; Binding: separate cover, thread-sewn. Pamphlet

Dryad Press
Leicester

A Catalogue of Books and other Publications on Handicrafts; The Dryad Press; 1930–31; 215 x 138 mm; 32 pp; Monotype Gill Sans, Monotype Baskerville, Stephenson Blake Baskerville, Ludlow Tempo; Stock: toned wove; Binding: separate cover, wire stitched. Pamphlet.

CRAMPTON C., MOCHRIE E., *Rush Work;* The Dryad Press, Leicester; 1926 and 1931; 214 x 135 mm; 36 pp; Monotype Garamond; Monochrome line and half-tones; Stock: toned wove and art; Binding: separate cover, thread-sewn. Pamphlet

Dryad Handicraft Materials, No 1—basket making, willow work, stool seating, rush work, rafia work; Dryad Handicrafts, Leicester; 1931–32; 215 x 137 mm; 33 pp; Ludlow Tempo, Monotype Imprint, Monotype Bold Face; Monochrome half-tones and line; Stock: toned wove; Binding: separate cover, wire stitched. Pamphlet

Henry Hope and Sons Limited
Birmingham

A Burning Question [publication no 100]: Henry Hope and Sons Limited; 1932; 212 x 135 mm; 36 pp; American Type Founders Cloister, Monotype Garamond; Colour line illustrations; Stock: toned, book wove; Binding: separate cover, thread-sewn. Pamphlet

Hope's Cottage Casements for Hanging to Wood Frames; Henry Hope and Sons Limited; 1923; 290 x 220 mm; 12 pp; Stephenson Blake Caslon, Monotype Caslon; Monochrome half-tones; Stock: toned, art; Binding: self-cover, single leaves, brass studs; Leaflet

Hope's Departments; Henry Hope and Sons Limited; circa 1920; 202 x 122 mm; 4 pp; Monotype Garamond; Monochrome half-tones; Stock: toned, art; Binding: single sheet folded x 1; Leaflet

Hope's Double Patent Glazing; Henry Hope and Sons Limited; 1953; 266 x 177 mm; 8 pp; Monotype Perpetua Titling, Monotype Perpetua; Monochrome half-tones and line illustrations; Stock; toned, art; Binding: self cover, thread-sewn. Leaflet

Hope's Glass Roofing; Henry Hope and Sons Limited; 1950; 266 x 180 mm; 48 pp; Fry's Baskerville, Monotype Baskerville, Stephenson Blake Caslon; Monochrome illustrations; Stock: toned, book wove; Binding: separate cover, thread-sewn. Pamphlet

Hope's Hardware; Henry Hope and Sons Limited; 1921; 282 x 220 mm; 72 pp; Hand drawn letters; Stephenson Blake Caslon, Monotype Caslon; Monochrome half-tones; Stock: toned, art; Binding: separate cover, thread-sewn. Pamphlet

Hope's Lok'd-bar Sash; Henry Hope and Sons Limited; 1927; 248 x 178 mm; 4 pp; Stephenson Blake Caslon, Monotype Garamond; Monochrome half-tones and line illustrations; Stock: toned, art; Binding: single sheet folded x 1; leaflet

Hope's Patent Glass Roofing; Henry Hope and Sons Limited; 1926; 223 x 126 mm; 4 pp; Monotype Cloister, American Type Founders Cloister; Monochrome half-tones; Stock: toned, art; Binding: single sheet, folded x 1; Leaflet

Hope's Standard Casements with Leaded Glass; Henry Hope and Sons Limited; 1926; 223 x 126 mm; 6 pp; American Type Founders Cloister, Monotype Imprint; Monochrome half-tones and line illustrations; Stock: toned, art; Binding: single sheet folded x 2; Leaflet

Hope's Standard Casements and Leaded Glass [list no 51]; Henry Hope and Sons Limited; 1927; 202 x 124 mm; 14 pp; Monotype Baskerville; Colour illustrations, monochrome diagrams; Stock: toned wove; Binding: separate cover, thread-sewn. Pamphlet

Hope's Standard Lanterns and Skylights; Henry Hope and Sons Limited; 1953; 266 x 178 mm; 6 pp; Fry's Baskerville, Monotype Baskerville; Monochrome half-tones and line illustrations; Stock: toned, art; Binding: folded x 2. Leaflet

Hope's Standard Steel Curtain Walling; Henry Hope and Sons Limited; 1967; 210 x 297 mm; 4 pp; Blue duo-tones and black line illustrations; Stock: toned, art; Binding: folded x 2. Leaflet

Hope's Standard Windows; Henry Hope and Sons Limited; 1927; 202 x 127 mm; 8 pp; Monotype Baskerville; Monochrome line illustrations; Stock: toned, wove; Binding: self cover, thread-sewn. Leaflet

Hope's Work at Wembly (pamphlet number 102)*;* Henry Hope and Sons Limited; 1924; 202 x 130 mm; 12 pp; Monotype Garamond; Monochrome half-tones; Stock: toned, art; Binding: separate cover, thread-sewn. Pamphlet

Henry Hope and Sons Limited, Works Advisory Committee; Henry Hope and Sons Limited; *circa* 1952; 140 x 110 mm; 8 pp; Monotype Perpetua, Monotype Times; Stock: toned, book wove; Binding: separate cover, wire stitched. Pamphlet

When You Build [publication no 200]; Henry Hope and Sons; 1930; 300 x 210 mm; 44 pp; Monochrome half-tones and line illustrations, Stock: toned wove; Binding: separate cover, thread-sewn. Pamphlet

Your Windows—the eyes of your home; henry Hope and Sons Limited; 1928; 202 x 124 mm; 32 pp; American Type Founders Garamond, Fry's Baskerville, Monotype Baskerville; full-colour illustrations by Mrs G Baraclough, monochrome half-tones; Stock: toned, book wove; Binding: separate cover, thread-sewn. Pamphlet

Hope's 'Z' Standard Windows—a new range for modern buildings; Henry Hope and Sons Limited; 1953; 264 x 176 mm; 6 pp; Monotype Albertus, Monotype Baskerville; Monochrome half-tones; Stock: toned, art; Binding: folded x 2. Leaflet

Kynoch Limited   *The Kynoch Smokeless Sporting Powder*; Kynoch Limited; 1898; 286 x 225 mm; 4 pp; De Vinne, Grotesque, Script; Monochrome trade mark; Stock: toned wove; Binding: self cover, 1 x folded. Leaflet

Kynoch Limited Price List of Military and Sporting Cartridges and Gunpowders, Revolver Cartridges, Percussion Caps, Gun Wads; Kynoch Limited; circa 1898; landscape; 74 pp; De Vinne, Antique No 5, Caslon, Grotesque, Caledonian Italic, Floral Letters No 5; Monochrome half-tones, line illustration, tables. Price list

Kynoch Limited Price List of Military and Sporting Cartridges and Gunpowders, Revolver Cartridges, Percussion Caps, Gun Wads; Kynoch Limited; 1898–99; landscape; 74 pp; De Vinne, Antique No 5, Caslon, Grotesque, Caledonian Italic, Floral Letters No 5; Monochrome half-tones, line illustration, tables. Price list

Kynoch Limited, Military and Sporting Cartridges and Gunpowders—price list; Kynoch Limited; 1901–1902; 70 pp; De Vinne, Grotesque; Monochrome and colour illustrations and diagrams, tables. Price list

Kynoch Limited Price List; Kynoch Limited; 1902–3; 48pp; Stephenson Blake Caslon, Old Face Bold; Monochrome and colour illustrations, tables. Price list

Kynoch Limited Price List of Sporting and Military Cartridges, Powders, Wads, Caps, Air Rifles and Sundries; Kynoch Limited; 1911; 46 pp; Stephenson Blake Caslon; Monochrome and colour half-tones, line illustrations, diagrams and tables. Price list

Kynoch Limited Price List of Sporting and Military Cartridges, Powders, Wads, Caps and Sundries; Kynoch Limited; 1913; 24 pp; Stephenson Blake Caslon; Monochrome and colour half-tones, line illustrations, diagrams and tables. Price list

An Account of the Activities of Kynoch Limited; 1920s; 140 x 108 mm; 8 pp; Monotype Baskerville; Stock: toned wove; Binding: separate cover, wire stitched. Pamphlet

Catalogue de la Machinerie Necessaire a la Fabrication de Cartouches de Fusil; Kynoch Ltd; 1919; 284 x 224 mm; Stephenson Blake Caslon; Monochrome half-tones; Stock: toned art; Binding: Separate cover. gummed. Pamphlet

CHAMBERLAIN, Arthur, *Free Trade and Protection* (a few words to the Witton work people of Kynoch Limited, 21st December 1905); Kynoch Limited, Lion Works, Witton; 1905; 226 x 135 mm; 4 pp; Stephenson Blake Caslon, Windsor; Stock: toned, wove. Binding: folded x 1. Leaflet

Cycle Fittings; Kynoch Limited; 1898; 266 x 213 mm; 20 pp; Monochrome line illustrations; Stock: toned art; Binding: separate cover, wire stitched. Pamphlet

General Factory Rules; Kynoch Limited, Lion Works, Witton, Birmingham; October 1899; 135 x 108 mm; 8 pp; Stephenson Blake Caslon, De Vinne; Stock: toned wove; Binding: self-cover, wire stitched. Leaflet

A Handbook on Clay Target Shooting; Nobel Industries Limited; circa 1921; 217 x 137 mm; 72 pp; Caslon; Monochrome half-tones and line illustrations; Stock: toned art: Binding: separate cover, thread-sewn. Pamphlet

Kynoch Cycles; Kynoch Limited; pre-1920; 220 x 143 mm; 12 pp; Stephenson Blake Caslon; Monochrome half-tones; Stock: toned art; Binding: separate cover, thread-sewn. Pamphlet

Kynoch Bearings and Shaft Fittings; Kynoch Limited; pre-1920; 220 x 143 mm; 30 pp; Stephenson Blake Caslon; Monochrome half-tones; Stock: toned art; Binding: Separate cover, wire stitched. Pamphlet

The Nobeloy Stream-line Bullet; Nobel Industries Limited; January 1924; 214 x 138 mm; 24 pp; Caslon; Monochrome half-tone, line illustrations, diagrams and tables; Stock: Abbey Mills toned laid. Pamphlet

Visit of the Gunmakers Association to the Kynoch Factory; Lion Works Witton; 24 February 1898; 285 x 224 mm; 32 pp; De Vinne, Grotesque; Monochrome half-tones; Stock: toned art; Binding: separate cover, thread-sewn. Pamphlet

Kynoch Press CARRINGTON Noel (ed), *Portmeirion Explained—with pictures*, 1st edition (essays by several hands, with pictures); Kynoch Press; 1931; 184 x 132 mm; 62 pp; Stevens Shanks Fat Face, Stempel Ratio Free Initials, Monotype Bembo; Monochrome half-tones; Stock: toned laid and art; Binding: separate cover, thread-sewn. Pamphlet

CARRINGTON Noel (ed), *Portmeirion Further Explained—with still more pictures*, 2nd edition (essays by several hands, with pictures); Kynoch Press; 1932; 184 x 132 mm; 66 pp; Stevens Shanks Fat Face, Ludlow Caslon, Stempel Ratio Free Initials, Monotype Bembo; Monochrome half-tones; Stock: toned laid and art; Binding: separate cover, thread-sewn. Pamphlet

CARRINGTON Noel (ed), *Portmeirion Still Further Explained—with yet more pictures* (essays by several hands, with an introduction by C. WIlliams-Ellis, third edition revised and enlarged); Kynoch Press; 1935; 180 x 130 mm; 66 pp; Stevens Shanks Fat Face, Ratio Free Initials, Monotype Imprint, Monotype Bembo; Monochrome half-tones, map and tipped-in hotel tarrif; Stock: toned, book wove and art; Binding: separate cover, thread-sewn. Pamphlet

CARRINGTON Noel (ed) *Broadway and the Cotswolds* (with an introduction by H. W. Timperley); Kynoch Press for the Lygon Arms, Broadway; 1933, 1935 and 1938; 215 x 138 mm; 64 pp; Stevens Shanks Fat Face, Ludlow Bodoni, Monotype Bembo; Monochrome half-tones; Stock: toned, book wove and art; Binding: separate cover, thread-sewn. Pamphlet

A Few Notes on Computers and Printing: The Kynoch Press; 1970; 297 x 70 mm [folded], 297 x 210 mm [flat]; 6 pp; Monotype Univers; Stock: white wove; Binding: 2 x folded, Leaflet

Have You Seen This Man?; Kynoch Press; 1960s; 210 x 153 mm; 6 pp; Monochrome half-tones, 3-colour jig-saw puzzle; Stock: high white card; Binding: 2 x folded. Publicity leaflet

IMI Kynoch Press—printers for 100 years; Kynoch Press; 1976; 208 x 210 mm; 90 pp;

Monotype Univers; Stock: high white wove; Binding: hard-cased, thread-sewn; Address book

Integration of Computer Based Information with Printing Techniques; The Kynoch Press and Oriel Computer Services Limited; 1970; 194 x 98 mm [folded] 194 x 776 mm [flat]; 8 pp; Monotype Univers; Stock: white wove; Binding: 4 x folded. Leaflet

Instructions to Compositors and Readers at The Kynoch Press; ICI Kynoch Press; 1935; 152 x 94 mm; 20 pp; Monotype Imprint, Monotype Old Face; Stock: toned, wove; Binding: separate cover, wire stitched. Pamphlet

Kynoch Communications—presents a radical approach to the literature of commerce and industry; Kynoch Press; 1960s; 210 x 153 mm; 12 pp; Monotype Univers; 2-colour graphics; Stock: high white; Binding: self cover, wire stitched. Publicity leaflet

The Kynoch Press Composing Room Chapel Rules; The Kynoch Press; 1947; 124 x 176 mm; 4 pp; Bauersche Giesserei Beton, Monotype Imprint; Stock: toned, card; Binding: folded x 1. Leaflet

*The Kynoch Press—Handbook (*Kynoch International Print, copy preparation, style of the house, proof correcting, typefaces, international paper sizes, business languages, conversion tables); Kynoch Press; 1966; 295 x 107 mm; 50 pp; Monotype Univers; Stock: white board; Binding: separate cover, spiral bound; Pamphlet

The Kynoch Press, Witton, Birmingham, England; 1950s; 224 x 95 mm [folded], 224 x 285 mm [flat]; 6 pp; Monotype Plantin, Monotype Grotesque No 1; Stock: white wove card; Binding 2 x folded. Leaflet

The Kynoch Press, Witton, Birmingham; Kynoch Press; circa 1927; 213 x 160 mm; 12 pp; Stephenson Blake Open Titling, Monotype Baskerville; Monochrome halftones; Stock: toned, wove; Binding: self cover, thread-sewn. Leaflet

Summary of the Paper on the Integration of Computer-based Information with Printing Techniques; Kynoch Press Seminar held at Imperial Chemical House, London; April 1970; 297 x 210 mm; 50 pp; Monotype Grotesque No 1, typescript; Stock: toned wove; Binding: separate cover, glued. Pamphlet

A Specimen of Garamond Type; The Kynoch Press; 'This leaflet was set on the Monotype Machine and sent to you from the Kynoch Press.'; 191 x 128 mm; 4 pp; Monotype Garamond; Stock: toned wove; Folded x 1; Leaflet

Institute of Industrial Supervisors

MORTON Frederick John Burn, *The Supervisor and the Specialists;* Institute of Industrial Supervisors; 1950; 205 x 135 mm; 20 pp; Monotype Times; Stock: toned, wove; Binding: separate cover, thread-sewn. Pamphlet

The Status of the Foreman; Institute of Industrial Supervisors and Industrial Administration Group; 1949; 205 x 135 mm; 20 pp; Monotype Times; Stock: toned, wove; Binding: separate cover, thread-sewn. Pamphlet

Murex Welding Process Limited
London

The Study of Welds and Weld Metal (Leaflet No M3); Murex Welding Processes Limited, London; 1937; 246 x 182 mm; 32 pp; Monotype Garamond; Monochrome halftones; Stock: toned, art; Binding: self cover, wire stitched. Leaflet

Arc Welding on Tram Ways (Leaflet No M5); Murex Welding Processes Limited, London; 1937; 246 x 182 mm; 16 pp; Monotype Garamond; Monochrome halftones; Stock: toned, art; Binding: self cover, wire stitched. Leaflet

Rural Industries Bureau

The Rural Industries of England, Scotland and Wales—an illustrated guide; The Rural Industries Bureau; 1933/34; 215 x 138 mm; 20 pp; Monotype Imprint, Stevens Shanks Fat Face; Monochrome half-tones, cover illustrations by Eric Ravilious; Stock: toned art; Binding: separate cover, wire stitched. Pamphlet

How to Cost a Workshop Plant [leaflet number 31]; Rural Industries Bureau; 1930; 244 x 151 mm; 12 pp; Monotype Gill Sans and Baskerville; Stock: toned wove; Binding: separate cover, wire stitched. Pamphlet

Looking Forward—a few ideas for woodworks, better business with a better plant; Rural Industries Bureau; 1930s; 242 x 152 mm; 4 pp; Monotype Gill Sans, Monotype Baskerville; Stock: toned wove; Binding: self-cover, 1 fold. Leaflet

Rural Industries Catalogue; The Rural Industries Bureau; 1931; 277 x 206 mm; 12 pp; Monotype Gill Sans, Monotype Baskerville; Monochrome half-tones; Stock: toned art; Binding: separate cover, wire stitched. Pamphlet

Trade and Industrial Development Association

London; The Trade and Industrial Development Association of Great Britain and Northern Ireland; 1930; 177 x 110 mm; 64 pp; Monotype Bembo and Gill Sans, Ludlow Tempo, Bauersche Giesserei Beton, Ravilious Initials; Monochrome half-tones, 2-colour cover illustration by John Farleigh; Stock: toned art; Binding: separate cover, wire stitched. Pamphlet

Victoria and Albert Museum
London

A Picture Book in Colour I (Pamphlet No. 197); Victoria and Albert Museum and The Board of Education; 1931; 165 x 105 mm; 62 pp; Monotype Gill Sans; Full-colour half-tones; Stock: toned, art; Binding: separate cover, thread-sewn. Pamphlet

A Picture Book in Colour II (Pamphlet No. 198) Victoria and Albert Museum and The Board of Education; 1931; 110 x 160; 48 pp; Monotype Gill Sans; Full-colour half-tones; Stock: toned, art; Binding: separate cover, thread-sewn. Pamphlet

TRENDELL P. G., *Guide to the Collection of Lace*; Victoria and Albert Museum Department of Textiles, The Board of Education; 1930; 240 x 150 mm; 58 pp; Stephenson Blake Caslon; Monotype Imprint; Monochrome half-tones; Stock: toned, book wove and art; Binding: separate cover, thread-sewn. Pamphlet

[Henry] Wiggins and Company Limited

WIGGINS H., *Laboratory Ware in Pure Nickel*; Henry Wiggins and Company Limited; 1928; 244 x 170 mm; 12 pp; Monotype Gill Sans; Monochrome half-tones; Stock: toned, art; Binding: self cover, thread-sewn. Leaflet

WIGGINS H., *Proprietes et Emplois du Nickel Malleable*; Henry Wiggins and Company Limited; 1928; 244 x 170 mm; 24 pp; Ludlow Tempo, Monotype Gill Sans, Monotype Imprint; Monochrome half-tones; Stock: toned, art; Binding: self cover, thread-sewn. Leaflet

PERIODICALS   *The Crabtree;* J. A. Crabtree and Co., Walsall—electrical equipment of enduring quality; Published every little while by Crabtree Sales Development Department; [volume 5, 1943, no 25–30; volume 7, 1945, no 1–6; volume 8, 1946, no 1–6; volume 9, 1947, no 1–6]; 210 x 134 mm; 12 pp; Monotype Falstaff, Monotype Baskerville, Monotype Bodoni, Monotype Cloister; Monochrome and colour half-tones, 2-colour diagrams, monochrome tables; Stock: toned art; Binding: self-cover, wire stitched

The Crabtree; J. A. Crabtree and Co., Walsall—electrical equipment of enduring quality; Published every little while by Crabtree Sales Development Department; [volume 14, 1952, no 1–16; volume 15, 1953, no 1–3; volume 16, 1954, no 1–3; volume 17, 1955, no 1–4; volume 19, 1957, no 1–3] Monotype Falstaff, Monotype Times [Bauersche Giesserei Cartoon, Stephenson Blake, Chisel, Playbill and Grotesque No 9 for adverts]; Monochrome and colour half-tones, 2-colour diagrams, monochrome tables; stock: toned art; Binding: self-cover, wire stitched

Design for Today; Design and Industry Association, Weekend Publications Limited; May 1933–January 1934; 284 x 210; 38 pp; Bauersche Giesserei Shaded Black, Klingspor Prisma, Monotype Baskerville, Monotype Gill Sans; Monochrome half-tones, monochrome line-illustration; Stock: toned, art; Binding: separate cover, thread-sewn

Endeavour (a quarterly review designed to record the progress of the sciences in the service of mankind): Imperial Chemical Industries; 1942–62; 272 x 196 mm; 1963–76 292 x 205 mm; 48 pp; 1942-62 Monotype Perpetua, Monotype Baskerville, 1963–76 Grotesque and Baskerville; Monochrome half-tones and line illustrations, graphs and tables, full-colour half-tones; Stock: 'readers may be interested to know the advance in applied chemistry which has made its possible to manufacture, from raw materials available in Great Britain, the quality of paper used in Endeavour. Straw has replaced espato grass, and waste wood has replaced imported wood pulp, for no less than 85% of fibrous material. The coating on the paper used for the illustration is, as normally, English china clay from Cornwall.' Binding: separate cover, thread-sewn

Head Office News—a monthly publication issued free to members of Head Office; ICI; 367 x 270 mm; 4 pp; Monochrome half-tones; Stock: news print; Binding: single fold

ICI Magazine; ICI; 1928–1982; 237 x 175 mm [1928–1949]; 273 x 205 mm [1950–1966]; 292 x 205 [1967]; 307 x 220 mm [1969–1971]; 292 x 205 mm [1972–1979]; Monotype Baskerville, Monotype Times, Monotype Imprint, Monotype Univers; Full-colour and monochrome half-tones and line illustrations; Stock: toned art; Binding: self cover, wire stitched

IMI Progress—a review of recent developments; IMI Limited; 1937; 297 x 210 mm; 12 pp; Full-colour half-tones; Stock: toned, art; Binding: self-cover, wire-stitched

The Kynoch Journal—concerning guns and ammunition, LEWIS J.F. P. (ed) Volume I, Nos 1–6; Kynoch Limited; 1889–1900; 287 x 230 mm; 152 pp; Monochrome half-tones and line illustrations; Stock: toned, art; Binding: separate cover, thread-sewn

The Kynoch Journal—concerning guns and ammunition, LEWIS J.F. P. (ed) Volume 11, Nos 7–12; Kynoch Limited; 1900–1901; 287 x 230 mm; 140 pp; Monochrome half-tones and line illustrations; Stock: toned, art; Binding: separate cover, thread-sewn

The Kynoch Journal of Technical Research Volume I, II, II; Kynoch Limited; 1918; 258 x 195 mm; 152 pp, 200 pp, 182 pp; Monochrome half-tones and line illustrations, full-colour diagrams; Stock: toned, wove, unbleached Arnold paper; Binding: separate cover, thread-sewn

The Kynoch Press Notebook and Diary; Kynoch Press; 1929–1963; 1929 D. E. Milner; 1930 Tom Poulton; 1931 J. B. Fletcher; 1932 electrotyped woodblocks; 1933 Eric Ravilious; 1934 Albert Rutherston; 1935 Edward Bawden; 1936 Agnes Miller-Parker; 1937 Mary M. Kessell; 1938 Joan Hyde; 1939 Richard Beck; 1940 Gordon Cullen; 1941 Robert Gibbings; 1942 Russell Leslie; 1947 R. J. Beeching; 1948 John O'Connor; 1949 Douglas Woodall; 1950 Geoffrey Wales; 1951 Elizabeth Skilton; 1952 Doreen Roberts; 1953 Mary Burrows; 1954 Roy Chambers; 1955 Derrick Harris; 1956 Ian Ribbons; 1957 Peggy Morgan; 1958 John Tavener; 1959 Jane Poole; 1960 Colin Sorensen; 1961 Colin Sorensen; 1962 Jean Slee-Smith; 1963 Alan T. May

The Monotype Recorder Volume 22 Number 195 (includes some notes of the 'modern serif and typefaces by Stanley Morison); Monotype Corporation; May and June 1923; 280 x 210 mm; 36 pp; Monotype Bodoni, Monotype Garamond; Monochrome half-tones; Stock: toned, art; Binding: separate cover, thread-sewn

Metals Monitor—supplement; ICI Metals Division; 1956; 271 x 206 mm; 12 pp; Stephenson Blake Chisel, Monotype Bodoni, Monotype Times; Monochrome half-tones and line illustrations; Stock: toned, art; Binding: self-cover, wire stitched

Metals Monitor—supplement, Royal Visit to the Kynoch Works; ICI Metals Division; 271 x 206 mm; 8 pp; Monotype Perpetua Titling, Monotype Bodoni, Monotype Grotesque No 9, Monotype Times; Stock: toned, art; Binding: self cover, wire stitched

Outlook on Agriculture, Volume 1, No 1–6; Editor, E. J. McNaughton; ICI; 1956–57; 266 x 200 mm; Monotype Times, Monotype Garamond; Monochrome and full-colour half-tones, tables and graphs; Stock: toned art and wove; Binding: self-cover, thread-sewn

Plastics Today No. 14, B A R T L E T T K. B., (ICI *Plastics Today* is published quarterly by ICI Plastics, for the interest of all users and potential users of plastics materials and articles made there form. Its purpose is to keep its readers abreast of development in the technology and the uses of the wide range of plastics made by ICI) ; ICI Plastics Division; 1962; 297 x 210 mm; 24 pp; Monotype Grotesque No 1, Monotype Russian Gill; full-colour half-tones; Designed by Fletcher | Forbes | Gill; Stock: toned, art, the coating of which contains 'Butakan' Latex ML501; Binding: Separate cover, wire stitched

Review [Volume 1, No 15] (a brief review of the development of the zinc, copper, and brass industries of Great Britain from AD 1500 to 1900, by W. O. Alexander); Murex Limited, Rainham, Essex; 1955; 216 x 140 mm; 50 pp; Monotype Times; Monochrome line and half-tone; Stock: toned art; Binding: self-cover, wires stitched

End notes

CHAPTER 1

pages 1–9

1   Information relating to George Kynoch and his company was found in the following publications: *Imperial Chemical Industries—a history*, volumes 1 & 2, W. J READER, Oxford University Press, 1970; *Under Five Flags—the story of the Kynoch Works*, Kynoch Press, 1962; and various articles in the *ICI Magazine*—'A short history of Kynoch Limited', July 1928, pp. 27–30; 'Our Mr K', 1962, pp. 149–155.

2   Information on the history of Birmingham was found in the following publications: A *Short history of Birmingham—from its origins to the present day*, CONRAD GILL and CHARLES GRANT ROBERTSON, City of Birmingham Information Bureau, 1938; *Victorian Cities*, ASA BRIGGS, Penguin Books, 1990; *The history of Birmingham—1865–1938*, Volume II, ASA BRIGGS.

3   The extract from Charles Dickens, *The Pickwick Papers*, is taken from the World Classics edition by Oxford University Press, 1988, p. 633.

4   'In 1864 they decided to convert the Enfield rifle into a breech loader, and two years later the model designed by Snider was accepted. This was nearly still-born because no existing cartridge would perform satisfactorily in it, so the Government admitted their need for a "strong gastight cartridge containing its own means of ignition". The answer was the famous Boxer cartridge, which had a case made of thin coils of brass held together with paper, and a brass cap chamber. It was a development of extraordinary importance to Kynoch and Co., both directly and indirectly—first because it initiated an interest in metals as raw materials, second because it paved the way for the solid drawn cartridge case which was to prove Kynoch's most strikingly successful enterprise.' (*Under Five Flags—the story of the Kynoch Works, Witton, Birmingham, 1862–1962*, Imperial Metal Industries, June 1962, pp. 17–18.)

5   The extracts from George Bernard Shaw's *Major Barbara* are taken from the Penguin Books edition, 1957.

6   The importance of the influence of the nonconformist families on Birmingham life cannot be underestimated, as Asa Briggs highlights: 'In Victorian Birmingham they (the dissenters) did much to mould the economic, social and political life of the town. In particular, Unitarians and Quakers occupied important positions in business and politics. Unitarian families, like

the Chamberlains, Kenricks, Martineaus and Nettlefolds, provided a compact and tireless leadership in all branches of local life . . . These Unitarian families were as important to Birmingham of the nineteenth century as were the village squires and parsons to the older rural England . . . They were families, as much as individuals, conscious of their birthright, and well established in local life.' (*History of Birmingham 1865–1938*, Volume II, ASA BRIGGS, Oxford University Press, 1952.)

7   'In furtherance of the policy of making the works as independent as possible for the manufacture of ammunition, the company extended its activities in 1888 and successive years. Plant for the manufacture of fuses, steel shell, etc., was installed, while the rolling mill in Water Street, near by, from which the company drew its supplies of brass and copper, was purchased. With increasing business, this mill proved of insufficient capacity, and in 1889 the lease was acquired of another rolling mill in Lodge Road, Birmingham, thus the company had two sources of supply. Fully equipped now for work on the metal side of the business, the company next directed its attention to the supply of explosives, and in 1893 the Wosboro' Dale Black Powder Mills were purchased . . . In 1894 Kynoch Limited erected a factory for the manufacture of cordite at Arklow in Co. Wicklow, Ireland . . . the demand for the increased quantity of explosives led to the erection of a factory on the Thames, later known as Kynochtown, for the manufacture of guncotton, high explosives and smokeless sporting powder, and by 1899, Kynochs had become the largest manufacturer of cordite in the world.' ('A Short History of Kynoch Ltd.' *ICI Magazine*, July 1928, pp. 27–30.)

CHAPTER 2
pages 10–15

1   'The Three elements of modern civilisation, Gunpowder, Printing and the Protestant Religion' THOMAS CARLYLE, *Critical and Miscellaneous Essays [1839], I,* 'State of German Literature.'

2   The Silk and Terry imprint can be found on a number of items emanating from the Kynoch Works and which are now housed in the Birmingham Reference Library and ICI archives.

3   No official records of the formation of the Press remain. Such documentation that does exist can be found in the turn of the century in-house magazine *The Kynoch Journal* which frequently indulged in retrospective articles on the Kynoch empire. Later, publications such as the *ICI Magazine* also ran historical items. For their information, the *ICI Magazine* was dependent upon the recollections of two employees: Mr George Williams and Mr Nutt from the composing room. Both men commenced their employment with the press in 1896, eighteen years after the press started production. Refer to 'A Short History of the Kynoch Press', *ICI Magazine*, March 1931, pp. 229–237.

4   Information regarding the accommodation of the Press was found in the following publications: *The Kynoch Journal*, 1889–1900, p. 11; 'The Kynoch Press', *ICI Magazine*, March 1931, pp. 229–237; 'The Kynoch Press', *ICI Magazine*, May 1937, pp. 458–549; 'Kynoch Press has 75th Birthday', *ICI Magazine*, October 1953, pp. 298–300.

5   Information regarding the staff employed by the Press was found in the following publications: *The Kynoch Journal*, Volume I, 1889–1900, p. 11; 'The Kynoch Press', *ICI Magazine*, March 1931, pp. 229–237; 'The Kynoch Press', *ICI Magazine*, May 1937, pp. 458–549; 'Kynoch Press has 75th Birthday', *ICI Magazine*, October 1953, pp. 298–300.

6   Information regarding the equipment employed by the Press was found in the following publications: *The Kynoch Journal*, Volume I, 1889–1900, p. 11; 'The Kynoch Press', *ICI Magazine*, March 1931, pp. 229–237; 'The Kynoch Press', *ICI Magazine*, May 1937, pp. 458–549; 'Kynoch Press has 75th Birthday', *ICI Magazine*, October 1953, pp. 298–300.

7   There are few surviving examples of Kynoch ammunition catalogues and none appears to exist in library or museum archives. All are in the collections of interested individuals who may be contacted through the United Kingdom Cartridge Club. The scarcity of the catalogues makes them prohibitively expensive for the majority of collectors. In most instances, therefore, it has not been possible to view the originals, the material proffered has been in the form of photocopies. Whilst these have been of great use I cannot remark upon the dimensions, substrate, sizes of type, colour or binding of the catalogues. My descriptions and comments are, therefore, rather general.

8   Few examples of the *Kynoch Journal* exist. Those which have survived may be found either in the Birmingham Reference Library; the Royal Armouries, Leeds; The British Library; or with private collectors. No complete collection of the *Journal* can be found with any single individual or institution.

9   'The Kynoch Press', *The Kynoch Journal*, Volume 1, October 1899–1900, p. 11.

CHAPTER 3
pages 16–25

1   For more information on Donald Hope refer to 'The Kynoch Press, 1876–1981, Appendix 2, Interviews' [Michael Hope] Caroline Archer, Ph.D. thesis, University of Reading, 1999.

2   Donald Hope was appointed a Director of Kynoch Ltd at a board meeting held on 20 May 1901 (on the recommendation of the Chairman, Mr Arthur Chamberlain). On 27 June 1922, Hope resigned from the Board of Kynoch Ltd when Nobel Industries became its sole Director and Manager. However, on the same day he was appointed to a 'local board' of Kynoch Ltd. This appears to have become a Delegate Board in 1927 after Nobel Industries became part of ICI Hope tendered his resignation from Kynoch Ltd Delegate Board on 18 September 1928. (Information available from the ICI archives in the Birmingham City Library Archive Department.)

3   Donald Hope's family business, Henry Hope and Son, was founded by Thomas Clark in 1818 in Lionel Street, Birmingham. The firm was originally known as Jones and Clark, with the Clark's being principal owners. Donald's father, Henry Hope, joined the firm as a boy from school, and spent a lifetime in the business working as a draughtsman of domestic and commercial conservatories and was, by all accounts, of unsurpassed ability. In 1864, Henry Hope was taken into the partnership and the firm's name was changed to Clark and Hope. In 1875, following the death of Thomas Clark, Henry Hope became

sole owner and from then on the firm traded under his own name. In 1898 the business was incorporated as a limited company of Henry Hope and Sons; the first directors were Henry Hope and his sons H. Donald Hope, J. Arthur Hope and Ralph W. Hope. In 1908 Henry Hope retired and was succeeded by Donald who, through his energetic leadership, was responsible for the company's great expansion away from the manufacture of metallic hothouses and towards the production of central heating and metal windows and their accessories. These commodities were extremely popular at the turn of the century, and Hope's products were particularly favoured as their workshops had championed the designs and spirit of Ruskin and Morris for which Hope's windows acquired a world-wide reputation. (Refer to *A Short History of Henry Hope and Sons Limited*, Curwen Press, London, 1958.)

4   Obituary for H. Donald Hope, *Birmingham Post and Mail*, 20 February, 1953.

5   Information relating to the arts and crafts movement in Birmingham can be found in: *A History of British Design 1830-1970*, FIONA MACCARTHY, Chapter 2, 'Arts and Crafts 1860–1915', George Allen and Unwin, 1979, and *By Hammer and Hand—the arts and crafts movement in Birmingham*, edited by ALAN CRAWFORD, published by the Birmingham Museums and Art Gallery, 1984, pp. 27–30, 103–6, 119–22.

6   The Birmingham Guild of Handicraft was founded in 1880. It grew out of the Birmingham Kyrle Society which existed to help working people find enjoyment in something higher than the gin palace and more refined than the music hall. The Guild practiced several crafts—furniture making, metal work and, under Arthur Gaskin and James Richardson Halliday, printed books and magazines. Prominent amongst its members were the wealthy Birmingham Unitarian families—the Chamberlains, Dixons, Kenricks, Napier-Claverings, Martineaus and Nettlefolds—who played an important part in the political and cultural life of late nineteenth-century Birmingham. All were united through marriage. The voluntary directorship of the Guild was filled for many years by Arthur Stanfield Dixon, son of George Dixon MP. By 1899 it was under the directorship of Claude Napier-Clavering, the first paid Managing Director of the Guild. Clavering married Millicent Kenrick whose father, William, made substantial investments in the Guild, was Chairman of the board of Directors and whose family was responsible for the Chamberlain move to Birmingham. William Kenrick was head of a forceful Liberal, Unitarian family and connected to the Birmingham printing firm of Kenrick and Jefferson.

7   'The Kynoch Press', *ICI Magazine*, p. 458, 1937.

8   Examples of the work produced for Henry Hope and Sons can be found in the Archive Department and the Local Studies Department of the Birmingham Reference Library. Additional material is in private collections.

9   Ben Day tints were the shading mediums used by chromolithographers, and were available in line, stipple, grain or other textures.

10   Refer to ' The Kynoch Press, 1876–1981, Appendix 2, Interviews', Caroline Archer, Ph.D. thesis, University of Reading, 1999.

11 The Birmingham Typographic Association records an initial Kynoch Press membership of thirteen men at December 1920. This had doubled to 27 by 1921, the year in which Donald Hope surrendered his contacts with the Press. The Press maintained a strong representation on the committee of the Typographic Association with an almost unbroken succession of one compositor and one pressman from the Press taking his place on the Committee — a more persistent and sustained representation than from any other Birmingham printer. Its representation reflects the fact that Kynoch went on to have the largest composing room in Birmingham and the second largest membership of the Association. (Records of Kynoch Press T.A. membership can be found at the offices of the Birmingham Typographic Association, 9 William Street North, Birmingham B19 3QH.)

CHAPTER 4
pages 26–49

1 There is little written documentation giving evidence of Herbert Simon's personality, inspirations or tenets. His book, *Song and Words* (George Allen and Unwin Ltd, 1973), recounts the history of the Curwen Press (of which he was later a director), but is devoid of autobiography. Refer also to T*he Double Crown Club Register of Past and Present Members*, compiled by JAMES MORAN, May 1949; *Artists at Curwen*, PAT GILMOUR, The Tate Gallery, London, 1977; *Printer and Playground*, OLIVER SIMON, Faber and Faber, 1956.

2 'Herbert Simon Hon FSIA' STUART ROSE *The Designer,* March 1975.

3 *Printer and Playground*, Oliver Simon, Faber and Faber, London, 1956.

4 *Printer and Playground*, Oliver Simon, Faber and Faber, London, 1956.

5 'Mr Herbert Simon leaves the Kynoch Press', *Magazine of the Midland Master Printers' Alliance*, September 1933, p.11.

6 'The Kynoch Press', *ICI Magazine*, July 1928

7 Information on the Kynoch Press Monotype installation was taken from the Monotype sales ledgers, the Type Museum, 100 Hackford Road, London SW9 0QU.

8 Information about staffing at the Kynoch Press was available from the Birmingham Typographic Association, 9 William Street North, Birmingham.

9 Refer to 'The Kynoch Press, 1876–1981, Appendix 2, Interviews' [Roger Denning], Caroline Archer, Ph.D. thesis, University of Reading, 1999.

10 External customers of the Kynoch Press included: Aluminium Development Association; Barrows Stores; Best and Lloyd; Birmingham Art Advisory Committee; Birmingham Chamber of Commerce; Birmingham Civic Society; Birmingham Education Authority; Birmingham Guild of Handicraft; Birmingham Law Society; Bournville Dramatic Society; Brierely Crystal; Brockhouse; Bickford Smith; British Broadcasting Corporation; British Gas Council; British Nuclear Fuels; British Titanium Products; Bovis; Cadbury; City of Birmingham Corporation; Crabtree and Co.; Crown Agents; Copper Development Association; Coronation Planting Committee; Coventry Cathedral; de la Rue; Design and Industries Association; Dryad Press; Edwin

Lowe; Forth Road Bridge; G.E.C.; Gordon Russell; Henry Hope and Sons; Institute of Industrial Supervisors; International Union of X-ray Crystallography; Kodak; Lord Mayor's Parlour; Library Association; Limmer and Trinidad Co Limited; Magnesium Elektron Limited; Magadi Soda Company; Manders; Murex Welding Processes Limited; Pilkingtons; Rolls Royce; Rubber Research Institute; Rural Industries Bureau; Severn Road Bridge; Seismological Centre; Tarmac; Tufnol; Unilever; University of Birmingham; Victoria and Albert Museum; Wednesbury Corporation; Wolverhampton Archaeological Society.

11   *Printing Types*, a broadsheet issued by the Kynoch Press, 1924.

12   Kynoch Press produced books for the following publishing houses: Bernard Sleigh, Cornish Brothers, Effingham Wilson, Elkin Matthews, Fleuron, Nonesuch Press, Norman Gale, Porpoise Press, Selwyn and Blount, Society of Saint Peter and Paul, Architectural Press, Allen and Unwin, Bodley Head, Cassells, Design and Industries Association, Dryad Press, Stanley Nott, Bulletin Press, Butterworths, Oliver and Boyd, James Moran, Oxford University Press.

13   *Printing Explained*, Herbert Simon and Harry Carter, The Dryad Press, Leicester, 1931.

14   The *ICI Magazine* was edited by: R. Lloyd Roberts (editor-in-chief) [1928–]; H. R. Payne (editor) [1928–]; Y. M. Reeves (assistant editor) [1928–]; Anthony Sutcliffe [–1947]; Henry Maxwell [1947–51]; Richard Kean [1951–67]; Francis Odle [1967–79]; Ian Allen [1980–]. Circulation commenced at 30,002 in 1928; by the end of the decade it had reached 40,002; at the end of the 1940s it had risen to 43,000; in the 1950s circulation topped 87,000. No figures are available for the 1930s, 1960s or 1970s. Format: 237 x 175 mm [1928–1949]; 273 x 205 mm [1950–1966]; 292 x 205 mm [1967]; 307 x 220 mm [1969–1971]; 292 x 205 mm [1972–1979].

15   Information relating to the relationship between the Kynoch Press and ICI was found in the following documents: 'Report on the Kynoch Press' C. N. SHEARER, ICI Purchasing Department, 3 May 1929; 'Extensions to the Printing Department', P. FRANK, ICI Finance Department, 29 May 1929; 'Report on the Kynoch Press' W. H. HOLLAND, ICI; Minute no 271 of the Metal Group Delegate Board Meeting, 23 June 1931.

16   *ICI Magazine*, 1933.

CHAPTER 5   1   All biographical detail relating to H.V. Davis has been taken from 'The
pages 50–53   Kynoch Press', *ICI Magazine*, October 1933, p. 62..

2   Information about staffing at the Kynoch Press was available from the Birmingham Typographic Association, 9 William Street North, Birmingham.

CHAPTER 6
pages 54–63

1   All biographical detail relating to Michael Clapham has been taken from: *Perishable Collections*, MICHAEL CLAPHAM, The Cloanthus Press, London, 1996; For more information refer to 'The Kynoch Press, 1876–1981, Appendix 2, Interviews' [Michael Clapham]; Caroline Archer, Ph.D. thesis, Reading, 1999.

2   *Perishable Collections*, MICHAEL CLAPHAM, The Cloanthus Press, London, 1996.

3   *Perishable Collections*, MICHAEL CLAPHAM, The Cloanthus Press, London, 1996.

4   Minutes of the meeting of the Kynoch Press Committee, March 1939.

5   Michael Clapham writing in the ICI Magazine, January 1939.

6   The Kynoch Press Notebook and Diary, 1947.

7   The Kynoch Press Notebook and Diary, 1943.

8   Dr E. J. Holmyard, *Editor* [1942–54]; Dr Trevor I. Williams, *Editor* [1955–76]; Dr Trevor I. Williams, *Deputy Editor* [1946–54]; W. A. Osman, *Deputy Editor* [1959–67]; Dr. J. A. Wilcken, *Foreign Editor* [1947–56]; G. N. J. Beck, *Foreign Editor* [1957–76] were recruited for their wide knowledge of foreign languages and their scientific terms and were aided in their task by a team of translators from both the United Kingdom and abroad who were selected not merely for their linguistic and scientific ability, but also their literary adroitness. he extent of the publication commenced at forty-four pages and gradually rose with each volume until it reached its maximum extent of sixty-four pages in 1957. This extent was more or less maintained until 1961, after which the publication slowly declined in size until it reached 48 pages in the late 1970s. The frequency of issue between 1942–1962 was quarterly [January, April, July and October], thereafter, publication was reduced to three times a year [January, May, September].

9   'Breaking the rules—the story of ICI's company advertising'. Sydney Rogerson, *ICI Magazine*, September 1952.

10   Letter written by Michael Clapham, 9 August 1987.

CHAPTER 7
pages 64–77

1   For more information on the Kynoch Press during the 1950s, refer to 'The Kynoch Press, 1876–1981, Appendix 2, Interviews'; Caroline Archer, Ph.D. thesis, 1999. Also see 'Kynoch Press has 75th birthday' JOHN KENNEDY, *ICI Magazine*, October 1953, pp. 298–300.

2   'The Kynoch Press, 1876–1981, Appendix 2, Interviews' [David Hopewell]; Caroline Archer, Ph.D. thesis, University of Reading, 1999.

3   'The Kynoch Press, 1876–1981, Appendix 2, Interviews' [Bert Pace]; Caroline Archer, Ph.D. thesis, University of Reading, 1999.

4   'The Kynoch Press, 1876–1981, Appendix 2, Interviews' [David Hopewell]; Caroline Archer, Ph.D. thesis, University of Reading, 1999.

5   'The Kynoch Press, 1876–1981, Appendix 2, Interviews' [Bert Pace]; Caroline Archer, Ph.D. thesis, University of Reading, 1999.

6   'The Kynoch Press, 1876–1981, Appendix 2, Interviews' [David Hopewell];
     Caroline Archer, Ph.D. thesis, University of Reading, 1999.

7   'The Kynoch Press, 1876–1981, Appendix 2, Interviews' [Roy Kilminster];
     Caroline Archer, Ph.D. thesis, University of Reading, 1999.

8   For information on graphic reproduction techniques at the Kynoch Press refer
     to 'Improvements in colour masking systems for photo-mechanical reproduc-
     tion processes' and 'The simulation of colour proofs by optical means', ROY
     KILMINSTER, paper issued by the Kynoch Press, July 1958.

9   'The Kynoch Press, 1876–1981, Appendix 2, Interviews' [Roger Denning];
     Caroline Archer, Ph.D. thesis, University of Reading, 1999.

10   'The Kynoch Press, 1876–1981, Appendix 2, Interviews' [Roger Denning];
     Caroline Archer, Ph.D. thesis, University of Reading, 1999.

11   'Bob Gill, internationally known graphic designer has been retained to head a
     new design unit—Kynoch Graphic Design. Gill was born in New York and
     studied in Philadelphia. He arrived in the United Kingdom in 1960.' (Kynoch
     Press press-release, 26 August 1968.) Alan Fletcher, Colin Forbes and Bob Gill
     joined together to form the partnership Fletcher | Forbes | Gill Ltd., in London.
     They were consultants to a number of British and International industrial
     companies, and they also designed for advertising, publishing, exhibitions,
     films and theatre. It was a not uncommon practice for designer/printers to
     retain the services of an outside designer; the Curwen Press, for example
     retained John Miles as design consultant in 1969.

12   'The Kynoch Press, 1876–1981, Appendix 2, Interviews' [Len Harvey];
     Caroline Archer, Ph.D. thesis, University of Reading, 1999.

13   'The Kynoch Press, 1876–1981, Appendix 2, Interviews' [Alex King];
     Caroline Archer, Ph.D. thesis, University of Reading, 1999.

14   'The proof-reader', *ICI Magazine*, 1952, pp. 276–277.

15   'The Kynoch Press, 1876–1981, Appendix 2, Interviews' [Alex King];
     Caroline Archer, Ph.D. thesis, University of Reading, 1999.

16   'The Kynoch Press, 1876–1981, Appendix 2, Interviews' [David Hopewell];
     Caroline Archer, Ph.D. thesis, University of Reading, 1999.

17   Martin J. Buerger, John S. Kasper (USA), Norman F. M. Henry, Kathleen
     Lonsdale (UK), Caroline H. MacGillary (Netherlands).

CHAPTER 8
pages 78–100

1   For more information on the Kynoch Press during the 1960s and 1970s, refer
     to 'The Kynoch Press, 1876–1981, Appendix 2, Interviews'; Caroline Archer,
     Ph.D. thesis, University of Reading, 1999.

2   'The Kynoch Press, 1876–1981, Appendix 2, Interviews' [Wallis Heath];
     Caroline Archer, Ph.D. thesis, University of Reading, 1999.

3   'The Kynoch Press, 1876–1981, Appendix 2, Interviews' [Wallis Heath];
     Caroline Archer, Ph.D. thesis, University of Reading, 1999.

4   'The Kynoch Press, 1876–1981, Appendix 2, Interviews' [Wallis Heath]; Caroline Archer, Ph.D. thesis, University of Reading, 1999.

5   'The Kynoch Press, 1876–1981, Appendix 2, Interviews' [Wallis Heath]; Caroline Archer, Ph.D. thesis, University of Reading, 1999.

6   'On a long-term basis a £95,000 research contract has been placed with the University of Newcastle-upon-Tyne for a three-to-four-year programme on computer applications in printing. The aim of the operation is to provide industry with a series of adaptable programmes that perform all copy editing, preparation and actual type composition. An investigation will be made on the output problem of processing information from computers into publishable form without intermediate stages.' From 'Government report into the use of computers in British Industry', circa 1969, p. 42.

7   *A few notes on computers and printing*, Kynoch Press, 1969.

8   'The Kynoch Press, 1876–1981, Appendix 2, Interviews' [Dick Hurst]; Caroline Archer, Ph.D. thesis, University of Reading, 1999.

9   'The Kynoch Press, 1876–1981, Appendix 2, Interviews' [Dick Hurst]; Caroline Archer, Ph.D. thesis, University of Reading, 1999.

10 'The Kynoch Press, 1876–1981, Appendix 2, Interviews' [Colin Baines]; Caroline Archer, Ph.D. thesis, University of Reading, 1999.

11 'The Kynoch Press, 1876–1981, Appendix 2, Interviews' [Wallis Heat]; Caroline Archer, Ph.D. thesis, University of Reading, 1999.

12 'The Kynoch Press, 1876–1981, Appendix 2, Interviews' [Wallis Heath]; Caroline Archer, Ph.D. thesis, University of Reading, 1999.

13 'The Kynoch Press, 1876–1981, Appendix 2, Interviews' [Len Harvey]; Caroline Archer, Ph.D. thesis, University of Reading, 1999.

14 'The Kynoch Press, 1876–1981, Appendix 2, Interviews' [Roger Denning]; Caroline Archer, Ph.D. thesis, University of Reading, 1999.

15 Kynoch Press Notebook and Diary, 1963.

16 'The Kynoch Press, 1876–1981, Appendix 2, Interviews' [Len Harvey]; Caroline Archer, Ph.D. thesis, University of Reading, 1999.

17 'The Kynoch Press, 1876–1981, Appendix 2, Interviews' [Len Harvey]; Caroline Archer, Ph.D. thesis, University of Reading, 1999.

18 'The Kynoch Press, 1876–1981, Appendix 2, Interviews' [Bert Pace]; Caroline Archer, Ph.D. thesis, University of Reading, 1999.

CHAPTER 9
pages 101–108

1   Information relating to the sale and closure of the Press was found in the following documents: Agreement for the sale and purchase of the business IMI Kynoch Press, 26 September 1979; Minutes of a meeting held between Kynoch Press and Gilmour and Dean, at Kynoch Press, 11 July, 1979; 'Future plans and investments.' Minutes of a meeting held on Thursday, 19 July 1979 between IMI Kynoch Press, Gilmour and Dean and the Print Unions;

Statement from the majority of staff to IMI and Kynoch Press management and through them to Gilmour and Dean, issued 16 July 1979; Report to Branch Committee Meeting, 14 July 1979, re proposed acquisition of Kynoch Press by Gilmour and Dean Group, Scotland; Minutes of the meeting with the Litho Chapel, 23 July 1979; Minutes of the meeting with the Composing Room Chapel, 24 July 1979; Minutes of the meeting with the Letterpress Chapel, 24 July 1979; Announcement to all Kynoch Press Employees issued on 4 July 1979, by Mr R. G. Tennant, IMI; Minutes of a meeting held on Wednesday 11 July 1979 between IMI Kynoch Press, Gilmour and Dean and the print unions; 'Kynoch goes to Scottish Buyer', *Birmingham Post*, 14 November 1979; Report to Branch Committee Meeting, 14 July 1979, re: the proposed acquisition of Kynoch Press by Gilmour and Dean Group, Scotland.

2   Gilmour and Dean were a long-established group of companies with head-quarters in Scotland and who operated three specialised and very modern printing plants. They were formed in 1846 when the engraving skills of Alexander Davidson Dean and the considerable business acumen of William Gilmour were brought together and became bank-note printers. The Gilmour and Dean plant produced high-quality labels and cartons; Chorley and Pickersgill Ltd, Leeds, joined the Group in 1962 and produced greetings cards, building society passbooks, calendars and catalogues; Gilmour and Dean Business Forms Division, which comprised Alexander Pettigrew (Scotland) and E. K. Lickfold (Gloucestershire) produced multi-part sets, continuous stationery, computer cheques, tax and share certificates and word processing stationery.

CHAPTER 10
pages 109–125

1   For notes on the typefaces held by the Kynoch Press refer to pages 157–168 of this book.

Bibliography

AMERY W. H., 'A few notes on typefaces', *Penrose's Annual*, Volume 20, Lund Humphries, London, 1915, pp.103-107.

'An award winning in-plant', *Litho Printer*, April 1972, pp. 30–33.

ARCHER Caroline, *The Kynoch Press, 1876–1981*, Ph.D. thesis, The University of Reading, 1999.

ATKINS William (general editor), *The Art and Practice of Printing—a work in six volumes: the composing department; letterpress printing; lithographic printing; photo engraving; bookbinding and ruling; printing office management*, Sir Isaac Pitman and Sons Limited, London, 1932.

ATTERBURY Rowley, 'The Contributors' being the paper of a talk delivered to the Wynkyn de Worde Society at Stationers' Hall on 16 May 1974.

AYNSLEY Jeremy, *Nationalism and Internationalism—Design in the 20th Century*, Victoria and Albert Museum, London, 1993.

BANN David, *The Print Production Handbook*, Macdonald Illustrated Books, Quarto Publishing, London, 1986.

BARNETT Michael P., *Computer Typesetting—experiments and prospects*, The MIT Press, Massachusetts Institute of Technology, Cambridge, Massachusetts and London, England, 1965.

BENNETT Paul A., *Books and Printing—a treasury for typophiles*, Forum Books, the World Publishing Company, 1963.

BERRY W. Turner, JASPER W.P., JOHNSON A.F., *Encyclopedia of Typefaces*, third edition (further revised and enlarged), Blandford, London, 1991.

'The BFMP Congress: a plan for effective growth', *British Printer*, July 1965, pp. 92–95.

BIRD Vivian, *Portrait of Birmingham*, Robert Hale and Co., London, 1979.

BLACKWELL Lewis, *Twentieth Century Type*, Laurence King Publishing, London, 1992.

BLUHM Andrew, 'The French printing revolution', *British Printer*, June 1965, pp. 82–93.

BRAUN A. A., 'An analysis of foreign types and some reasons for their popularity', *Penrose's Annual*, Volume 30, Lund Humphries, London, 1928, pp. 50–60.

BREWER Roy, 'The international computer typesetting conference 1964—the report of the proceedings', *British Printer*, April 1965, pp. 69.

BRIGGS Asa, *History of Birmingham 1865–1938*, Volume II, Oxford University Press, Oxford, 1952.

BRIGGS Asa, *Victorian Cities*, Penguin Books, first published 1963, this edition 1990.

BRODIE L., 'Britain's printing prospects in relation to a future European Free Trade Area', *British Printer*, January 1960, pp. 88–91.

CARRINGTON Noel, *Industrial Design in Britain*, George Allen and Unwin (Publishers) Ltd., London, 1976.

CARTER John, *ABC for Book Collectors*, Oak Knoll Press, Werner Shaw, 6th edition, 1994.

CARTER Harry, 'Printing for our time', *Design for Today*, Design and Industries Association, 1933, pp. 60–63.

CARTER Sebastian, *Twentieth Century Type Designers*, new edition, Lund Humphries, London, 1995.

CARTWRIGHT H. M., 'Methods of colour correction', *The Penrose Annual*, Volume 47, Lund Humphries, London, 1953, pp. 109–111.

CARRUTHERS J., 'Survey of Specimens: an objective review of current work: problems in the production of technical literature', *British Printer*, May–June 1951, pp. 54–55.

CARRUTHERS J., Survey of specimens, an objective review of current work: Diary and Notebook for 1951', *British Printer*, May–June 1951, pp. 58–59.

CHAMBERS David, *Specimen of Modern Printing Types by Edmund Fry, 1828*, a facsimile with an introduction and notes by David Chambers, Printing Historical Society, London, 1986.

'Changing trade conditions call for customer re-education', *British Printer*, March–April 1952, pp. 27–28.

CHILD John, *Industrial Relations in the British Printing Industry—the quest for security*, George Allen and Unwin Ltd., London, 1967.

CHURCH R. A., *Kenricks in Hardware—a family business 1791–1966*, David and Charles, London, 1969.

CLAPHAM Michael, *Perishable Collections*, The Cloanthus Press, London, 1996.

'Comps and computers', *British Printer*, September 1964, p. 55.

'Commercial and classical printing—the Kynoch Plan,' *The Monotype Recorder*, Monotype Corporation, England, 1923, p. 20.

'Conference Report: computer typesetting', *British Printer*, September 1966, pp. 71–75.

CONWAY Hazel (ed), *Design History—a student's handbook*, Routledge, London and New York, 1994.

COPPIN F. W., HEPHER M., LEE J., WELLS D. J., 'A comparison of colour masking and hand correction in the four-colour half-tone process', *The Penrose Annual*, Volume 44, Lund Humphries, London, 1950, pp. 88–90.

Computer typesetting conference, preprints, University of Sussex, July 15–16 1966, Institute of Printing.

CORRIGAN Andrew J., 'Changing trade conditions call for customer re-education', *British Printer*, March–April 1952, p. 27.

CRAWFORD Allan (ed), *By Hammer and Hand—the arts and crafts movement in Birmingham*, Birmingham Museums and Art Gallery, 1984.

CURE G. A. C., 'New markets for print at home and abroad' *British Printer*, March 1966, pp. 91–93.

CURWEN Harold, *The Stencil Process at the Curwen Press*, The Curwen Press, London [n.d.].

DAISH A. N., 'Shooting at a sitter', *British Printer*, November–December 1951, pp. 48–52.

DAVIS Alec, *Package and Print—the development of container and label design*, Faber and Faber, London, 1967.

DAVIS Alec, *Type in Advertising*, Raithby, Lawrence & Company, Leicester, 1951.

DAVIS Alec, 'Printing for exporters', *British Printer*, October 1964, pp. 104–110.

DAY Kenneth, 'Types of the sixties', *Pernrose's Annual*, Volume 61, Lund Humphries, London, 1968, pp. 241–256.

DENMAN Frank C., 'When you buy that specimen book—what should go in and also what should be left out', *American Printer*, February 1931, pp. 45–49.

DICKINSON Ken, 'A decade of type design', *Pernrose's Annual*, Volume 56, Lund Humphries, London, 1962, pp. 16–23.

Design in the Festival, introduction by Gordon Russell, HMSO for The Council of Industrial Design, London, 1951.

'Design service is no longer and optional extra', *British Printer*, February 1962, p. 75.

'The Double Crown Club—register of past and present members', May 1949.

DOWDING Geoffrey, *An Introduction to the History of Printing Types, from 1440 up to the present day*, The British Library, London and Oak Knoll Press, New Castle, DE, 1997.

DREYFUS John, 'Notes on some new types and revivals', *Penrose's Annual*, Volume 44, Lund Humphries, London, 1950, pp. 18–22.

DREYFUS John, *Into Print—selected writings on printing history, typography and book production*, The British Library, London, 1995.

'Electronic systems for printing and publishing', *British Printer*, June 1966, pp. 95–101.

EVANS, Bertram, 'Typography in England, 1933—frustration or function', *Pernrose's Annual*, Volume 36, Lund Humphries, London, 1934, pp. 57–61.

'Exportise', *British Printer*, October 1964, pp. 55.

'Fatfaces and Elephants—early nineteenth-century display types still in active service', *British Printer,* January 1959, pp. 81–84.

GARLAND Ken, *Graphics, Design and Printing Terms—an international dictionary*, Lund Humphries, London, 1989.

GARRETT Albert, *A History of Wood Engraving*, second edition, Bloomsbury Books, London, 1986.

GASKELL Philip, *A New Introduction to Bibliography*, Oxford at the Clarendon Press, reprinted with corrections, 1974.

GASCOIGNE Bamber, *How to Identify Prints*, Thames and Hudson, London, reprinted 1988.

GILL Bob, *Forget all the Rules you never learnt about Graphic Design—including the ones in this book*, Watson-Guptill, New York, 1981.

GILL Conrad, GRANT-ROBERTSON Charles, *A Short History of Birmingham—from its origin to the present day*, City of Birmingham Information Bureau, 1938.

GILL Eric, *An Essay on Typography*, with a new introduction by Christopher Skelton, fifth edition, Lund Humphries Publishers, London, 1988.

GILMOUR Pat, *Artists at Curwen*, The Tate Gallery, 1977.

GRAY Nicolete, NASH Ray, *Nineteenth Century Ornamented Typefaces*, new edition, Faber and Faber, London, 1976.

GRAY Nicolete, *Nineteenth Century Ornamented Types and Title Pages*, Faber and Faber, London, 1938.

GRAY Nicolete, 'Lettering in Coventry Cathedral' *Typographica*, 6 December 1962, pp. 33–41.

HARLEY Basil, *The Curwen Press—a short history*, The Curwen Press, London, 1970.

HARLING Robert, 'Necessities and novelties', *Pernrose's Annual*, Volume 39, Lund Humphries, London, 1937, pp. 65–68.

HARLING Robert, 'Victorian revival', *Pernrose's Annual*, Volume 41, Lund Humphries, London, 1939, pp. 73–76.

HARLING Robert, 'Experiments and alphabets', included in *Printing in the twentieth century—a Penrose Anthology*, (Ed) James Moran, Northwood Publications, London, 1974, pp. 152–156.

Hazells in Aylesbury 1867–1967— scrapbook to commemorate the first hundred years at the printing works, Aylesbury, Hazell, Watson and Viney, London, 1968.

HAZZLEWOOD John W., 'The growth of the house magazine', *Penrose's Annual*, Volume 47, Lund Humphries, London, 1953, pp. 67–69.

HAZZLEWOOD John W., 'Company magazine', *Penrose's Annual*, Volume 53, Lund Humphries, London, 1959, pp. 43–47.

HOCK Johann, 'How the letterpress printer can make the most of current technical advances', *British Printer*, December 1965, pp. 103–106.

HOCK Johann, 'Magazine publishers discuss the possibilities of computer control', *British Printer*, August 1965, pp. 86–89.

HOLLIS Richard, *Graphic Design—a concise history*, Thames and Hudson, London, 1994, reprinted 1996.

HORN, Frederick A., 'Old types with a new significance', *Pernrose's Annual*, Volume 36, Lund Humphries, London, 1934, pp. 17–22.

HORNE Alan, *The Dictionary of Twentieth Century British Book Illustrators*, Antique Collectors Club, 1994.

HOYEM George A., *The History and Development of Small Arms Ammunition*, Volume III, Armoury Publications, Oceanside, USA, 1991.

HUMPHRIES Eric, 'New techniques in printing, an era of machines controlled by machines', *British Printer*, September–October 1950, pp. 34–35.

HUSS Richard E., *The Development of Printers' Mechanical Typesetting Methods, 1822–1925*, University of Virginia Press, Charlottesville, 1973.

HUTCHINGS R. S., *The Western Heritage of Type Design—a treasury of currently available typefaces*, Cory, Adams & Mackay Ltd., London, 1963.

'Industrial Publishing', *British Printer*, April 1961, pp. 70–78.

'In-plant unit expands into commercial printing', *British Printer*, September 1967, pp. 63–67.

'In-plant printing at Rolls-Royce', *British Printer*, September 1967, pp. 68–70.

INNES Brian, 'Foreign language typesetting—an eye on the future', *British Printer*, August 1962, pp. 89–90.

JAFFE Erwin, *Halftone Photography for Offset Lithography*, third edition, Graphic Arts Technical Foundation Inc., USA, 1964.

JOHNSON A. F., *Type Designs—their history and development*, new and revised edition, Andre Deutsch, London, 1966.

JOHNSON A. F., 'English type specimen books', *Pernrose's Annual*, Volume 35, Lund Humphries, London, 1933, pp. 19–22.

JOHNSON J., GREUTZNER A., *Dictionary of British Art, Volume V—British Artists 1880–1940*, Antique Collectors Club, 1994.

JULIER Guy, *The Encyclopedia of Twentieth Century Design and Designers*, Thames and Hudson, London, 1993.

KEEFE H. J., *A century in Print—the story of Hazell's 1839–1939*, Hazell, Watson and Viney, London, 1939.

KINROSS Robin, *Modern Typography—an essay in critical history*, Hyphen Press, 1992.

'Kynoch Press export service—BP news of the month', *British Printer*, 6 October 1965.

LAMBERT Frederick, *Graphic Design Britain*, Peter Owen Ltd, London, 1967

LAWSON Alexander, *Anatomy of a Typeface*, Hamish Hamilton, London, 1990.

LEWIS John, *Such Things Happen—the life of a typographer*, Unicorn Press, 1994.

LEWIS John, *Printed Ephemera—the changing use of type and letterforms in English and American Printing*, W. S. Cowell, Ipswich, and Faber and Faber, London, 1990.

LESSER Samuel, 'A plan for avoiding the expense of individual type-specimen books', *Inland Printer*, January 1931, pp. 71–72.

'Let's take a look at Birmingham as a printing centre', *British Printer*, September 1960, pp. 74–82.

MacCARTHY Fiona, *A History of British Design 1830–1970*, revised edition [formerly published as *All Things Bright and Beautiful*] George Allen and Unwin Ltd., London, 1979.

McLEAN Ruari, *Jan Tschichold—typographer*, Lund Humphries, London, 1997.

McLEAN Ruari, *How typography happens*, The British Library, London, and Oak Knoll Press, New Castle, DE, 2000.

Miller and Richards Typefounders Catalogue (for 1873), re-printed in facsimile by Bloomfield Books, Owston Ferry, Lincolnshire, 1974.

MORAN James (ed,) *Printing in the Twentieth Century—a Penrose Anthology*, Northwood Publications, London, 1974.

MORAN James, 'Design and the printer', *British Printer*, January 1962, pp. 92–108.

MORISON Stanley, *First Principles of Typography*, Cambridge University Press, 1967.

MORISON Stanley, 'Picture-printing and word-printing', *Penrose's Annual*, Volume 50, Lund Humphries, London, 1956, pp. 21–26.

MORRISON W. A., 'The worker's place in a developing industry', *British Printer*, September–October 1950, pp. 22–23.

'News of the Month—government grant for computer setting work' *British Printer*, August 1965, pp. 1.

'New computer series: possibilities in the printing field', *British Printer*, November 1964, pp. 83–85.

'On-line computer typesetting—two recent applications', *British Printer*, August 1966, pp. 76–81.

'One million characters per hours from Digiset Photosetter', *British Printer*, February 1966 pp. 108–113.

OTT, J. Steven and CLARK Milo G., 'OCR' *British Printer*, November 1965, pp. 80–85.

'Outlook for computer setting', *British Printer*, September 1965, pp. 73–76.

PEPPIN Brigid and MICKLETHWAIT Lucy, *Dictionary of British Book Illustrators of the Twentieth Century,* James Murray, London, 1983.

PEVSNER N., *Pioneers of Modern Design—from William Morris to Walter Gropius,* Penguin Books, London, 1960.

PHILLIPS Arthur, *Computer Peripherals and Typesetting—a study of the man-machine interface incorporating a survey of computer peripherals and typographic composing equipment,* Her Majesty's Stationery Office, London, 1968.

PICKERING Charles, 'The future of the typographer', *Penrose Annual,* Volume 44, Lund Humphries, London, 1950, pp. 48–50.

POLIPHILUS, 'Layout and style—the roots of the British national style in typographic design', *British Printer,* July–August 1951, pp. 33–40.

PLANT Marjorie, *The English Book Trade—an economic history of the making and sale of books,* second edition, George Allen and Unwin Ltd., London, 1974.

'A printed image for Coventry Cathedral—Kynoch Press pioneers a new approach to graphic design for the Church', *British Printer,* August 1962, pp. 105–106.

'Printer's guide to computer typesetting terminology', *British Printer,* October 1964, pp. 59.

'Printer's bookshelf: Alphabet: International Annual of Letterforms', *British Printer,* July 1964, pp. 65.

'Printers to the world of science', *British Printer,* April 1964, pp. 68–70.

'Proceedings of the automatic typesetting congress, TPG '65', *British Printer,* September 1965, pp. 61–63.

'Prospects and problems of computer typesetting', *British Printer,* April 1966, pp. 79–82.

'Report of the committee appointed to select best faces of type and modes of display for government printing', HMSO, London, re-printed 1933.

ROBERTS Bernard, 'Is typography becoming a secret?', *British Printer,* March–April 1951, pp. 18–21.

ROSE Stuart, 'Printers need a design policy', *British Printer,* November–December 1950, pp 54.

ROSNER Charles, 'Entente cordiale', *Penrose's Annual,* Volume 49, Lund Humphries, London, 1955, pp. 21–24.

A Short History of Henry Hope and Sons Limited, Curwen Press, London, 1958.

SHAND James, 'Modern printing—a reply' *Design for Today,* Design and Industries Association, 1933, p. 194.

SHAND James, 'Tradition or experiment in printing design', *British Printer,* 1950, pp. 57–61.

SIMON Herbert, *Song and Words—a history of the Curwen Press,* George Allen and Unwin Ltd, London, 1973.

SIMON Oliver, *Printer and Playground*, Faber and Faber, London, 1956.

SIMON Oliver, *Introduction to Typography*, Faber and Faber, London, 1963.

Some Account of the Oxford University Press 1468–1921, Oxford at the Clarendon Press, 1922.

'Some practical problems of establishing a design service in a smaller printing house—experience of H. Hacker Design Group Ltd', *British Printer*, January 1962, pp. 110–115.

SOUTHWARD John, *Modern Printing—a handbook of the principles and practice of typography and the auxiliary arts*, Volume I & II, 6th edition, Raithby, Lawrence and Co., Leicester, 1933.

SOUTHWORTH Miles, SOUTHWORTH Donna, *Colour separation on the desktop*, Graphic Arts Publishing, Livonia, NY, 1993.

SOUTHWORTH Miles, SOUTHWORTH Donna, *Colour Reproduction—communication and control*, Graphic Arts Publishing, Livonia, NY, revision 3.1, 1993.

SPARKE Penny, *An Introduction to Design and Culture in the Twentieth Century*, Routledge, London, 1992.

SPENCER Herbert, *Design in Business Printing*, Sylvan Press, London, 1952.

SPENCER Herbert, *Pioneers of Modern Typography*; second revised edition, Lund Humphries, London, 1982.

SPENCER Herbert, 'Old types, new layouts', *Pernrose's Annual*, Volume 51, Lund Humphries, London, 1957, pp. 42–43.

'Standardised production of scientific print', *British Printer*, February 1964, pp. 100–104.

SUTTON James and BARTRUM Alan, *Typefaces for books*, The British Library, London, 1990.

SYMONS A. J., FLOWER Desmond, MEYNELL Francis, *The Nonesuch Century*, 1936.

SYMONS A. J., 'The book and its making', *Design for Today*, Design and Industries Association, 1933, pp. 117–118.

TARR John C., 'What are the fruits of the new typography?', *Printing in the twentieth century—a Penrose anthology*, James Moran (ed), Northwood Publications, London, 1974, pp. 145–151.

'Three latest computer-printing projects', *British Printer*, April 1964, p. 61.

THORPE Joseph (ed), *Design in Modern Printing—the Yearbook of the D.I.A.*, (introduced by Sir Lawrence Weaver), Design and Industries Association, 1927–28.

'The Time Colour Scanner', *British Printer*, September 1950, pp. 38–39.

TOMPKINSON G.S., *A Selected Bibliography of the Principle Modern Presses, Public and Private in Great Britain*, First Edition Club, 1928.

TRACY Walter, *Letters of Credit—a view of type design*, Gordon Fraser, London, 1986.

'Thompson "Computerset" will speed up newspaper production', *British Printer*, May 1965, pp. 90–91.

TSCHICHOLD Jan, *The Form of the Book—essays on the morality of good design* (translated from the German by Hajo Hadler, edited with an introduction by Robert Bringhurst) Hartley and Marks Publishing Inc., Washington, USA, 1991.

TWYMAN Michael, *Printing, 1770–1970—an illustrated history of its development and uses in England*, The British Library, Oak Knoll Press, Reading University Press, 1998.

TWYMAN Michael, *The British Library Guide to Printing, History and Techniques*, The British Library, London, 1998.

'Typesetting by computer—a report on the Institute of Printing conference', *British Printer*, September 1964, pp. 70–75 .

'Typography in Britain', *Typographica* No 7, New Series, May 1963, pp. 2–22.

Under Five Flags—the story of Kynoch Works, Witton, Birmingham, 1862–1962, Imperial Metals Industries (Kynoch) Ltd., 1962.

The Victoria History of the Counties of England—a history of Warwickshire, Volume VII, The City of Birmingham, published for The Institute of Historical Research, By the Oxford University Press.

Vincent Figgins Type Specimens 1801–1815, edited with an introduction and notes by Berthold Wolpe, London. Printing Historical Society, 1967.

WALLIS L. W., *A Concise Chronology of Typesetting Developments 1886–1986*, The Wynkyn de Worde Society in association with Lund Humphries Publishers Ltd, London, 1988.

WALLIS L. W., *Type Design Developments, 1970–1985*, National Composition Association, Arlington, Virginia, 1984.

WALLIS L. W., *Modern Encyclopedia of Typefaces 1960–90*, Lund Humphries, 1990.

'What I look for in a type book', *British Printer*, September/October 1930, pp. 123–124.

Who's Who in Art, twenty-sixth edition, The Art Trade Press Ltd., Havant, Hampshire, 1994.

WILKINSON Gerald, 'A typographer's trade', *British Printer*, March–April 1952, pp. 47.

WOLPE Berthold, (edited and introduction notes) *Vincent Figgins Type Specimens 1801 and 1815*, Printing Historical Society, London, 1967.

WOODRUFF A. B., 'Photo—lithography today, a quick survey', *British Printer*, November–December 1950, pp. 44–49.

Index